<u>THE</u> SCIENCE OF SALES SUCCESS

A PROVEN SYSTEM FOR HIGH-PROFIT, REPEATABLE RESULTS

Josh Costell

⁂AMACOM

American Management Association

New York • Atlanta • Brussels • Chicago • Mexico City • San Francisco
Shanghai • Tokyo • Toronto • Washington, D.C.

This publication is designed to provide accurate and authoritative information in regard to the subject matter covered. It is sold with the understanding that the publisher is not engaged in rendering legal, accounting, or other professional service. If legal advice or other expert assistance is required, the services of a competent professional person should be sought.

Library of Congress Cataloging-in-Publication Data

Costell, Josh, 1953–
    The science of sales success : a proven system for high-profit, repeatable results / Josh Costell.
        p.   cm.
    Includes bibliographical references and index.
    ISBN 978-0-8144-7192-0 (hardcover)
    ISBN 978-0-8144-1599-3 (paperpack)

    1. Selling.   I. Title.

HF5438.25.C675   2003   2003015183
658.85—dc22

Printing number

10   9   8   7   6   5   4   3   2   1

Contents

This book is dedicated to Pierre Pilon. He represented all that's good about a professional salesperson: he was trustworthy, motivating, candid, dedicated, customer-centric, problem solving, fun, personal, an attentive listener, enthusiastic, competitive, and value driven. He also happened to be one of my most-trusted friends and confidants—a person who made your life more enriched just to know him.

Foreword

Think about the title of book you are holding: *The Science of Sales Success*. Does that title make sense to you? Can selling really be "scientific"?

Well, if you are a professional salesperson, you probably hope so. After all, the opposite of science is magic, and if you're counting on magic to make your numbers, this could be a very difficult year for you.

Unfortunately, most sales methodologies are like diets. They generate a lot of hope and enthusiasm, but they produce little in the way of lasting results. They perpetuate clichés and assumptions that are about as valid as the notion that the sun revolves around the earth.

For example, you may have been taught that an effective salesperson uncovers the customer's needs. Sound familiar? *Josh Costell shows you why focusing on needs may actually make the sales process more difficult.*

Similarly, you've probably been taught to link product or service features with benefits. *Josh shows you how some features may actually dilute the persuasiveness of your message and cause the customer to view your offering as a commodity, not a solution.*

Finally, you may have read or been taught that a strong salesperson qualifies the opportunity, finding out if customers have a need for your products, if they have the budget to afford them, whether they have the authority to make the buying decision, and what their timeline is. *Josh demonstrates how using this approach to qualifying customers will delay the sales process and cause your customer to see you as little more than a vendor at best, and as an adversary at worst.*

This book is different in some other ways, too. For one thing, it's based on sound principles, not anecdotes and war stories. Josh clearly shows you how to use the same disciplined, logical approach characteristic of scientific investigations to manage a selling opportunity. More important, he gives you plenty of practical examples of what he's talking about, examples that you can easily follow and apply to your own opportunities. And he gives you step-by-step guidelines that will produce successful outcomes for both you and your customer.

Recently I had the opportunity to interview professional salespeople who are responsible for selling complex technical solutions. "Why do decision makers hesitate to proceed with a deal?" I asked them. Many of them answered the same way: "Lack of information. I have to provide them with the facts they need, then they can move forward."

Unfortunately, their answers all veered toward explanations of the technology, of product applications and features. "Help them understand how it works, why it works, and they'll go forward."

No, actually they probably won't. People don't buy technology for its own sake, they buy it to achieve positive results in their organization. You can dump tons of information on them, but if it's not the right kind of information, it won't do either of you much good. And for both you and your customer, a rare opportunity—to achieve important outcomes, to solve significant problems, to deliver huge gains to the organization, and to make a big sale—has been squandered.

The beauty of *The Science of Sales Success* is that it pinpoints exactly which facts your customer needs to have at each stage of the sales process in order to feel confident about moving to the next stage. It shows you how to make the right observations and gather the right information, how to transform information into a statement of value that's intimately tied to your customer's goals and your own unique strengths, and then how to get out of the way so they can convince themselves.

So what does "scientific selling" involve? It means that you apply the principles of the scientific method to your activities as a salesperson. Like a scientist, you first obtain the most accurate data you can from careful observation and inquiry. And like a trained scientist, you don't waste your time gathering data that is irrelevant. (Josh shows you the nine specific types of information you need to

THE SCIENCE
OF SALES
SUCCESS

gather and how to find them.) Next, you formulate a theory or hypothesis that takes all of the data into account and makes sense of it. You don't discount the facts that don't fit, you don't ignore the uncomfortable ones, and you don't bend reality to fit the theory. Once you have an approach that makes sense of all the facts, that passes what Josh calls the "test of reasonableness," you move to the next phase—an agreement with the customer. Incremental agreements result in closed business in a natural, logical path.

One of the strengths of taking a scientific approach to selling is that it makes the process much easier to manage. Josh firmly believes that what you cannot measure, you cannot manage; so he shows you how to measure your progress at each stage of the sales process against objective benchmarks to guarantee that you are moving in the right direction.

When you use this approach, both you and your customer work collaboratively to engage in rational decision making. You feel confident about the recommendations you're making. The customer feels confident about the probability of achieving important goals. And both of you feel that the process has been based on thoughtfulness and honesty, not manipulation or pressure.

Josh Costell demonstrates that professional sales is the epitome of knowledge work. No number of expensive client lunches, no quantity of tickets to a hot sports event, will ultimately overcome the power of knowledge. In *The Science of Sales Success*, he shows you what facts you need to know, when you need to know them, and what to do with these facts once you have them.

So are you ready to be a scientific salesperson? Then make an experiment. Apply Josh's techniques and look for the results. And here's a hint: you'll find them in your pay envelope.

Tom Sant, Ph.D.
Former CEO and founder of The Sant Corporation
Inventor of ProposalMaster and RFPMaster
Author of Persuasive Business Proposals

Acknowledgments

When I started this book, I never thought it would take twenty years to finish. Neither did the following people, who were a constant source of encouragement and advice. First and foremost, my incredible wife and biggest supporter, Carole, and my energetic five-year-old son, Justin Pierre (who we thought would be old enough to read the book by the time I was finished), for their patience and understanding; and my family, both blood and extended, whose support has been unwavering. Now, in no particular order: Johnny D'Espostio, who was my eight-mile-an-hour editor and sounding board on our runs along the beach; Stefanie Hicks, who has been my trusty and loyal assistant, proofreader, jack-of-all-trades, and friend for more than a decade; Rich Jann, a life-long friend, who has an absolutely brilliant and opinionated sales mind that challenges every assumption made about selling; Paul Boudreau, Nikole Kroll, and Steve Puntolillo, who brought my ideas to the world of high-tech sound and graphics while fine-tuning them; Kenny Weiss and Carrie Cantor, my original editors, who made my thoughts actually make sense on paper; Mary Miller, my copyeditor, who tweaked the book to make it a much more enjoyable read; Bruce Gerber and Jim Daly, who went through years of printing changes and always make the "latest" seminar workbook look great; Robert Trommler, who pushed me to make the book's concepts be crystal-clear so they would empower salespeople; Peter Englezos, my brother-in-law, who always reminded me not to lose faith and that I was on the right track; Rich Barry, who for four summers listened to every book idea (at least twice) and always found a way to act like he was hearing it for the first time; Vic McCloskey and Sherman Turner (York International Company), John Burke and Jim Severs (Rittal Corporation), Jim Bujold (Johnson Controls), and Matt Dugan and Joe Kubala (The Trane Company), who gave me the opportunity to teach the book's processes to their sales forces on local and national levels; my mentor, H. L. Singer, who set an excellent example to follow for almost thirty years; Cliff Dorsey and Bob Emenecker, whose friendship and encouragement have served me well for more than two decades; Ellen Kadin (AMACOM Books), who was committed to getting the book published from the get-go; and Erika Spelman (AMACOM), who made sure the flow of the book kept readers engaged.

Yes, there's one more group to acknowledge: the thousands of sales professionals and their customers worldwide, who let me share in the excitement of helping them sell and buy measurable value for the ultimate "win-win" scenario.

Introduction

Think about it. Who are the top-performing salespeople you know? They are the ones with the most long-term customers. Over the years, top performers earn long-term customers by fulfilling their expectations measurably better than competitors can. In return, these superstars earn their expected profit levels for doing so. This book will teach you how to make sure you are one of those sales superstars.

The Science of Sales Success shows you how to ensure that customers' expectations are not moving targets. It will show you how to fast-forward the sales process to get prospects and new customers to act like long-term ones. They will be eager to share the measurable dollar benefits of their goals and the nine critical details of their purchasing decisions. Customers will see how sharing purchasing criteria with you empowers them.

Now, you can reach the pinnacle of sales success, which is called *relationship selling,* in a matter of two to three sales calls. You no longer need to invest dozens of sales calls over months or years to achieve that status. You (and your customers) will make well-informed, advance-or-abandon decisions at what will feel like the speed of light. When you and customers do not waste each other's time, everyone wins—and your productivity explodes as a result. Rest assured, there are no gimmicks and this is not science fiction. Logic and science are what power this book.

The Big Picture

This book explains the objective benchmarks you need to use to manage your selling efforts and duplicate success on a planned basis. It provides all the tools a salesperson needs to outvalue the competition. You'll help customers manage their expectations so that the potential for unfulfilled ones disappear. Customer satisfaction rises along with profits, so everyone wins. Yet, it is a blueprint, not a wrecking ball. It *builds* on your foundation of skills, style, talents, knowledge, personality, and customer relationships to accomplish this goal. Its plug-and-play framework inserts your sales knowledge into a format that makes it easy to retrieve and apply. The faster you can look up answers, the more efficient and productive you will be.

The Science of Sales Success also pieces together all the key components of the sales and marketing puzzle. It shows how the different pieces interact to create *customer value*. When you understand these interactions, you can harness their power to make your sales soar. (See Exhibit I-1.)

Measuring Up

The Science of Sales Success uses the MeasureMax selling system as its plug-and-play framework for you to custom-tailor the book's

Exhibit I-1. Connecting all the pieces in selling.

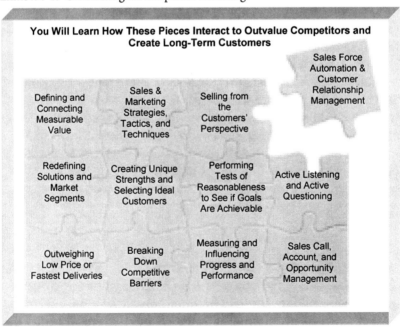

You Will Learn How These Pieces Interact to Outvalue Competitors and Create Long-Term Customers

Sales Force Automation & Customer Relationship Management

Defining and Connecting Measurable Value

Sales & Marketing Strategies, Tactics, and Techniques

Selling from the Customers' Perspective

Redefining Solutions and Market Segments

Creating Unique Strengths and Selecting Ideal Customers

Performing Tests of Reasonableness to See if Goals Are Achievable

Active Listening and Active Questioning

Outweighing Low Price or Fastest Deliveries

Breaking Down Competitive Barriers

Measuring and Influencing Progress and Performance

Sales Call, Account, and Opportunity Management

concepts to your sales situations. MeasureMax is short for "Measure to Maximize." The powerful business axiom, "You can only manage what you can measure," is its engine. By using this unique selling system, you learn how to help customers measure in financial terms the value they receive from achieving their goals via your products and services. Some examples are shown in Exhibit I-2.

Exhibit I-2. Comparing traditional selling to the MeasureMax selling system.

With traditional selling, customers *venture*:	With the plug-and-play format of MeasureMax, customers *state*:
• "I need to improve reliability by 5 percent over last year."	• "My goal is to prevent annual production losses of $50,000 due to unscheduled downtime."
• "I need to reduce operating expenses significantly."	• "My top priority is to save $30,000 on administrative paperwork."
• "I need to increase revenues by 15 percent."	• "My number one objective is to add $1,000,000 to net profits."
• "I need to gain market share."	• "My top-ranked goal is to generate $5 million in sales for every one percent of increased market share."
• "I need to upgrade quality."	• "My most pressing priority is to reduce mean time between failures to lower warranty costs by $250,000."

This selling system also provides you with the means to influence results by measuring the progress of your sales opportunities while they are occurring. No more postmortems on lost sales after it's too late to do anything. You and customers learn how to take the guesswork out of advance-or-abandon decisions. Some examples are shown in Exhibit I-3.

This book also shows you better methods for applying best practices. Best practices are the strategies and tactics from past sales successes that you repeat in similar situations. Logic seems to dictate that if they worked in one situation they should work in similar ones. Yet, how do you know these sales situations share enough similarities to make these best practices apply?

You probably rely on gut instinct and common sense. *The Science of Sales Success* adds to your insight by providing you with the means to put to use not only anecdotal war stories involving how "Joe sold Mary" but also analytical evaluations. You learn not only *what* best practices worked but also *how* and *why* they worked. You learn to predict and duplicate success so sales orders become planned events, not random occurrences.

Exhibit I-3. Comparing traditional selling to the MeasureMax selling system.

With traditional selling, salespeople *venture*:	With the plug-and-play format of MeasureMax, salespeople *state*:
• "I have a great chance to get the sale."	• "In this market segment and dealing with a vice president of manufacturing, I can demonstrate that our two unique strengths will achieve her goal of improving productivity by 15 percent or $2,000,000 annually."
• "Both of my sales opportunities are in the qualifying stage."	• "For the first sales opportunity, I only have six of the nine critical purchasing criteria measurable. In the second opportunity, I only have four of the nine purchasing criteria measurable. My first opportunity is definitely more qualified at this stage."
• "My proposal should meet all their requirements."	• "I can connect seven different features to the customers' three measurable benefits; four with measurable value; three with an external focus, and two of them are unique strengths. I can definitely value-justify their investment (and our price)."
• "It looks like our products and services will be a good fit for this customer."	• "In this market segment, manufacturing managers' primary goal is to reduce the number of returns. They typically use a system of evaluation that measures warranty expenses on a dollar-cost-per-incident basis."
• "I am pretty sure the customer will be able to afford our products."	• "The way they are measuring the benefits from achieving their goals to increase production by $3,000,000 annually makes me question whether they will be able to justify their investment."
• "I seem to be making good progress."	• "I have made three in-person sales calls without understanding how they will know whether they achieved their goal of 'increasing market share.' If I cannot find out what measurements they will use on the next sales call, I'm going to invest my selling efforts elsewhere."

The common denominators you will use to make best practices analytical are:

• Customers' goals and benefits
• Market segments that share those goals
• Strongest features or unique strengths that achieve those goals
• Systems of evaluation used to calculate the value of those goals, and the "costs" of doing nothing
• Positions of customers that determine their goals
• Competitive offerings that match up to customers' goals
• Profit levels earned from achieving customers' goals

Note that each common denominator contains the word *goals*. *The Science of Sales Success* revolves around helping your customers achieve their goals, thereby making you the person they want to do business with. Its selling system increases in value the more you use it, as your database of sales knowledge increases.

The Science of Sales Success will work for you because it encourages you to answer, in very specific terms, the following four questions:

1. What do you know about new sales opportunities from your past experiences that will help you to earn higher profits for providing measurable value?
2. What do you need to find out to determine the potential for success in any particular sales opportunity?
3. How well did you find out from customers the specifics involving your sales opportunities?
4. What do you still need to find out or do next in your sales opportunities based on what you have already found out?

A Systematic Approach

This book's systematic approach embodies Peter Drucker's comments from his book *Innovation and Entrepreneurship* when he states that, "Every practice rests on a theory, even if the practitioners themselves are unaware of it."[1] Typically, salespeople concentrate mainly on how they conduct sales calls—not on what comes before or after the calls occur. Yet, for the most part, the probabilities for success are set before salespeople even contact customers. To determine those probabilities, you need to take a systematic approach to the theory that governs your sales opportunities from five perspectives before, during, and after sales calls.

Before Making Sales Calls

In sales, like most professions, success is 90 percent planning the work, and 10 percent working the plan. You need to make sure that you understand who the ideal customers are—and who are not. You need to ensure that you select your customers, not settle on them, if you are going to sell *compensated value*—that is, provide more measurable dollar benefits than competitors or the cost of doing nothing (status quo is often a salesperson's biggest competitor)—and receive your expected profit margins for doing so. The five perspectives, or viewpoints, from which a salesperson views opportunities are illustrated in Exhibit I-4.

An overview of the four selling phases of the MeasureMax system used to sell compensated value is illustrated in Exhibit I-5 on page 8.

Change the Order to Get the Order

The way in which customers' emotions affect their purchasing decisions has been the subject of countless books. The consensus is that you can venture only educated guesses about the influence of emotions; however, the outcomes of guesses are unpredictable. Yet, duplicating sales success is all about predictability—knowing what should happen next—and being prepared when it does (or does not) happen.

While you cannot make a sale void of emotions, use the processes and tools in this book to dilute the randomness of their impact. As Dr. Jack Katz wrote in his book *How Emotions Work,* "intellectual analysis seems to nullify emotions."[2] You appeal to customers' intellect when you make the value they receive from achieving their goals measurable in dollars. Motivate customers to change the order of their decision-making process so that everyone thinks clearer and reaps benefits. Make facts come first, emotions second. You can enhance the way you sell by enhancing the way customers buy. After all, customers do not willingly make illogical purchasing decisions. Yet, they will unwillingly make illogical decisions if they aren't aware they are missing information that would make them decide differently.

Note: Ironically, you usually find out the facts after you lose a sale or do not fulfill a customer's expectations. You know emotions drove the customer's decision when either one of you says, "If I had only known that, I would have . . ."

Creating High-Return Opportunities

Sales opportunities involve either business-to-business or business-to-consumer transactions. Yet, not every sales opportunity affords

Exhibit I-4. The five viewpoints of the MeasureMax selling system.

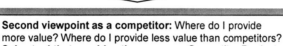

----- Before Making Sales Calls -----

Do your research to quantify the value that your customers seek and your products and services provide, as well as competitors . . .

> **First viewpoint as a marketing manager:** What do I offer that no else does (unique strengths)? Which customers place the most value on my products and services? **Sales tool that provides the answers:** *Product Profile* sheet, Chapter 2.

> **Second viewpoint as a competitor:** Where do I provide more value? Where do I provide less value than competitors? **Sales tool that provides the answers:** *Competitor Product Profile* sheet, Chapter 9.

> **Third viewpoint as a customer:** If I were my customer, what would make me say yes? How would I measure and compare value? **Sales tool that provides the answers:** *Market Profile* sheet, Chapter 3.

------- While Making Sales Calls ------

Because of your planning, you are ready to conduct a customer-oriented sales call. Every question you ask will serve a business purpose and make sense for the customer to answer. You are able to view the sales call from your most comfortable perspective . . .

> **Fourth viewpoint as a salesperson:** How do I produce more compensated value? **Sales tools that provides the answers:** *Connecting Value* sheet and *Pushed Through vs. Pulled-Through Test*, Chapter 7.

------- After Making Sales Calls ------

Now is not the time to rationalize how well the sales call went using subjective benchmarks. "I think (or feel) I did okay" will not get you to superstar status. Objective self-evaluations and absolute benchmarks will. This last perspective will ensure that you do . . .

> **Fifth viewpoint as a sales manager:** How well am I conducting my sales calls to find out measurable specifics? What can I do to be more productive? **Sales tool that provides the answers:** *Quick-Entry Sales Management* sheet; Chapters 6 and 9.

Exhibit I-5. The four phases of MeasureMax. (Note: MP stands for Measurable Phases, while MPC stands for Measurable Phase Changes.)

MP 1: Spark Interest (salesperson viewed as a customer expert on initial contact)
   Step 1: Research and Membership (salesperson confirms valid business reasons exist for contacting customer)
   Step 2: Take Your Pick (customer selects a potential goal[s] he or she is interested in achieving from the ones you suggested)
   Step 3: Track Record (salesperson documents success from same industry)
MPC 1: Interest Confirmed (customer agrees to meet to determine ability to achieve goals)

MP 2: Measure Potential (salesperson helps customer gauge ability to achieve his or her stated goal[s])
   Step 1: Market Focus (salesperson reinforces industry expertise and knowledge)
   Step 2: Purpose and Goals (salesperson reinforces that meeting is to help customer determine ability to achieve stated goals)
   Step 3: Eliminate Unknowns (salesperson's questioning helps customer provide measurable purchasing information)
   Step 4: Yellow Light (salesperson summarizes the measurable purchasing criteria required to achieve the customer's stated goal[s])
MPC 2: Potential Confirmed (customer agrees goals are worth pursuing)

MP 3: Cement Solution: (salesperson connects solution to customer's goal[s])
Before meeting customer:
   Step 1: No Blanks (salesperson sees what measurable purchasing data is missing and determines strategy to find them out)
   Step 2: Benchmarks (salesperson connects features of products and services to the measurable benefits of customer's goal[s])
   Step 3: Oops! (salesperson determines what measurable benefits cannot be achieved and develops strategies to address them)
At the customer meeting:
   Step 4: Purpose & Summary (salesperson reinforces that meeting is to present how selected solutions achieve customer's goals and recaps measurable benefits)
   Step 5: Connect the Dots (salesperson connects measurable benefits of customer's goals to features of selected solutions)
   Step 6: Conditions Met (salesperson demonstrates how all requirements of customer's purchasing decision are satisfied)
MPC 3: Solution Confirmed (customer agrees that solution achieves goals)

MP 4: Implement Agreement (salesperson inks the deal)
   Step 1: Deal (salesperson confidently asks customer to purchase agreed-upon solutions)
   Step 2: Logistics (salesperson goes over details needed to start business relationship)
MPC 4: Agreement Confirmed (customer agrees to enter into a contract and inks the deal)

you the ability to provide additional compensated value. Typically, these high-return opportunities involve the following "two-plus" requirements:

- There are two or more decision makers.
- They require two or more in-person sales calls to complete.

The more "two-plus" requirements you have, the greater the opportunity to sell compensated value. Individuals seeking only the lowest price or the quickest delivery would not need to make this type of investment in people or time.

Note: In business-to-consumer transactions, there might be only one decision maker. However, if a sale involves more than one in-person sales call, it still allows the opportunity for you to use *The Science of Sales Success*'s processes, tools, and selling system.

Shattering Myths

When you add measurability to selling, it shatters the following ten common sales myths:

1. Selling is an art, not a science.
2. Customers buy primarily for emotional reasons, not logical ones.
3. Most salespeople are customer focused, not product focused.
4. Lost sales results from competitors' lower prices, not from higher value.
5. More sales calls equal more orders.
6. Great salespeople know how to handle obstacles.
7. More product features produce more benefits for customers.
8. Salespeople can more easily sell value to existing customers than to new ones.
9. Strategies drive salespeople's tactics, not the other way around.
10. A salesperson knows how well a sale is going at any given time.

The Building Blocks

Each chapter follows this format to make it an easy read:

- *Reading Section.*
- *Example Boxes:* Relate concepts to identifiable selling situations.
- *Exhibits:* Consist of illustrations to visualize key concepts and charts to show how to put into practice the book's concepts.

- *Two Case Studies* (Chapters 2 to 8): One addresses processes on conceptual levels while the other case highlights tactical and strategic perspectives.
- *Summary.*

Overview of Chapters

Chapter 1—Measurability Matters. Explains and demonstrates how to make key aspects of selling measurable so your productivity explodes.

Chapter 2—Defining Value. Explains and demonstrates how to make your products and services generate value.

Chapter 3—Receiving Value. Explains and demonstrates how customers determine the value they receive from achieving their goals.

Chapter 4—Tests of Reasonableness. Explains and demonstrates how nine preexisting factors determine if customers or you can achieve their goals.

Chapter 5—Every Question Counts. Explains and demonstrates how to use listening and questioning skills to encourage customers to provide measurable answers.

Chapter 6—Leave the Brochures Behind. Explains and demonstrates how to make sales calls that measure your potential to outvalue competitors—without mentioning *specific* products or services.

Chapter 7—Every Reason to Say Yes. Explains and demonstrates how to create proposals that vividly connect to customers' goals.

Chapter 8—When the World Isn't Perfect. Explains and demonstrates how to handle customers' concerns by determining how they affect their goals.

Chapter 9—Using MeasureMax Your Way. Explains and demonstrates how you use this unique selling system to fit your sales opportunities.

Glossary. Lists the terms used throughout the book.

Bibliography. Lists further resources.

Note: No quick fixes or "learn how to sell smart in sixty minutes" schemes exist when it comes to high-value sales and high-level decision making. In *The Science of Sales Success*, details replace anecdotes; logic replaces war stories. Understand its key points because each chapter builds on the previous one. Everything connects and continues to become clearer the further along you read, Scout's honor.

The Rewards

You will increase productivity, exceed customer expectations, build long-term relationships, create golden referrals, motivate frustrated competitors to seek new career opportunities, own a cat-that-ate-the-canary smile, and earn a higher dollar W-2 to name a few benefits. You will also:

INCREASE YOUR KNOWLEDGE OF PRODUCTS AND SERVICES BY LEARNING HOW YOU:

- Define value by how *customers* measure it.
- Focus on your unique strengths and make them measurable.
- Ensure you do not dilute your products' strengths.
- "Create" new products and services with unique strengths.

INCREASE YOUR KNOWLEDGE OF YOUR CUSTOMERS BY LEARNING HOW YOU:

- Segment and prioritize markets by how they value your unique strengths.
- Help customers define and assign value to their goals.
- Spark interest in your customers to pursue specific goals.
- Determine customers' and your ability to achieve their goals.

IMPROVE COMMUNICATION SKILLS BY LEARNING HOW YOU:

- Use active listening to encourage customers to provide detailed information.
- Ask questions that make sense for customers to answer.
- Make presentations that customers accept.
- Ask questions that illustrate your customers' expertise.

IMPROVE ABILITY TO HANDLE UNEXPECTED BARRIERS BY LEARNING HOW YOU:

- Prevent them from forming.
- Handle them so customers remove them for you.
- Dilute the adverse affects of obstacles that do not go away.

IMPROVE CLOSING RATE BY LEARNING HOW YOU:

- Qualify solutions so you know customers accept them before you make your presentations.
- Make the close nothing more than the logical conclusion to a series of previous customer commitments.

INCREASE PRODUCTIVITY (THE W-2 FACTOR) BY LEARNING HOW YOU:

- Use a process that is structured enough to repeat success and avoid failures, yet flexible enough to accommodate different styles.
- Qualify the business potential faster to determine whether your and your customer's investment of time, effort, and resources is worth the expected return; and figure out what would have to change if it is not.
- Use the attainment of predetermined customers' agreements to measure and manage your progress.
- Make every sale a reference for the next one, and build competitor-proof, long-term professional relationships.

Eliminating the Tower of Babel Effect

Traditional selling methods focus on nonmeasurable concepts such as relating, prospecting, qualifying, and closing. This book makes these topics and others key ones measurable (review Exhibit I-1).

Because this approach is new, no terms exist yet to allow you to measure concepts such as *qualifying* or *prospecting*. This approach required creating new terms that are logical and measurable. Now, everyone involved in a sales opportunity can evaluate it the same way. Otherwise, you end up with a Tower of Babel with everyone using different benchmarks to determine the status of sales opportunities.

It's Your Choice

If you prefer to use your own sales methods, MeasureMax's flexible framework accommodates that choice. However, this book treats sales methods (including MeasureMax) like diet plans. Claims are one thing, results another. *The Science of Sales Success* works like a scale for whichever ones you choose to use. You weigh yourself throughout sales opportunities to see how well the methods you are using work. If past results mean anything, you will be surprised at which method works, and which ones do not.

Making the gray areas of selling black and white by injecting measurability takes discipline. It also takes courage to stifle our ability to self-rationalize. Not everybody can do it—only superstars. Yet, as a soon-to-be superstar, you know that when selling goes from a subjective and random-occurring art to a manageable and predictable science, the improvements in your performance will be phenomenal.

One last thought on what makes this book powerful. You can give a copy of it to your customers and never be concerned or embarrassed about what has been written. *The Science of Sales Success* empowers you to help selected customers make well-informed, value-driven purchasing decisions to choose your solutions. Everyone wins.

Notes

1. Peter Drucker, *Innovation and Entrepreneurship* (New York: Harper & Row Publishers, 1985), p. 26.
2. Jack Katz, *How Emotions Work* (Chicago: University of Chicago Press, 1999), p. 49.

Chapter One

Measurability Matters

Every sales opportunity has two columns that customers use to weigh out their purchasing decisions. Both of these columns have items with actual or perceived dollar figures assigned to them. After adding up the items, customers use the totals of the two columns to decide whether they will buy something and from whom. While customers can assign a dollar value to the Column 1 items on their own, Column 2 requires a salesperson's assistance. You want that salesperson to be you.

In Column 1, customers always (informally) insert the dollar value of the differences between these four items:

1. *Purchase Prices of Competitors' Products and Services.* Customer will use actual values to calculate this difference.
2. *Delivery Dates.* Customer will use actual or perceived values to calculate this difference.
3. *Personal Relationships with Suppliers.* Customer will use perceived value to calculate this difference.
4. *Costs of Changing to New Products, Services, or Suppliers.* Customer will use actual or perceived values to calculate this difference.

Note: The cost of change always favors the salesperson working for the existing supplier. Salespeople often mistakenly form elevated opinions about the effectiveness of their selling skills in situations where the cost of change favors them. The real test of their selling skills occurs when they are in sales opportunities involving competitors' customers (where the cost of change works against them).

Column 2 only has one item: the measurable benefits customers receive from achieving their goals. When it comes to selling value, this one item can more than compensate for the four items found in Column 1. Column 2 *always* starts out empty. Only you can help customers (formally) fill in their dollar amounts to outvalue the dollar differences from Column 1.

Your ability to sell value depends on whether you have the opportunity to fill out Column 2. To compound matters, you have only a limited number of in-person sales calls you can make in a year. Sales calls are your currency; where you invest them will determine your return. Therefore, invest more of your sales calls in Column 2 opportunities rather than those in Column 1. Using the quantifiable value of benefits and the other metrics of the Measure-Max selling system will help you concentrate your efforts on the former, but when necessary, also help you to obtain the most value out of the latter. (See Exhibit 1-1.)

The chart in Exhibit 1-2 illustrates how customers would assign value to the Column 1 items if you were not the existing supplier. If the customer only uses the dollar value of Column 1, you will lose the sale because the existing supplier's perceived value is worth $10,000 more than yours. Personal relationships and costs of change always favor the existing supplier (more on this subject in later chapters). However, if the customer considers both columns, you will win the sale (as long as you help the customer make Column 2 measurable). Your products and services are worth $15,000 ($25,000 minus $10,000) more than the existing supplier's. You outvalued the competition—and can justify a $3,000 higher price.

Using the measurements of MeasureMax, you achieve the following three key sales goals:

1. Provide more value than competitors.
2. Receive higher profits for doing so (with performance-based compensation becoming the norm, as a sale's profit level increases, so will your commissions and bonuses).
3. Earn long-term customers by fulfilling their measurable expectations.

Exhibit 1-1. Column 2 makes value measurable.

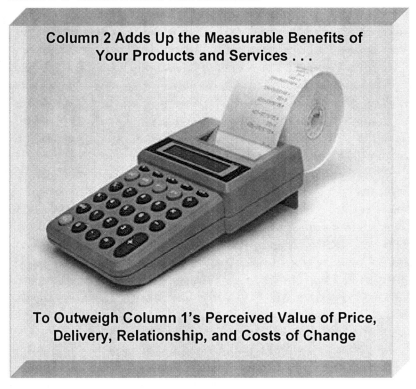

Column 2 Adds Up the Measurable Benefits of Your Products and Services . . .

To Outweigh Column 1's Perceived Value of Price, Delivery, Relationship, and Costs of Change

Achieve all three goals and you are a consistent, top-performing salesperson. Chapter 1 shows how using measurability to sell value:

- Drives your strategies and tactics
- Affects customers and your mode of selling
- Influences every sales opportunity
- Works in negotiated and bid sales

Note: Although this section provides an overview of these topics, later chapters are dedicated to detailing them. The learning strategy is to progress from broad concepts to detailed descriptions, analyses, and applications—one chapter at a time.

Strategy First, Tactics Second

Successful selling depends on your strategy driving your tactics, and not vice versa. Before you make sales calls do you think, "If my

Exhibit 1-2. Using Column 2 to win over competitors' customers.

Column 1	Your Products	Existing Supplier Products	$ Value to Existing Supplier	Column 2	Your Products	Existing Supplier Products	$ Value You Provide
1. Purchase Price	$73,000	$70,000	$3,000	Measurable benefits customers receive from achieving their goals via your products	Quantifies that products save customer $25,000 worth of lost production	Customer is not sure how much products save in lost production	$25,000
2. Delivery Date	1 week	2 weeks	(-$1,000)				
3. Personal Relationship	New	Existing Supplier	+$3,000				
4. Cost of Change	-$5,000	$0	+$5,000				
Column 1 Value to Existing Supplier			**+$10,000**	**Column 2 Value to Existing Supplier**			**-$25,000**

customer says this, I will say that" or, do you think, "This is what *we* need to find out, and what *we* need to agree on to continue the sale." The former means you rely on tactics and reactive techniques (that is, handling objections) to win debates. The latter means you rely on strategies to plan and manage your selling efforts to win orders.

Another surefire method exists for determining which approach you use. If you discuss specific products on your first sales contact, tactics drive your strategies. Product presentations rely on canned techniques to highlight your features and benefits. Your so-called strategy is to use product presentations to flush out customers' likes and dislikes. To convince customers to buy, you name every feature you believe produces great benefits. With tactics-driven selling, customers typically request proposals on the first sales call that never go anywhere.

When tactics drive this shotgun approach, you need knowledgeable customers. You count on them to know how to pick out what features they like while disregarding the ones they do not. Never sure how customers will react, you rely on your ability to react to the unexpected. When you use tactics, you become proficient at verbal jiujitsu. You learn how to spar with customers when situations arise that do not favor your products or company.

Example

Eileen Watkins is the information technology (IT) administrator for a large life insurance agency. Bob Thompson sells security, storage, and backup software for networks to prevent the loss of information. Eileen contacts Bob's company and requests that they send someone out to discuss her electronic data protection needs. Lucky Bob, Eileen is in his territory. Bob confirms on their initial phone call that Eileen wants to know what products and services his company can provide to increase data protection during power outages and prevent incidents of illegal access (hacking). Bob is certain that he can help Eileen solve her problems.

On his first in-person sales call to Eileen, Bob relies on tactics. They exchange pleasantries and brief histories of one another's background and companies. Bob asks Eileen if she has any other concerns ("pain") in addition to power outages and hacking. She says no.

Bob launches his well-polished PowerPoint presentation to outline features, benefits, and price ranges to gauge the extent of Eileen's preferences, sense of urgency, and available budget. He explains how his products and services help companies like Eileen's to protect their electronic data. He provides various dollar amounts these companies avoided losing by preventing data loss and illegal access.

Eileen sends out numerous buying signals. Their discussions focus on the different product costs and projected benefits. Bob also confirms that Eileen is the decision maker, has a $150,000 budget, and wants a solution in place within three months. Eileen requests that Bob work up three different combinations of products and services for her to review. Bob goes for the trial close. He asks Eileen if his products solve her outages and hacking problems, while also satisfying her budget and completion date, would she buy them? She says yes. Bob immediately agrees to present three proposals later in the week. Why not? Bob knows he has an interested and qualified customer (expressed need, available funding, set deadlines, and affirmed trial close), right?

Maybe not. Bob did a good job qualifying whether Eileen has the ability to *buy his products*. However, key metrics and details are still missing about whether Eileen can *achieve her goals*—and whether Bob can help in her endeavors. These measurable details could delay or lose the sale. In addition, the missing metrics and details would eliminate the need for Bob to present three different proposals that include details such as:

- What does "increasing data protection" really mean in dollar terms?
- What does it cost Eileen's company per hour or minute of downtime?
- What is the company currently doing to address these situations?
- Are there any other competitors or alternatives involved?
- How many incidents of hacking has the company had, and what was the cost?
- How will Eileen justify the expense of any new software?
- Which is more important: illegal access or outages, and why?

- What are the reasons the company proceeded with or abandoned this type of project in the past?
- Why is the company pursuing these issues now?

Most important, what measurable benchmarks will Eileen and Bob use to determine if she achieves her goals of data protection? After all, Bob wants to turn Eileen into a long-term customer by fulfilling her measurable expectations—a hit-or-miss proposition if he does not know the answer to this question. Bob might even find out that he cannot help Eileen to achieve her measurable benefits. If so, he would explain why he cannot help her at this time—and pass on this opportunity. If you get the sale but disappoint the customer with unfulfilled results, you will lose the opportunity to develop a repeat, long-term customer. A lost sale always beats a lost customer.

In *The Science of Sales Success*, you learn how to motivate customers to answer all these questions with specific and measurable details.

In tactics-driven selling, once salespeople throw out enough features and benefits to hit customers' hot buttons or "pain," they tend to end sales calls. When success seems likely, it is tempting to avoid finding out additional information that might jeopardize sales opportunities. "If I do not bring up something negative, hopefully customers will not either," they think. This approach often results in time wasted on unqualified opportunities for everyone.

Tactics Result in Unequal Motivation

Relying mainly on tactics, you become more motivated than your customers are. Nothing productive happens when you want to accomplish something for customers more than they want to achieve it for themselves. Do not fall into the trap of focusing on why you would buy your products, believing customers share the same sentiments. While it is important how much you think your products or services can help someone, it's more important how much customers think your products or services can help them.

Common symptoms of this more-motivated-than-the-customer situation are numerous. Customers may conceal information, avoid your calls, and give you an eventual, but long-drawn-out no. Customers, sales managers, and you try to figure out why you made the proposals in the first place. When you find out why your proposals failed, you also realize something of significant value. This information was as available on the first or second call as it was on the tenth. All you had to do was have the right strategy.

Strategy

In using a selling system such as MeasureMax, your strategy is simple: Seek measurable details about customers' purchasing decisions. Help motivate them to perform tests of reasonableness on whether they first, you second can achieve their goals. You do this before you mention any specific products. Then, working with measurable expectations, you see how well your products and services can produce the value they seek.

Note: If you chose your market segment per MeasureMax requirements, the connections to customers between their goals and your products will be evident. Now they will be as motivated as you are to pursue those connections.

Example

Let us turn back the clock to our previous sales call. This time Bob, upon hearing Eileen's interest in increasing data protection, alters his sales call from a tactical one to a strategic one by asking her to:

1. Explain what she means by increasing data protection—for example, decreasing the number of lost data incidents by 50 percent to only thirty per year.

2. Elaborate on what measurable value increasing data protection would generate—for example, thirty lost data incidents cost $2,000 each, which results in $60,000 savings annually.

3. Explain how Eileen will know if she achieves her goal of data protection.

With this information, Bob determines which products and services best achieve Eileen's goals. However, without a goal-oriented strategy of defining what customers want to—and are able to—achieve, the results are up for grabs as is their choice of business partners. You will also see how you can gain competitive advantages when your customers (and competitors) do not know how to answer questions like the ones presented to Eileen, but you do. You become valuable to customers when they acknowledge you as their industry expert.

Customers, Selling Modes, and Measurability

In any sales situation, you use one of three selling modes as the vehicle to seek the metrics and details for the questions highlighted in the Eileen and Bob examples. The modes (in order of least productive and desired to most productive and coveted) are brinkmanship, courtship, or relationship selling. Because the courtship mode comprises both the relationship and brinkmanship modes, they will be discussed in the following order: relationship, brinkmanship, and courtship. Each one influences the amount and depth of details you gather. These details will ensure that your sales strategy drives your selling tactics.

Relationship Selling

The salesperson with the most long-term (that is, loyal) customers wins. You win because you made it to the coveted third and highest stage of a salesperson's career, which is relationship selling. You enjoy the rewards of your professional and personal relationships with customers. Years of meeting or exceeding customers' expectations will earn their loyalty.

Purchase orders become foregone conclusions. Customers have confidence that you listen to and act upon what they say and always put their best interests first. The benefits of relationship selling are huge: Customers willingly share their needs, deadlines, competitive data, decision-making process, and budgets with you. There are no secrets among trusted allies.

You answer each other's questions with vast amounts of valuable (that is, measurable) details. Everyone knows that by sharing information you can select the best solutions. You coach each other on the best way to make sales happen. With patience reserved only for long-term business partners, customers help to fine-tune your proposals until the right needs-solutions-price combinations shake out. They take your advice on how to sell proposals to their organizations, knowing they will receive fair market pricing. You can count on them to return with signed proposals. Surprises or disappointments do not often happen with long-term customers.

You can even measure the value of relationship selling. Review what differential they paid for your relationship when competitors offered similar products. Past surveys suggest somewhere between a 5 percent and 8 percent premium. You will find that the measurable benefits of Column 2 justify a much larger price differential than the 5 to 8 percent that customers are willing to pay for your relationships. Measurable benefits are always worth more financially to your customers than your personal relationship is. The key is to motivate customers to understand both the value of your personal relationship and the value of the measurable benefits you provide. You now have earned a long-term customer.

Furthermore, relationships are a two-way street. At what point do you recommend competitors' products because they provide more value in a given situation? You do so only when customers have measurable benefits that connect to competitors' unique strengths (products only they provide). After all, you would rather lose an opportunity than a customer. Do not worry; when you choose your market segments as outlined in Chapter 3, that occurrence will be rare. After all, the selling methods in this book are not concerned with becoming a referral service for competitors.

In Chapters 2, 3, and 4, you also see the significant benefits of acknowledging to customers where your strengths lie—and where they do not. In return, appreciative customers do not ask you to work up proposals they will not seriously consider. In relationship selling, you and your customer place a strong premium on not wasting each other's time. You will see in these chapters that the value differential between yours and the competitors' measurable benefits—when known—can break down the barriers of mainly personal customer relationships.

Understandably, long-term customers demand and consume a lot of your time. Yet, they are your best customers because they compensate (higher profits) you for the time you invest in solving their problems. They are the basis of the so-called 80/20 rule: 80 percent of your business comes from 20 percent of your (long-term) customers. Just make sure they consume less than 80 percent of your time so you get a fair return on your investment (more on this point in later chapters).

You cherish relationship selling. You probably welcome the day when the repeat business from long-term customers means you never have to make another cold call (other than out of boredom) to exceed quota. However, if relationship selling is the prize, what are the other two stages of selling you must go through to win it? These stages are brinkmanship and courtship selling.

Brinkmanship Selling

Brinkmanship selling occurs with new prospects. It is the most challenging type of selling. You must uncover many unknowns while trying to establish rapport with strangers (not unlike the singles' bar scene). Adding to your difficulty, you have only about fifteen minutes in which to make it happen.

You attempt to discover the prospect's "pain," or at least the prospect's sense of urgency, deadlines, competition, decision makers, and budgets. Your goal is to obtain enough specifics to qualify or disqualify the prospect as quickly as possible. You do not want to waste time presenting products or services that might not satisfy the prospect's purchasing requirements or your pricing levels.

Conversely, prospects also want to determine whether you can help their situation. Therefore, they seek to gather product or company information such as prices, delivery dates, technical specifications, and warranties. The cat-and-mouse game begins. You ask qualifying questions; they ask product questions. You are both careful about how much information you provide each other. You treat selling as a race that you win when you gather information that is beneficial to you faster then you give out information that is detrimental to you. You delay giving out prices until you know their budgets. Prospects delay giving out budgets until they know your prices.

The cat-and-mouse game continues until price or budget amounts surface. You bring each other to the brink. You then see if anyone blinks. The call either continues with some chance of success or someone mercifully ends it.

As is so often the case with first meetings, it is anybody's guess how they will end up. Do you walk away with another meeting, a follow-up call in six months, send more literature, a purchase order, or is it a waste of time? If you decide it is best to wait for the prospect to be fired or quit before you try again, you can safely assume the sales call did not go well.

Courtship Selling

Courtship selling occurs with new buyers who do not yet qualify as long-term customers. It is the most confusing type of selling because you deal with customer schizophrenia. Sometimes these new customers act like long-term customers (and share details)—and sometimes they act like new and fickle prospects (and clam up). Courtship selling is a blend of brinkmanship and relationship selling. Your challenge is to know which selling mode you need to use and when.

Since they just bought something from you, initially you treat them as long-term customers and use relationship selling, exchanging information freely. You stay in this selling mode until you lose a sales opportunity to a competitor. You then shift to brinkmanship selling with all its challenges. Eventually, customers either evolve into long-term customers or regress into prospects again. If you are willing to let another salesperson handle their account, it is safe to say you do not consider them to be potential long-term customers.

Note: A common mistake is to evaluate your selling skills by your successes with long-term customers. Using the relationship selling model, which depends on time, past results, and personal bonds, will not work effectively on new customers and prospects when those factors do not apply.

It Takes Time

Time powers your progression from brinkmanship to courtship to relationship selling. As the time of doing business together with a customer increases, everyone's risk goes down. Conversely, trust levels and the value you provide (through better understanding of the customer's business) and receive (through higher profits) goes up. As you will see, the element of time becomes both a benefit and a liability to your pursuit of relationship selling. (See Exhibit 1-3.)

Exhibit 1-3. It's all about time.

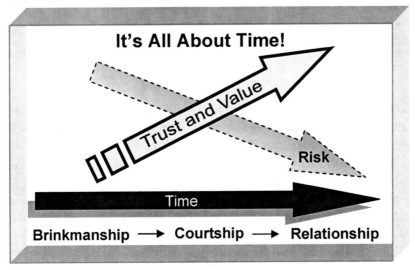

Getting Rid of the Wait

While it is easy to see the benefits of long-term customers and relationship selling, they do have one major drawback: *They are dependent on time.* You must accept that relationships often take years to develop. Fulfill your commitments, do not disappoint your customers, mingle socially, and let nature take its course.

In other words, if you wait long enough, you will have long-term customers that embrace relationship selling. With the selling system in this book, you can short-circuit the time requirements and still have all the benefits of relationship selling. As previously mentioned, it works like a time machine.

You quickly progress from brinkmanship to courtship to relationship selling over the course of several sales calls, not in a matter of months or years. MeasureMax dramatically shrinks the time it takes for prospects and new customers to act like long-term ones. As time speeds up, so does your productivity.

You need fewer sales calls to get more orders because *measurable* information flows freely. Customers benefit too. At an accelerated pace, they also know whether they can receive the value necessary to make working together worthwhile. Together, you both quickly gauge the potential of a business opportunity. You know whether to stay with this sales opportunity or to move on to one with a higher potential for success.

Shrinking Time

The principle behind how MeasureMax shrinks time is simple. It makes the five key components found in every sales opportunity visible and *measurable* to customers and you. When these key components become measurable, trust is not a function of repeated successes over time, but of short-term, quantifiable results. These five components determine whether customers act like new ones or long-term ones. They operate the same way laws of nature, such as gravity or centrifugal force, do. They have measurable effects on the outcome of sales opportunities whether you or your customers are aware of them or not.

The five waiting-to-become-measurable components are as follows:

1. The dollar value the features of your products or services generate by achieving customers' goals (Chapter 2 explains this topic)
2. The dollar value customers gain from achieving specific goals (Chapter 3 explains this topic)
3. The ability of customers to achieve their goals (Chapter 4 explains this topic)
4. The progress customers and you are making in achieving their goals, which tells you whether it is worthwhile to continue investing in the sales opportunity (Chapter 6 explains this topic)
5. Your ability to achieve customers' goals and receive higher profit margins for doing so (Chapter 7 explains this topic)

Note: The fact that the word *goals* appears in every one of them again tells you that this selling system concentrates on making customers' goals measurable. (See Exhibit 1-4.)

When you are *unaware* of these components, they stay invisible. Even if you wait until you win, lose, or abandon sales opportunities, you still might not know what they are. However, you are the only one with the power to make them visible by making them measur-

Exhibit 1-4. Measurability shrinks time.

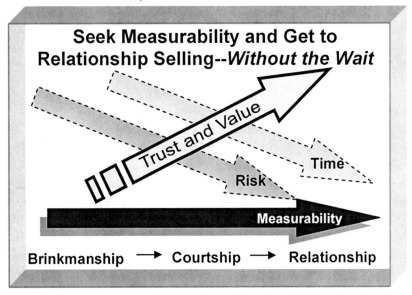

able. Once they become measurable, you are in the relationship-selling mode. You also doom competitors to brinkmanship or courtship selling—even if these opportunities involve their current customers.

Take these two selling scenarios. While slightly exaggerated for effect, they highlight how a salesperson seeking measurable details can go from brinkmanship to relationship selling in one sales call. You probably can put faces and names to both of these scenarios—unfortunately more often on the first than the second, but that will change shortly.

In the first scenario, Carole Nelson, a top-performing salesperson, is on a first call with Pete Sommers, a new prospect. She is in full brinkmanship selling mode, with her focus on obtaining Column 1 details. The second scenario illustrates what would happen if Carole's questions sought measurability and motivated Pete to act like a long-term customer. The difference in Column 2 details that Pete provides Carole jumps out at you, as she is at the height of relationship selling.

Scenario One: New Prospect (Brinkmanship Selling)

Carole is meeting with Pete Sommers for the first time. Although they spoke briefly on the telephone a week ago, Carole is not certain what to expect or how the sales call will turn out. (Her thoughts are in italics and parentheses.)

> **Carole:** Good morning, Mr. Sommers. *(Should I call him Pete? Should I make a comment about the picture of the sailboat on his wall?)* It's nice to meet you.

> **Pete:** Yeah, you too. I tried to contact your office to let you know that a last-minute meeting popped up. Therefore, I only have fifteen minutes, not thirty. So, what can you show me quickly about your products and services?

> **Carole:** Uh, did you get the brochure I sent? It explains our sales-training program, and how it can increase productivity for companies like yours. *(With only fifteen minutes, I better spare the small talk and get right to the point.)*

> **Pete:** I got it, but I didn't get the chance to read it. It's somewhere in this pile. Can you give me a quick rundown?

> **Carole:** Okay. *(I won't hand him a brochure now. The last thing I need is Mr. Pete reading my brochure while I'm talking to him.)* When we spoke last week, you mentioned that you are responsible for the company's sales-training programs. You said something about increasing sales training and productivity, but also decreasing the costs for training each salesperson. Is that right? *(Whew, am I ever glad I practiced my opening line on the drive over.)*

> **Pete:** Exactly.

> **Carole:** Well, in what areas do you see opportunities for cost savings? *(That ought to get Pete talking.)*

> **Pete:** I'm sure there are opportunities everywhere since we have not done a major review of our sales-training programs in more than three years.

> **Carole:** Okay, let me suggest that we focus first on the costs of training new hires. They usually consume the largest portion of a company's training budget and provide the greatest savings opportunities. *(Am I good or what?)*

> **Pete:** New hires are definitely our largest expenditure. So, how does your program reduce the costs of training new hires? By the way, how much does your training program typically cost?

> **Carole:** We reduce training costs by . . . (blah, blah, and blah).

The fun begins as Carole starts reciting countless features and benefits to see which ones (if any) interest Pete. She also slips in some qualifying questions to gather purchasing information. Finally, Carole tries to put off answering the how-much-does-it-cost question until she finds out his budget. Who knows? The sales call might turn out to be a good opportunity rather than a waste of time. It is anybody's guess.

Scenario Two: New Prospect (Relationship Selling)

In this second scenario, Carole gets the opportunity to make the same sales call over again (à la Bill Murray in the movie *Groundhog Day*, in which one day is continually relived until the main character gets it right). Only this time, although Pete Sommers begins the sales call like a typical new prospect, Carole's questions motivate him to act like a long-term customer would and share measurable details.

Carole: Good morning, Mr. Sommers *(Should I call him Pete? Should I make a comment about the picture of the sailboat on his wall?)*. It's nice to meet you.

Pete: Yeah, you too. I tried to contact your office to let you know that a last-minute meeting popped up. Therefore, I only have fifteen minutes, not thirty. So, what can you show me quickly about your products and services?

Carole: When we spoke last week, you mentioned that, as director of learning services, you are responsible for sales-training programs. I understood that your two primary goals are to reduce your training costs and yet increase sales productivity. Are there any others? *(I'm glad I remembered to confirm the customer's position, and then start with his or her goals, not my products.)*

Pete: No, that's it.

Carole: Pete, which of those two is your highest priority? *(Getting Pete to rank them will open the floodgates on details.)*

Pete: Definitely reducing the costs of sales training.

Carole: Why's that? *(Come on, Pete; give me the details.)*

Pete: About a year ago, we noticed that our training costs increased about 10 percent per employee.

Carole: What did that relate to in dollars? *(Keep building on what Pete tells me.)*

Pete: Our expenses rose from $50,000 to about $55,000 per person.

Carole: How many people do you train in a year? *(I need to get to a dollar figure.)*

Pete: We train two hundred new hires a year.

Carole: Wow, that's an additional million dollars in training expenses on top of your $10 million training budget yearly. What are you currently doing to reduce those expenses? *(Well, at least Pete knows that I can multiply; I still need to find out more details before I mention specific products or services.)*

Pete: We're talking about cutting back on the number of people we train.

Carole: How many people are you looking to postpone training for? *(Let me help Pete think through the ramifications.)*

Pete: Approximately 15 percent or thirty people.

Carole: Besides delaying the spending of $1,650,000 in training costs, how will that affect your business from a sales standpoint? *(I need to help Pete realize not only what he can save but also what it costs to delay training to help him justify any purchase. Also, he's a quick learner when it comes to understanding the importance of providing measurable details.)*

Pete: We figure that a trained salesperson produces $100,000 more in profits annually than an untrained one.

Carole: Thirty untrained people could cost your company $3 million in profits. In what other ways are you looking to reduce your training expenses? *(I want Pete to know that I'm listening to him as I seek more details as I build the Column 2 measurable benefits.)*

Pete: We contacted your major competitor, Advanced Training Systems, to give us a proposal.

Carole: When you seek proposals from sales-training companies, in general, what area do you feel is most important for them to highlight? *(No negative sell from me, Pete. I want to make sure my questions seek to understand what you're trying to accomplish—not what competitors have to offer.)*

Pete: A payback that makes sense for us to proceed.

Carole: What does that involve? *(We're getting closer to understanding Pete's measurable expectations.)*

Pete: We want to make sure that we get at least a two-year payback, and don't exceed our budget.

Carole: What dollar amount have you established to reduce your sales-training expenses? *(Funding is always easier to ask about when you can relate it back to their goals.)*

Pete: We've set aside $2 million in our operating budget.

Carole: Who, besides yourself, will be involved in approving this project? *(Thanks for the excellent opportunity to find out about the decision makers.)*

Pete: My boss, Mary Jones, who's the vice president of operations. She can approve it unless it goes over budget, then corporate gets involved. They take six months to a year to do anything.

Carole: Pete, I noticed my fifteen minutes are up. When will be a good time to continue our discussion? *(Let Pete know I respect his time.)*

Pete: I can't believe all the ground we covered. I look forward to continuing our conversation next Thursday at 9 A.M. How does that work for you?

Carole: Sounds great. That will give me enough time to review my notes and prepare for our next meeting. I think there might be a way to cut the costs of your training system without affecting its quality. On Thursday, I think we should concentrate on understanding how you'll know whether you achieve your goal of decreasing sales-training costs. In addition, we need to examine what sort of sales productivity gains in *dollar* terms you are looking to accomplish. In the interim, I'd like to send you an article on methods that directors of learning services use to calculate the costs associated with training programs, and the different ways to measure productivity. How does that sound to you? *(I'm glad I remembered to set the purpose of the meeting so Pete knows exactly what to expect and can be prepared to discuss these items.)*

Pete: It's a good plan. I look forward to seeing you next week.

As Carole leaves the meeting, she cannot help but hear a sound. Only this time it is not the sound of a door closing. Instead, it is the "cha-ching" of a cash register going off in her head as she starts calculating the savings and increased sales she can generate for Pete and his sales force. Not to mention her potential commission check.

Carole still needs to find out more information. However, like Carole, when you use the MeasureMax system, these quantifiable details change the entire feel of your sales calls. They go from having a product focus to having a customer focus (notice that no specific products or services were mentioned). In addition, these details help you to measure the progress and potential of sales opportunities while they are occurring. You know exactly where you left off, and what you must do next to provide more value than competitors and receive higher profits for doing so.

Sales Excellence Requires More Than Educated Guesses

For any activity you have excelled at, it is likely that you have been able to measure your progress in real time. Your progress determines what adjustments you need to make to improve your performance. Think about it: In golf, you keep track of strokes on each hole; with diets, the number of pounds lost per week; with school, your grades on tests; with stocks, your monthly return on investment; and the list goes on and on. Selling is no different if you want to excel at it. You must be able to measure your progress in real time as well.

Note: Most salespeople can explain why they lost sales. Yet, the key to duplicating success is to know why you won sales. Salespeople have a more difficult time explaining wins when they are more a function of persistence and style—or fall under the broad category of *relationships*—than structure, process, and substance.

Most selling methods divide the sales process into the following four basic stages:

1. Establishing rapport
2. Qualifying
3. Presenting/closing
4. Postsale support

You cannot use these stages to measure your progress. They are broad descriptions rather than specific events. Each salesperson determines when one stage ends and the next one begins. With ever-changing starting and ending points, salespeople (and their managers) find it difficult to evaluate the progress and potential of opportunities. For example, if you have two sales opportunities that are both in the qualifying stage, does that mean they are both at the same point with the same potential? Absolutely not!

Furthermore, these four stages can not help you to answer your most important question, which is "How did I do in my sales call?" This question lets you measure your progress and crosses your mind every time you conclude discussions with customers. Typical answers to this question usually consist of two after-the-fact responses and one well-intentioned guess.

- The call went great if you get the order or achieve a predetermined objective.
- The call went lousy if you let the sale slip away to the competition or the black hole of "maybe next year."
- The call went okay for everything other than what was "great" or "lousy."

The first two after-the-fact observations leave nothing to the imagination. You know the final score, and you either celebrate a great victory or learn from a lousy defeat. It is the third reply whose outcome remains in doubt—as does your ability to sell value and increased sales. Everything depends on how your undecided "okays" turn out.

Two conclusions jump out at you. First, your okay answers are really guesses. After all, okays in selling are always followed by a silent "I guess" or "I think." Second, uncertainty about your potential for a successful sale means possible wasted efforts and missed opportunities. (See Exhibit 1-5.)

Ask yourself what method you used to determine your answers. They probably range from personal or professional judgments to instincts or gut feelings to experiences or, simply, educated guesses.

Exhibit 1-5. Prevent wasted effort.

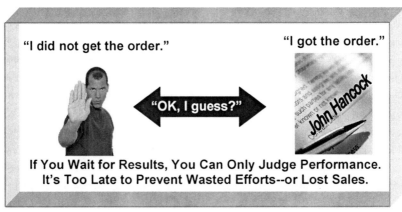

"I did not get the order."   **"I got the order."**

"OK, I guess?"

If You Wait for Results, You Can Only Judge Performance. It's Too Late to Prevent Wasted Efforts--or Lost Sales.

These replies, even though honed by time, remain subjective. They do not provide a measurable way to gauge and influence your progress. The value of these subjective indicators increases greatly if you use them after taking measurable readings, not before.

Note: You and customers share a common goal that helps to improve your productivity. They do not want to waste time either. However, your selling methods, which guide their buying framework, also do not let them measure their progress. Without that ability, customers cannot provide an accurate assessment of the potential for achieving their goals in a cost-effective manner.

Making the Sales Process Measurable

MeasureMax has four selling phases as shown in Exhibit 1-6. Unlike traditional selling stages, these Measurable Phases (MPs) include quantifiable steps that have definitive starting and verifiable ending points, which are referred to as Measurable Phase Changes (MPCs). MPs provide the framework to measure the how:

1. The number of sales calls you make in each MP determines your progress and your ability to be a consistent producer.
2. Their sequence creates the most measurable value for customers.
3. The length of time it takes to complete MPs gauges your efficiency.
4. The sequence of the MPs, as well as the pace needed to complete them, points you toward the most productive strategies to employ.
5. Their corresponding MPCs verify that the customers' pace and progress are in sync with yours.

MPs and MPCs also help you to determine whether the potential for achieving customers' goals is worth spending more time, energy, and resources. These sales mile markers ensure that you do not become lost. You know what steps lay ahead and how to stay on track. Use them to outvalue competition, earn higher profits margins, exceed customers' expectations, and retain long-term customers. Turn your "okay" guesses into measurable answers to determine whether "great" or "lousy" endings await you and your customers—so you both know whether to bail out sooner or hang in longer.

Exhibit 1-6. The four selling phases of MeasureMax.

MP 1: Spark Interest

MPC 1: Interest Confirmed

MP 1 Purpose:
Customers confirm an
interest in achieving
goals.

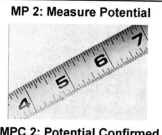

MP 2: Measure Potential

MPC 2: Potential Confirmed

MP 2 Purpose:
Customers confirm they
have the ability to achieve
goals.

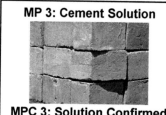

MP 3: Cement Solution

MPC 3: Solution Confirmed

MP 3 Purpose:
Customers confirm solutions
achieve their goals.

MP 4: Implement Agreement

MPC 4: Agreement Confirmed

MP 4 Purpose:
Customers agree to
achieve goals via your
solutions.

"Decommoditize" the Sale

The *C* word (as in *commoditize*) is a salesperson's greatest fear and failure. Customers consider your products or services to be a *commodity*. Customers see no measurable difference between your features and benefits and those of competitors. Although convinced they provided the most value, salespeople realize that the lowest price will win. Let the bidding wars begin.

Why didn't the most value win? In the minds of the customers, it did. They think lowest price equals the highest value. When salespeople do not give customers the means to measure value in terms other than price, they turn their products and services into commodities, not customers. That's good news.

What one takes away, one can give back. Armed with the proper tools and knowledge of the MeasureMax selling system, you can decommoditize sales. Just make sure to contact customers who want Column 2 filled out (if given the opportunity).

Note: When customers' technical knowledge of your products is equal to, or better than yours, they view your products as commodities. They feel they can accurately compare products without your input. They no longer depend on you to explain the technical differences between competitive offerings. You now lost a key opportunity to justify a higher price than that of your competitors. Fortunately, you can recapture this opportunity and lost value (and then some) when you make customers rely on you as an expert in their industry as outlined in Chapter 3.

Column 2 Selling

To fill in Column 2 with measurable benefits, you must contact individuals who do not equate price and delivery with value: *owners* and *beneficiaries.* The people who "own" the budgets that fund purchases are owners. The people who derive the most value or benefits from these purchases are beneficiaries. Owners reside at the top of the decision-making chain. When you sell to owners, you engage in top-down selling. You have the ability to negotiate price as a function of value.

In consumer or retail sales, top-down selling is easy. Consumers are the owners. In business-to-business selling, many more people are involved in purchasing decisions. Although the process is the same, finding the owners is difficult if you do not know where to look for them in organizations. Additionally, owners speak a language foreign and uncomfortable to most salespeople. Instead of speaking features and benefits, they use words associated with executive perspectives and economic value. Terms like *return on investment, corporate goals, net present value, company initiatives,* and *positive cash flow* pepper their vocabulary. Chapter 3 demonstrates how to find owners and speak their language.

Once you find out owners' goals and understand how they measure value, you can help them to fill out Column 2. In addition, you ask owners what role the beneficiaries play in the decision-making process. Often, salespeople make beneficiaries more important than the owners. Let the owners decide who is important. After all, it is their money.

Most salespeople prefer to contact beneficiaries first and engage in bottom-up selling. Beneficiaries understand the technical nuances of products better than owners do. They like to talk about features and benefits. They are the perfect matches for salespeople who are trained to talk technical and conduct product presentations. Yet, in between lengthy product discussions, sales problems can surface—ones that only meetings with owners can solve.

Problems arise when beneficiaries' goals and purchasing requirements differ from those of owners. The larger the differences, the greater the potential is for wasting your time, efforts, and resources on dead-end sales opportunities. Although you might be dealing with unknowns, beneficiaries have proven they know how to get purchase orders signed. Therefore, you gamble that they have the authority or influence to get more purchase orders signed.

You depend on them to either arrange for you to meet with owners or have them sell inaccessible owners on your proposals. Bottom-up selling works well in established relationships; however, it loses much of its effectiveness with new prospects or customers that do not have proven track records. Where you start the sales process is often where you end up. Always strive to start with owners.

While relying solely on beneficiaries possesses its share of challenges, it also has its fair share of rewards. It becomes harder to make that comment about the individuals found in Column 1 opportunities.

Column 1 Selling

Customers find it easy to fill in Column 1, because all they need to do is the following:

- View competitive products as commodities with equal product features and benefits.
- Receive proposals from at least two suppliers.
- Compare price and delivery differences between suppliers.
- Decide if these differences are large enough to warrant switching to a new supplier (overcome the value of an existing relationship) or proceed with the purchase (overcome the cost of changing products or services).

The people most likely to make buying decisions along these lines are purchasing agents or managers. Sometimes, to help them make purchases, companies hire third-party intermediaries such as contracting firms, engineering firms, architectural firms, and management firms. Like purchasing personnel, intermediaries rely on the bid system. It equates lowest prices or fastest delivery schedules to best buys. It concentrates on Column 1, almost completely ignoring Column 2. Therefore, intermediaries invite as many competitors as possible to bid. When it comes to driving prices down, they know the more the merrier.

Yet, bids still attract salespeople to them like mosquitoes to a bug zapper—often with the same results. Zap! Understandably, it is hard to pass up opportunities when you know customers are going to buy something from someone. Why not you? Yet, bids can become tremendous time robbers. All you need to do is look at bid documents to understand why.

Bid documents are at the heart of the bid process. They contain specifications that describe technical or operational features or capabilities your products must meet. Some are so specific that they are difficult to satisfy—for example, quarter-inch stainless steel, twenty widgets per minute, twenty-four-hour response time, and 200 horsepower. Others are so broad that it is almost impossible for you not to satisfy them. Terms such as "established credentials," "improve operations significantly," and "enhance performance," mean whatever anyone wants them to mean.

You mix these two extremes in one package and you have a lot of room for interpretations and disappointments. Yet, bid documents have a more fundamental flaw. They focus on product features (Column 1 details), not owners' measurable goals (Column 2 details). Without defined goals, it is difficult to determine whether any product meets owners' expectations. Everyone is trying to hit moving targets. Therefore, a catch-all goal surfaces in the bid process. Intermediaries award sales to companies that supply what is considered to be "the most value." Translation: Quick and cheap products win bids. Without measurable goals, everyone's products and services look the same.

However, even in a bid process, preferred salespeople exist. Intermediaries give them the inside track to help them win bids. Favored salespeople insert their products' unique strengths into the bid specifications and documents. The goal is to use their benefits to outweigh competitors' lower prices or faster deliveries. However, specifications tailored to your unique strengths can be a curse as well as a blessing for two reasons. First, you must count on competitors adhering to the bid specifications describing your unique strengths. If they choose to ignore them, ironic situations result.

Let's say you coauthored bid documents to end up as the only salesperson who can meet the specifications. This compliance raises your costs and lowers your price competitiveness. For instance, if you are the only one to supply titanium-tipped pens while competitors supply ballpoints, you are the only one adding costs to your bid. Without fear of penalties, competitors can win by simply ignoring specifications they cannot satisfy—the same way you would.

Therefore, you always want to find out what penalties, if any, competitors receive for noncompliance. In weak-enforcement bids, let competitors influence the specifications and be obligated to abide by them. Let them comment on the ironies of losing bids built around their unique strengths that you ignored.

Second, to keep unique strength specifications from becoming a negative, you must connect them to measurable goals to produce value. Otherwise, they look transparent and superficial. In bids where goals are vague, you cannot match them up. They appear to serve no purpose other than as artificial barriers to competition. This can hurt both your credibility and that of intermediaries.

Sharp-witted competitors will show owners where these so-called unique strengths only add costs, not benefits. Therefore, if comparisons between bids do not reward your unique strengths, they erode your competitiveness. They become unique weaknesses. For the most part, the bid process discounts the value of unique strengths.

Even if awarded the bid, you invest a great deal of time, effort, resources, and profits defending services or justifying costs. Thus, profit margins suffer. Still, it is not a bad outcome considering the alternative of losing the sale. However, no sale is a complete victory without compensation for the value of your unique strengths.

Change the Rules

The bid process distorts the sequence of the Measurable Phases along with your ability to sell value. With price being the main consideration, bids skip MP 1: Spark Interest and MP 2: Measure Potential, and instead begin the bidding process in the third phase, MP 3: Cement Solution. With bids, hard-fought, low-profit orders go to the last competitor willing to offer or match the lowest price. Everyone strives to be in a position to get the last shot at the order. Most important, if owners' goals do not consist of lowest prices or quickest deliveries, bids do them a great disservice. Many salespeople choose to play the bidding game, and take the risks that they will receive their fair share. Whenever possible, do not play along.

Act as if owners do not exist, and you play the price game. If you think owners desire no contact and do not influence purchasing decisions, you contend with bids. At least, until someone—make sure that someone is you—boldly asks if he or she really believes the following:

- Strong-ego executives abdicate 100 percent of their decision-making authority to third-party intermediaries.
- Owners buy products and services for the sole purpose of seeing how cheaply they can get them.

Of course not! They want to achieve specific goals that are cost effective but not necessarily in the cheapest manner possible. In fact, every sales opportunity—even bids—involves owners or beneficiaries wanting to discuss the best ways to measure and achieve goals. Great selling involves tapping into those discussions. Owners welcome discussions with professional salespeople who explain how to make their goals measurable. Do not disappoint them by making product pitches on the first call. If that is all you have to offer owners, the bid system works just fine.

Selling Measurable Value Is Habit Forming

Whatever sales techniques you employ become habit forming. The approaches you use out of habit in every sales opportunity become your overall mindset. If you mostly try to sell bid jobs, you tend to think that way. When you observe every opportunity through bid-tinted glasses, measurements of success will focus more on price differences than on value differences.

A great sale occurs when only one dollar separates your winning bid from the next lowest competitor's price. In bid lingo, you "left nothing on the table." You also received no compensation for providing a better table. In a bid-minded world, a Mercedes could be considered equivalent to a Yugo, and then judged only on price. So much for your opportunity to sell compensated value.

Nevertheless, one must wonder why companies with the fastest deliveries and lowest prices lose orders. Someone knows how to help customers select goals and measure value. Someone knows how to offer solutions whose value does not depend solely on lowest prices or fastest deliveries. Someone knows how to show customers that his or her solutions achieve their goals measurably better than do those of competitors. Someone knows that allocating selling time for maximum results requires thinking of Column 2 sales as the meat and potatoes with Column 1 sales as the gravy—not the other way around. Someone knows how to help customers fill out the measurable benefits of Column 2. The selling system outlined in this book will ensure that someone is you.

No Magic Wand

There is nothing magical about asking whether it makes sense for customers to conduct business with you and vice versa. When customers say yes to solutions that meet or exceed measurable expectations, it comes from logic not magic. The idea is to make a conscious decision not to waste anyone's time, efforts, or resources (especially your own). When you use a selling system like Measure-Max in your sales opportunities, you make that conscious decision.

SUMMARY

- Use measurability to influence performance, not judge results.
- Strategy determines structure and tactics, not vice versa; use a strategy to make customers' goals measurable so you can outvalue competitors, and receive compensation for doing so.
- Avoid wanting to accomplish something for customers more than they want to achieve it for themselves.
- You can only manage what you can measure.
- The salesperson with the most long-term customers wins.
- Relationship selling and long-term (and loyal) customers go hand-in-hand.
- You use brinkmanship and courtship selling with prospects and new customers, respectively.
- Time powers the progression from brinkmanship to courtship to relationship selling.
- Long-term customers and relationship selling do not need to depend on time.
- Introduce measurability into the sales process and you shrink time; prospects and new customers respond like long-term ones on the first sales call.
- You can make measurable the dollar value of features and goals, the ability of you and your customers to achieve their goals, and your sales progress.
- Measurable Phase Changes (MPCs) are like a road map of where you started, how far you have gone, how fast you travel, and how much farther you need to go to reach a sale. MPCs enable you to evaluate performance in a measurable manner so you influence and calculate chances for success.

- The four Measurable Phases (MPs) and associated Measurable Phase Changes (MPCs) are:

  MP 1: Spark Interest and MPC 1: Interest Confirmed

  MP 2: Measure Potential and MPC 2: Potential Confirmed

  MP 3: Cement Solution and MPC 3: Solution Confirmed

  MP 4: Implement Agreement and MPC 4: Agreement Confirmed

- Every sales opportunity has two columns that customers use to weigh their purchasing decisions. In Column 1, customers always assign the dollar value of price, delivery, relationship, and cost of change. In Column 2, which always starts out empty, only the salesperson can help customers assign dollar value to the measurable benefits of achieving their goals.

- Productivity jumps when you concentrate more on Column 2 sales situations than on Column 1, which can waste selling investments of time, effort, resources, and profits.

- Every sale involves an owner or beneficiaries with goals other than lowest price or fastest delivery.

- The customer's measurable goals must be clear before salespeople present solutions.

Chapter Two

Defining Value

If you do not define the Column 2 value your products or services generate, the easiest yardsticks for customers to use are Column 1's lowest prices or quickest deliveries. This chapter encourages you to think like your marketing managers and competitors by explaining:

- How features produce either benefits or liabilities
- How benefits create value for customers and for their customers
- How perceived and measurable value works for or against you
- How unique strengths build bridges to higher profits and barriers to competition
- How packaging and options help or hinder your selling efforts
- How Product Profile sheets highlight the strengths of your products for quick referencing

Features

You probably learned from basic sales courses that features, the attributes or key traits of products, produce benefits. However, saying what a feature does is not the same as defining it. This oversight probably explains why most salespeople view features and benefits as being interchangeable. They are not—and understanding how they differ helps you to better define value for customers.

In selling, the words you choose to communicate the value you provide are critical to your success. Because of the key role played by features and benefits, you must pay particular attention to the words you assign to them. Grammatically speaking, there is another way to distinguish features from benefits. Features are described with an adjective followed by a noun, such as *stainless steel* or *bullet-proof vests.*

The table in Exhibit 2-1 highlights two features of a high-tech cellular phone and a low-tech bottle of barbecue sauce. Try to limit features to two or three words for clarity and brevity, so they do not become narratives that confuse customers.

Exhibit 2-1. Column 1 vs. Column 2 values.

Cellular Phone Features (Adjective-Noun)	Attribute/Image
Digital Signal	State-of-the-Art
Hands-Free Operation	Safety Conscious

Barbecue Sauce Features (Adjective-Noun)	Attribute/Image
Hickory Flavor	Outdoorsy
Fat-Free Ingredients	Low-Fat

Basic selling courses also forget to point out that features can produce liabilities when they do not achieve customers' goals. This omission turned legions of salespeople into *features creatures.* You earn this designation when you think the sales pitch with the most features wins. To make matters worse, the more features you mention that do not achieve customers' goals, the more you dilute features and benefits that do.

In addition, these diluting features make customers become more conscious of price. No one likes paying for unnecessary features. A customer's price sensitivity becomes further aggravated when you explain how two dozen unwanted features are "free" because they come standard on your product. When customers feel they paid something for nothing, your prospects for repeat business become bleaker.

Example

You are shopping for a CD player for your car that can hold and play ten compact discs (your goal). You go into an audio equipment store and tell the salesperson you are interested in a ten-play CD player. The salesperson is a world-class feature creature on automatic pilot. He rambles on about how a particular ten-play unit offers random play, sequence order, and mix-and-match features.

Finally, about ten unwanted features later, he tells you the price is $500. You tell him: "Thanks anyway, but it's not exactly what I want. Five hundred dollars is a lot of money for a car unit." Especially one with a million gizmos you will never use. Off you go to the next store in your quest for the "perfect ten" unit.

Again, you state your interest in a ten-play CD unit (goal). This time the salesperson is not a feature creature. She explains only how the features of a particular model are designed specifically for ten-play. She focuses on how its *interchangeable cartridges* (feature) will also fit your home model, how easy they are to change, how they reduce handling wear and tear. She also highlights why a *ten-CD cartridge* (feature) has a higher resale value than units with five CD cartridges. The salesperson then tells you it costs $600. You say, "It's exactly what I want, I'll take it."

You go home and start thumbing through the operating manual. You find yourself saying, "Wow, it has this gizmo too," as you read about its peripheral features. The difference is that after the sale, secondary features build value; before the sale, they dilute value.

Note: Regardless of whether you sell a tangible product or an intangible service, both have features. Therefore, for the sake of brevity, the terms *products* and *services* will be used interchangeably throughout the book. For example, you could just as easily read the Product Profile sheet as a service profile sheet.

Describe Features Clearly

When you highlight features to customers, specific descriptions are better than general ones. The more specifically that you can describe features, the harder it is for competitors to claim they offer the same ones. Describe your features in a manner that clearly differentiates them from those of competitors. One of the most common challenges salespeople face is describing technical differences to nontechnical buyers. (Chapter 7 explains this concept in detail.)

Example

A stereo salesperson states that a certain model provides "great sound." The me-too competitors claim that they also provide great sound. General features make it difficult for customers to make objective comparisons between competitors making the same claims.

A better description for great sound would be "undistorted sound up to 200 decibels." However, you must ensure that the customer knows what a decibel is and in what range he or she listens to and appreciates (that is, places value on) undistorted sound. These technical details make it harder for competitors to mimic or customers to discount without a solid basis.

Benefits

Benefits are the value customers derive from features that achieve their goal(s). A benefit's value results from saving customers' time and money (ultimately, time translates into money too). Benefits are described with a verb or adverb followed by a noun or noun phrase such as *increases efficiency* or *reduces downtime*. Like features, limit benefits to five words or less to ensure clarity and to make them sound powerful and vivid.

Benefits produce two types of value: *perceived value* and *measurable value*. The former is fleeting; the latter is permanent.

Perceived Value

Customers use subjective evaluations like emotions, prejudices, preferences, and experiences to assign value to benefits. Benefits with perceived value are hard to prove or disprove.

Example

Does the Rocky Mountain flavor of Coors Light taste better than the Missouri Valley flavor of Budweiser? It depends on your individual preference. Therefore, taste is perceived value.

Note: Although subjective, benefits with perceived value can have perceived dollar amounts attached to them. For example, the "better" taste of one beer might be worth a dollar more of perceived value per six-pack than another beer.

Measurable Value

Customers use objective data to assign value to benefits. When benefits have measurable value, they require more efforts to calculate their worth. Yet, once calculated, the benefits of measurable value are easy to prove—and to sell.

Example

Does a bottle of Coors Light have fewer calories than a bottle of Budweiser? Absolutely. You can look up the calories on the labels and calculate that Coors Light has forty fewer calories.

The tables in Exhibit 2-2 and Exhibit 2-3 illustrate how benefits and value type apply to the cellular phone and the bottle of hickory-flavored barbecue sauce.

Note: When you use measurable value, make sure you can explain (if asked) how the feature technically achieves the benefit. For example, the digital signal extends talk time between recharges because it consumes less power to process voice transmission than does an analog signal.

Note: The same features can produce benefits with perceived and measurable value.

Exhibit 2-2. Features, benefits, and value type.

Cellular Phone Features (Adjective-Noun)	Benefits (Verb-Noun)	Value Type (Measurable or Perceived)
Digital Signal	Improves reception	Perceived value
	Increases battery life	Measurable value
	Extends talk time between recharges	Measurable value
Hands-Free Operation	Increases safety	Perceived value

Exhibit 2-3. Features, benefits, and value type.

Sauce Features (Adjective-Noun)	Benefits (Verb-Noun)	Value Type (Measurable or Perceived)
Hickory Flavor	Improves taste	Perceived value
	Eliminates costs of wood chips	Measurable value
	Eliminates time and expense of grilling	Measurable value
Fat-Free Ingredients	Reduces grams of fat intake	Measurable value

Advantages of Selling Perceived Value

When you sell benefits with perceived value, you do not need to prove the logical connection between the features and the benefits. The benefits might be what you say they are; you just cannot prove them. Conversely, customers and competitors cannot disprove them. It is your word against theirs.

Due to a high trust level, your long-term customers are more receptive to accept benefits with perceived value on face value than are new prospects and competitors. Therefore, use as many benefits with measurable value as possible when you sell to new prospects who cannot fully appreciate your trustworthiness yet.

Example

Does pouring hickory-flavored sauce on fried chicken produce as tasty a meal as does barbecuing the chicken with wood chips? Kentucky Fried Chicken claims it does and taste tests prove it (according to KFC).

Disadvantages of Selling Perceived Value

1. You damage your credibility if independent documentation casts doubts on your perceived value claims. In addition, when one claim gets disproved, all your claims come under scrutiny.

Example

A salesperson supplies an industry report proving his company's digital reception is 10 percent clearer than competitors who claimed their analog signal was just as good. Now, the competitors' other claims, such as extended battery life, are suspect as well.

2. Customers who eventually buy on perceived value change their minds often. You never know how their latest emotional attachments or personal preferences affect their purchasing decisions. Perceived value has no concrete proof, so conflicting claims create confusion. When enough confusion exists, customers use the certainty of lowest price or fastest delivery dates to clear it up. A take-them-to-lunch-and-lower-your-price strategy often surfaces in these situations as products become commodities.

Example

Another salesperson claims (without proof) that his new type of cellular phone offers the best reception but costs less. Customers try to figure out how companies can all offer the so-called best service. Price wars—and lunches—are right around the corner.

3. While you can (and do) win sales on perceived value, it is difficult to be compensated for providing more value than competitors—even if you do. You end up as being forced to match the lower price of a competitor who you know provides less value. Unfortunately, if you can't measure the difference, your customers can't either.

Note: The more you depend on selling perceived value, the more you must rely on your personal relationship with the customer. Conversely, the more you depend on selling measurable value, the less you need to rely on personal relationships. A double win is to have a strong personal relationship and measurable value.

Advantages of Selling Measurable Value

The value of measurable benefits is difficult to dispute or discount by customers and competitors alike.

Example

A salesperson explains how a digital signal (feature) requires 20 percent less power than an analog signal for processing. Therefore, its battery lasts 20 percent longer than the one in an analog phone. How this feature produces benefits is not only logical but also measurable to the customers. Grateful for the facts, they take the salesperson out to lunch.

You use industry standards or reports by independent experts to support the validity of your measurable benefits. You also use them to refute competitors' benefits that depend on perceived value. You demonstrate to customers your knowledge of the industry.

Example

A salesperson furnishes a Federal Trade Commission (FTC) report that highlights how a digital signal uses 20 percent less power than an analog signal. This report supports his battery life benefit. It also refutes counterclaims by analog telephone competitors that there is no difference between the battery life of analog and digital telephones.

Disadvantages of Selling Measurable Value

You must prove that your standards of measurement are valid. An erroneous "fact" jeopardizes your valid claims. When you sell on measurable value, ensure that your information is infallible. You should have two independent and measurable verifications in case one becomes suspect.

Example

The salesperson uses an outdated FTC report. He now needs another recognized authority (not counting his marketing manager) to substantiate the "20 percent less power" benefit.

You contend with conflicting claims that have their own proof. You constantly test your technical expertise when you sell measurable value. You must be sufficiently knowledgeable to prove your benefits while disproving competitors' counterclaims.

Example

A salesperson hands out an industry report that shows average customers do not recharge their analog telephones more than digital telephone users. The digital telephone salesperson must now offer proof to refute this report's claims.

Calculating the Value of Benefits

Benefits with both measurable and perceived value can produce either cost avoidance or dollar savings. You calculate the dollar value using indirect and direct savings. The former is more long-term and subjective, while the latter is more short-term and objective.

Indirect Savings

Indirect savings, such as that afforded by maintenance or insurance programs, has perceived value. Customers assign value to their benefits according to the negative events they avoid. The following two factors influence the value of indirect savings:

1. The probability these negative events will occur
2. The financial ramifications if they do occur

Note: As the probability and dollar ramifications increase, it is more likely that customers will place value on indirect savings.

Example

Doing an oil change every 3,000 miles supposedly makes your car engine last longer. Its value is hard to prove in dollars. If you never had engine problems, you might believe that a $20 oil change saves you a $2,000 engine rebuild. Additionally, as you put on more mileage (greater probability), the more valuable the oil change becomes.

Direct Savings

Direct savings have measurable value. You assign value to benefits without depending on cost-avoidance calculations. Customers measure the value of direct savings immediately.

Example

You buy a new car that uses regular gas instead of premium. Regular gas costs ten cents less a gallon. You calculate your cost savings instantly by taking the number of gallons and multiplying them by ten cents.

Note: Unless you are always the low-price supplier, you do not want the only direct savings to be Column 1's price difference between you and competitors.

It Matters Who Receives the Benefits

Benefits produce internal and/or external value to customers. The focus of these benefits plays a major role in how much value customers place on them. Additionally, whether benefits are internal or external determines what departments and positions you contact first.

Internal Benefits

Internal benefits produce value only for the *purchasers* of your products. They appeal more to departments with low customer contact such as accounting, purchasing, engineering, or manufacturing. Often, these departments are more concerned about Column 1 issues than Column 2 issues.

Example

You sell paint wholesale to painting contractors. One of the features of your paint is two-hour drying time. Painters can apply a second coat sooner, thereby reducing the time it takes to complete a job. They receive the internal benefits of reduced labor costs.

External Benefits

External benefits occur only when you sell to businesses, not consumers. They produce value for your customers' customers. External benefits appeal more to departments with high customer contact such as customer service, marketing, and sales. Often, these departments are more concerned about Column 2 issues than Column 1 issues.

Example

Painters use the quicker drying time of your paint to give homeowners faster completion dates. The quicker drying time produces an external benefit—faster completion dates—to the painters' customers: the homeowners.

Internal and External Benefits

As the name subtly implies, both your customers and their customers receive benefits. This combination produces the most value because everyone benefits (including you).

Example

The painting contractors pass along some of their cost savings to homeowners as lower prices. Everyone wins because painters increase their competitiveness and profitability, homeowners receive better prices and quicker completion dates, and you sell more paint.

The last column on the right in the table in Exhibit 2-4 demonstrates this concept for the cellular phone and the bottle of barbecue sauce.

Exhibit 2-4. Know the focus of the value.

Cellular Phone Features (Adjective-Noun)	Benefits (Verb-Noun or Adverb-noun)	Value Type (Measurable or Perceived)	Focus: Internal, External, or Both
Digital Signal	Improves reception	Perceived value	Both: you can reach customers more easily and for longer periods (I) Customers can reach you more easily and for longer periods (E)
	Increases battery life	Measurable value	Both: same as above
	Extends talk time between recharges	Measurable value	Both: same as above
Hands-Free Operation	Increases safety	Perceived value	Internal (external to other drivers)

Sauce Features (Adjective-Noun)	Benefits (Verb-Noun or Adverb-Noun)	Value Type	Focus
Hickory Flavor	Improves taste	Perceived Value	Internal
	Eliminates the costs of wood chips	Measurable Value	Internal
	Eliminates the time and expense of grilling	Measurable Value	Internal
Fat-Free Ingredients	Reduces the intake of fat grams	Measurable Value	Internal

Which Value Should You Use When Selling?

If you can prove your products are technically superior, sell on measurable value and direct savings to offset low-priced competitors. If your products are not technically superior but cost less than competitors, sell on perceived value and indirect savings to offset higher-value competitors. In the final analysis, your *unique strengths* determine whether you sell on perceived or measurable value.

Unique Strengths (Let the Big Dogs Eat)

Unique strengths are features of products that only your company offers. Use them to identify sales opportunities where you can out-value the competition. If competitors invest a lot of selling efforts with customers whose goals connect to your unique strengths, you will still receive the orders. Competitors' only short-term defense against your unique strengths is to lower their prices to the point at which price becomes the customer's only consideration.

Fortunately, no company can afford to lose money on every sale. Even not-the-sharpest-knife-in-the-drawer competitors eventually get smart and start looking for other places to sell. Fighting losing battles with you gets old quick. Unfortunately, competitors also have unique strengths—and the sword cuts both ways. You need to know your competitors' unique strengths and how to counterbalance or avoid them. (You will learn techniques for doing this in subsequent chapters.)

Note: Even if customers show your proposal containing unique strengths to existing suppliers, they will only enhance the value of your offer. Competitors will take a double hit: They will be forced to acknowledge that your measurable benefits are real and that they can't achieve them.

Deciding Whether a Feature Is a Unique Strength

Some companies think that if they are the only ones to provide specific features, they have unique strengths. They encourage sales-people to discuss these unique strengths on every sales call. You soon discover these so-called unique strengths turn out to be unique weaknesses. They become diluting features that add no measurable value, only costs to your products. The following four questions can help you to determine what constitutes a unique strength:

1. Do your customers consider it unique (not just your engineering or marketing departments)?
2. Does it achieve well-recognized customer goals?
3. Does it produce *measurable* value and direct savings in terms of money?
4. Does it build barriers to competition that force competitors to use measurable value (if they can) rather than perceived value?

Note: Even a single "no" answer disqualifies a feature as a unique strength. It can still create value and help you make a sale; it is just not a unique strength. In addition, like regular features, unique strengths only create value if they achieve the customer's goals.

Example

Apple Computer has less than 10 percent of the personal computer (PC) market, while Microsoft Windows has 90 percent worldwide. Apple Computer's unique strength is an easier-to-use operating system that works fantastically with graphics programs. Microsoft's unique strength is that it supports ten times more business software programs.

Therefore, Apple concentrates on customers whose goals are graphics creativity and ease of use—customers who do not need numerous business programs. Its ease-of-use operating system dominates the educational (nonbusiness) market, while its graphics superiority dominates the publishing world.

Ten times more business software does not matter to customers with nonbusiness applications. Apple's success results from knowing which customers place the most value on their unique strengths; and which ones do not.

What If Your Product Doesn't Have Any Unique Strengths?

Some products do not have any unique strengths. Customers view them as commodities, and price and speed of delivery become the main purchasing considerations. You offset this situation by accentuating the unique strengths of your company. These can be warranty policies, quality-assurance programs, turnaround times, stocking levels, number of distribution centers, ease of ordering, payment terms, size, number of documented successes or geographical locations. Again, apply the same litmus test to a company's unique strengths as you do to those of products. Think of a company's unique strengths as universal features that come standard on every proposal as long as they connect to customers' goals.

You can also win sales by making your sales approach a unique strength. When competitors use sales methods that depend on perceived value, it is difficult for them to connect their features to customers' goals. With your measurable value approach, customers can see how your features (even regular ones) achieve their goals quantifiably better than competitors.

The Power of Packaging Products Together

You probably sell your products mainly on an individual basis. Yet, if you group different products together and sell them as a single entity, you create "new" products. You usually do not need engineering or manufacturing to help you create them, just marketing. The major advantage of packaging is that you transform products without unique strengths into products with unique strengths.

Example

Home Depot sells assorted toolboxes and tools on an individual basis. Occasionally, they package selected tools with a toolbox as a new Handyman special product. The tool and toolbox selection will vary with the level of expertise of the targeted customer (weekend warrior or professional). The price of the package is less than if you purchased the tools and toolbox separately.

Home Depot made a competitive product with unique strengths out of commodity items.

How Product Options Affect Your Selling Efforts

Options are product accessories. They are the features offered to customers in the format of: "Would you be interested in . . . ?" If you need to ask your customers about options, it might indicate that many purchasing requirements remain unknown to you. If you fully understood their goals, you would not have to ask customers if this option or that one interests them. You would already know. You especially do not want to guess whether your unique strength makes sense for customers.

Of course, options benefit you when they are merely a matter of a customer's personal preferences, such as whether to order the telephone's leather case in brown or black.

Note: If you are not careful, a major pitfall with options lurks ahead. You might end up with the syndrome of "one from Column A, two from Column B." You spend all your time explaining to customers why one feature or product from "Column A" costs this much while two from "Column B" cost this much. Your product's value becomes how individual features stack up against each other or those of competitors. How your features achieve customers' goals gets lost in the shuffle. You can even end up competing with yourself, never a good situation.

Feature Value Rating

Fundamental to the principle of "you can only manage what you can measure," you assign features a numerical value. To represent their significant difference in value, unique strengths get a 5; regular features receive a 1. In Chapter 7's Connecting Value sheet, you select the features that produce the measurable benefits of customers' goals, and then calculate their value rating. You compare this rating to a value-neutral rating, which would mean all the features were a 1 because your products had no unique strengths that connect to customers' measurable benefits.

For example, if you selected five features that matched a customer's goal, their competitive neutral rating would be a 5 (5 × 1). If two features were unique strengths, and three were not, you multiply the two unique strengths by 5 and the three features by 1 for a total value rating of 13 (5 × 2 + 3 × 1). Your value rating would be 8 more than value neutral (13 − 5). What is the significance of this number?

A lot when you tie it into the gross margins (sell price minus material and labor costs) of your proposals. In future sales, you use past results to determine if you are receiving the margins you deserve for the value (numerical score of your proposals) you are providing. Use these ratings to *measure* the value your proposals produce for customers, how they compare numerically to competitors' proposals, and their relationships to historical gross profit margins.

For example, a value rating of 12 might coincide with a 40 percent gross margin while a rating of 8 might coincide with a 30 percent gross margin. If your proposals with similar value ratings have significantly lower gross margins, you are not receiving compensation for the value provided. You need to find out why not.

You can also assign a competitive value rating by filling out a Competitor Product Profile sheet. You only fill in competitors' unique strengths because all their other features would be the same as yours. You then compare the number of unique strengths you have with those of competitors that match up to customers' goals. This connection is critical to outvaluing competitors. For example, if you have two unique strengths while a competitor has only one, your competitive value rating would be plus 5 over theirs.

Analogies

Take the strongest feature or unique strength your product possesses and develop an analogy for it. Analogies are especially useful when selling technical products to nontechnical customers. You want to use everyday parallels to which your customer can relate (more on this topic in Chapter 7 also).

Example

You sell expensive collectors' watches. The strongest feature is their high resale value. You tell a customer to think of a collector's watch as not only a precision instrument and work of art but also an investment, like a mutual fund.

The worth of the watch increases the longer you own it—historically at a rate of 11 percent annually. You point out that this return is better than that of any savings account. Everyone can relate to the benefits of investing in a mutual fund, even one that tells time.

The Product Profile Sheet

The Product Profile sheet analyzes your products in terms of the concepts discussed in this chapter, such as:

- *Features.* List the key features of your product that add value to it. The more specific the description, the harder it is for competitors or customers to redefine them to your detriment.
- *Benefits.* Express them in terms of time or money savings. Express a benefit as a verb followed by a noun.
- *Value Type.* Decide whether the benefits are perceived or measurable.
- *Focus.* Determine if the benefits have an internal or external focus or both.
- *Unique Strengths.* Review the summary on unique strengths before you classify a feature as such.
- *Value Rating.* Assign a 1 for a feature everyone possesses, and a 5 for a unique strength only your company has.
- *Analogies.* What everyday event parallels your highest-value unique strength or strongest feature?

Use this data to decide which market segments your products best serve. You develop a Product Profile sheet for each product. A Competitor Product Profile sheet should also be filled out for each product. (Microsoft Word templates for the sales tools shown in Exhibit 2-5 and Exhibit 2-6 can also be found as downloadable files on www.measuremax.com.)

The example in Exhibit 2-5 shows how you record the Talk Free and Clear service package on a Product Profile sheet. The Market Profile sheet in Exhibit 2-6 on page 64 illustrates how a salesperson, Steven Smartsell, working for a fictitious company called Future-Tech, fills one out. The company provides high-tech products and services to computer manufacturers. (Subsequent chapters will fol-

Exhibit 2-5. Product profile sheet example.

Product: **Talk Free and Clear** Calling Program					
Features	**Benefit**	**Value Type**	**Focus:** Internal, External, or Both	**Unique Strengths**	**Value Rating**
Digital Signal	Improves reception	Perceived	**Both:** you can reach customers more easily **(I).** Customers can reach you more easily **(E).**	Yes	5
	Increases battery life	Measurable	**Both:** same as above	Yes	5
	Extends talk time between recharges	Measurable	**Both:** same as above	Yes	5
Hands-Free Operation	Increases safety	Perceived Value	Internal (external to other drivers)	No	1
Free Weekend Minutes	Reduces weekend costs	Measurable	Internal	No	1
Analogy: The difference in reception between digital and analog is like using a satellite dish to get your TV picture versus a set of rabbit ears antennae.					

low Steven's sales efforts throughout the process of using the selling system described in this book.)

It Only Takes One

It only takes one feature and benefit to make a customer to say yes. It just needs to be the one that achieves his or her top goals. Avoid reciting *diluting features* that diminish your products' value to customers. Always ask yourself first, "Does this feature help the customer achieve his or her goals?" If you answer "no," do not mention it unless the customer asks you to discuss it.

SUMMARY

- Features produce *potential* benefits before they connect to customers' goals, actual ones after they connect.
- Features that do not relate to customers' goals dilute your sales presentation and diminish your product's value.
- Specific descriptions of features make it difficult for customers or competitors to redefine them to your detriment.

Exhibit 2-6. Product profile sheet example.

Products/Services: Predicto Services, ProdoGain, and CodeCheck						
Products/ Service	Feature	Benefit	Value Type	Focus	Unique Strengths	Value Rating
Predicto Services	Variance Alerts	Prevents Unscheduled Breakdowns	Perceived Value	Both. It ensures uninterrupted shipments to their customers (E) and saves money from lost production (I).	Yes	5
	Tolerance Checks					
Analogy for *Variance Alerts*: It is like the low-fuel warning in your car. You look for a gas station before you run out of fuel.						
ProdoGain	Single-Operator Controls	Eliminates Need For Two Operators	Measurable Value	Internal	Yes	5
ProdoGain	200-Unit Capacity	Increases Capacity By 15%	Measurable Value	Internal (more revenue) and External (more available stock to their customers)	No	1
ProdoGain	5-Year Warranty	Eliminates Repair Costs	Measurable Value	Internal	No	1
Analogy for *single-operator controls*: It is like flying your own private plane; you do not need a copilot to help you get where you are going.						
The CodeCheck Program	Computerized Program	Analyzes Operations for Potential Violations	Perceived Value	Internal	Yes	5
Analogy for *Computerized Program*: It is like using a geopositional satellite to navigate you through a gigantic legal maze. It tells you how to stay on track, and how to get back if you get lost.						

- Internal benefits provide value to your customers; external benefits provide value to your customers' customers. When you have both types in a sale, you generate the most value.
- Value is either measurable or perceived, but the key to value is whether the customers accept its worth.
- Perceived value has no proof.
- Measurable value has proof and shows your expertise in the customers' industry.
- Indirect savings use cost-avoidance calculations and perceived value; direct savings use measurable value.

- Products without unique strengths are commodities that will be chosen based on Column 1's lowest price and fastest delivery—or Column 2's measurable benefits.
- When you know your unique strengths and those of competitors, you choose sales opportunities that give the best returns.
- Selling to customers that place the highest value on your unique strengths is the catalyst to success.
- Unique strengths must be considered unique by customers, not only by your company; produce measurable value and generate direct savings as cost justifications; and use measurable value to create barriers to competition.
- Packaging enables you to combine unique strengths of various products to form "new" products. It also helps you to create new products with unique strengths from products that did not have them separately.
- If you fully understood customers' goals, you would not need to ask them whether a particular option interests them.
- Use analogies so that customers can relate to your unique strengths through everyday experiences.
- Product Profile sheets analyze your products so that you can evaluate their strengths.
- Competitor Profile sheets analyze your competitors' products so that you can evaluate their strengths and weaknesses.

Chapter Three

Receiving Value

You and customers need only one thing in common to make sales happen: You both must be able to achieve their goals. When you help customers to achieve goals that produce expected value for them, you complete half your mission. You complete the other half when customers compensate you for providing that value.

This chapter crystallizes how customers think about receiving value by explaining:

- How the differences between needs and goals affect value
- How goals choose customers
- How customers assign value to goals
- How customers make their goals measurable
- How Market Profile sheets highlight the ways your products help customers achieve their goals and receive value

Note: Terms such as *suspects* or *prospects* are not used to describe potential buyers, only the word *customers*. Everyone is somebody's customer, and the only question is: "Does it make sense for him or her to be yours?"

Needs

It may sound like an exercise in splitting hairs. What is the big difference whether you use the word *goals* or *needs*? The answer is "plenty" when value-driven sales are at stake. It is more than just a question of semantics when you focus on goals and not needs. Goals motivate you to think first like customers; needs encourage you to think mostly like, well, products. It is the difference between you selling features or customers buying value. Goals and needs are not interchangeable terms or concepts.

In selling, these terms are diametrically opposed. As a point of interest, in the top-selling book of synonyms (talk about great vacation reading), *The Synonym Finder,* the word *goal* is not listed as a synonym for *needs* and vice versa. This probably explains why no one ever refers to *needs-satisfaction selling* as *goals-satisfaction selling.* You cannot help but think of needs-satisfaction as being a submissive mindset. Are you really in sales to satisfy needs the way Barbara Eden did in the TV show *I Dream of Jeannie* ("Your wish is my command, Master")? The answer is an emphatic no. Again, you are in sales to exceed customers' expectations and to receive higher profits for doing so.

According to *Funk & Wagnalls* dictionary, the word *need* means "to have urgent or essential use for [something lacking]." This definition implies that customers are urgently aware that something needs fixing. Because most people are urgently aware of pain, it is easy to understand why most sales methods equate needs with pain. For salespeople, the words *needs* and *pain* are interchangeable.

Therefore, a popular sales strategy is to ask customers, "What hurts or keeps you up at night?" in order to uncover their pain and then focus on remedying it. This strategy works on a simple principle: The greater the pain, the greater the urgency, and the bigger the sales opportunity. When you focus on pain, the logic behind the ease of selling water hoses to people with houses on fire is beyond dispute. Yet, not every customer's house is on fire; and you do not always have water hoses to sell. When you focus on needs, avoidable problems arise.

These problems arise because needs are very specific. Customers think they have a good idea of what they "need" to remedy their pain. Again, people with houses on fire know they need a water hose. Customers with evident pain make sure you—along with every other competitor they can remember—have ample opportunity to satisfy their needs. They need delivery dates and prices to compare so that they can find the cheapest prices and the fastest deliveries. You are now in a reactive, not a proactive selling mode. You are responding to specific and out-of-the-blue requests. It is difficult to build value when specific requests force you to join the crowd that competes on price and delivery.

These requests can be excellent sales opportunities if you have the exact products customers think they need. If they match, you just won the "needs lottery." Lady Luck is smiling on you. You might want to walk home and look for lost wallets along the way. More than likely, your products are not exactly what they had in mind. You end up trying to convince customers you have better products than the ones they and competitors are proposing. The features start flying, and besides finding yourself in the middle of bidding wars, another problem surfaces.

A narrow focus on needs also weakens one of your greatest strengths. You limit your expertise as a problem solver. When in an emergency or urgent pain, customers do not consider all the alternatives you could recommend out of experience. Their purchasing decisions revolve solely around quickest delivery dates. At this point, all products look like commodities; another reason why they want more than one supplier bidding on the sale. Understandably, customers discount long-term benefits when they focus on short-term emergencies.

Another difficult selling situation arises during emergencies even when customers are choosing your products. When you think better remedies exist, you gently try to "unsell" customers on their current (and deficient) product choices. However, you are careful to point out that if these new products you suggest do not interest them, you will gladly furnish them with a quote on their requests. With that vote of confidence, it is not surprising that you encounter resistance.

When you reach the point at which you might be jeopardizing your sale, understandably you stop. You resign yourself to a strategy based on thinking that "I tried. Now it's time to give customers what they think they need." No one wants to lose a sale. However, you are taking a big risk if the customer's poor selections do not fulfill his or her unclear goals. You might incur the blame, unless you think most customers blame themselves when the products they insisted on buying do not help them the way they thought.

Example

Janice Edwards, a manufacturing manager, has an old piece of production equipment and wants to make sure that if it breaks she has spare parts on-site. She calls the manufacturer and tells the salesperson, Robert Finley, she needs a redundant motor and gear set in case of breakdowns. Robert, with his customers' best interests at heart, wants to make sure Janice does not waste money on obsolete equipment. He knows that his newest machinery product line has 40 percent more production capability than her current unit. He can easily justify the price differences to her between a new, state-of-the-art machine and these two spare parts. A new machine will pay for itself in less than eighteen months.

Robert feels he knows exactly what Janice needs—a new piece of equipment. He starts to explain to Janice the significant difference in production output between the new models and her obsolete one. Janice tells Robert all she needs right now is a proposal for these components. She will talk about buying a new machine when things slow down. Though everyone's intentions are good, everybody loses. Janice misses an opportunity to spend her money more efficiently; Robert misses an opportunity to sell Janice a better solution. What went wrong?

Everyone equated needs with products. Janice felt she *needed* spare parts, Robert felt he *needed* to supply new equipment. He tried to sell his product on the payback resulting from improving production capabilities by 40 percent.

A more effective way to approach this sales situation would be to use the following steps:

1. Robert focuses first on Janice's goal of preventing breakdowns, rather than on the production differences between her machine and a new one.

2. He asks her how she feels a spare motor and gear set will help her prevent breakdowns.

3. Taking into consideration her answers, he explains how features of the new equipment help prevent breakdowns measurably better—that is, new diagnostics warn of impending problems before they occur so that the customer can take corrective actions, typically saving two hours of downtime.

4. Once Janice agrees that these are benefits, Robert can point out the additional financial benefits to be gained by increas-

ing production capabilities. (Remember the ten-play CD example from Chapter 2?) Secondary features and benefits increase value only *after* customers achieve their primary goals.

When you focus on needs, another problem arises. You miss sales opportunities because even people who are not in pain can have their lives improved—and there are more healthy people than sick people. Customers with no obvious pain often feel there are no opportunities to improve their situation. Salespeople who are pain magnets miss these opportunities to unleash hidden value.

These sentiments often arise when customers are unaware of new technological advances. For instance, think of the first time customers using carbon paper were introduced to copier machines. Talk about the goal of improving productivity in ways yet unknown. A more recent example is wireless technology. The majority of Internet customers are satisfied (no pain) communicating via telephone connections. They might not know how wireless products without the need for phone connections might help them improve their communications.

Finally, when you sell to needs, you give customers more credit than they deserve or want. While customers are always right about where they want to end up (goals); they are not always right on the best way to get there (products). This is where you excel. When you make sure customers always evaluate products in terms of achieving their goals, you reduce the potential for disappointments.

Goals

A goal (again according to *Funk & Wagnalls* dictionary) is "something toward which effort or movement is directed—an end or objective." Customers' goals always involve either achieving a positive result or avoiding a negative one. One of your primary sales responsibilities is to motivate customers to understand their goals. Making goals measurable provides customers with that motivation. Goals become the standards against which customers judge your products. As you will see later in this chapter, you make the goals customers want to achieve work in your favor. You let logic and measurable proof run their predictable course.

Know Customers' Goals Even If They Don't

Fortunately, most customers do not know what goals they want to achieve. They do not even think in terms of goals; they think in terms of needs. After all, they have mainly been exposed to sales methods that focus on needs, or pain. Yet, your *best* opportunities arise when customers do not know their goals. Soon they will— thanks to you. As an industry expert, know what your customers' goals should be in case they do not. Everyone wins (except competitors) when you help customers to set quantifiable and attainable goals that accurately reflect their priorities and connect to your unique strengths.

When you ask customers what goals they are trying to achieve, be prepared for blank looks as well as wonderment and appreciation. They will respond, "Gee, I have never been asked that question before." Needs-focused customers and product-focused salespeople do not discuss goals. This lack of goal discussions is to your advantage. Then, they will ask *you,* "What exactly do you mean by goals?" You must be able to answer their questions by knowing the typical goals of their industry. You will now have positioned yourself as a customer expert. You will have separated yourself from the typical product-packing salespeople. Caution: The rally killer of a sales call is two "What do you mean?" questions in a row. If the customer asks you, "What do you mean?" after you ask what his or her goals are, you can't answer, "What do you mean, what do I mean?" Make sure you know typical industry goals (the Market Profile sheet at the end of this chapter will ensure that you do).

Note: The University of North Carolina's Kenan-Flagler Business School conducted a survey of chief executives and senior management. They were asked what they considered to be the most important reason for meeting with a salesperson. More than 70 percent of them responded that a salesperson's knowledge of their industry and company would be the major reason why they would agree to an appointment. Knowing their goals makes you that salesperson.

Therefore, your initial emphasis in sales opportunities is to help customers define their goals. When you help customers set goals, you do not need to wait for them to have an obvious pain to act upon. You act as a catalyst to motivate customers to pursue and achieve measurable goals. You are in control of your own sales destiny when you act (as opposed to when you react).

Note: When a customer doesn't have clear-cut goals, ask what one thing would make his or her company more competitive. Know the competitors of your customers' strengths and weaknesses and you become a valuable asset to them.

One Big Product Reason to Focus on Goals, Not Needs

Often, customers will request a specific feature that your product does not possess. When you question customers on why they need that feature, it is difficult for them not to question your motive. After all, if you cannot provide the feature, it is in your best interests to discourage them from wanting it. Customers find it hard to view you as an objective participant. However, that perspective changes when you know the customers goals—and question them on how that feature helps them achieve their goals.

For instance, a customer says he wants framing material that consists of half-inch-thick titanium. He knows that you only provide quarter-inch-thick framing material. If you question him on why he needs a half-inch and not a quarter-inch thickness, suspicions may arise that you are placing your own interests (keeping the sale alive) over his interests. However, if you know his goal is to prevent rusting, you could then ask him how he thinks half-inch-thick titanium helps him prevent rust. Once you know the answer, you can determine whether the size difference achieves his goal, or just ends up adding costs as a diluting feature.

General Categories of Customer Goals

For examples of general corporate categories and specific customer goals, see Exhibit 3-1. (To create more categories and goals that are specific to your business, you can download Market Profile templates from www.measuremax.com.)

From Vendor to Supplier to Partner

When you focus on customers' needs, you are a vendor. Like a vending machine, you display your products and wait for custom-

Exhibit 3-1. Examples of general corporate categories and specific customer goals.

Broad Goal Categories	Specific Customer Goals
▪ Administrative	▪ Maximize organizational resources ▪ Ensure compliance with laws and codes ▪ Ensure longevity of organization
▪ Customer Service	▪ Improve customer satisfaction ▪ Improve corporate image
▪ Finances	▪ Improve cash flow ▪ Increase return on investment (ROI) ▪ Improve shareholder value ▪ Increase profits
▪ Competitiveness	▪ Increase market share ▪ Develop new products and services ▪ Maximize engineering, manufacturing, marketing, and selling resources ▪ Open up new markets ▪ Manage growth and change
▪ Operations	▪ Improve reliability ▪ Increase efficiency and productivity ▪ Improve work environment ▪ Reduce operating expenses ▪ Increase safety

ers to buy from you. You leave it up to customers with a commodity mentality to choose which goodie they want most. The customers' purchasing decisions are driven by availability of product and price. It is difficult to sell value as a vendor.

When you are a supplier, you concentrate on helping middle-management customers to achieve short-term, measurable goals with the products you supply. Short-term goals usually involve issues that have an immediate effect on only their department, such as improving operations or reducing administrative expenses. You have moved ahead of vendors on the value chain. You also have the opportunity to be compensated for the value your products generate. However, as customers better understand their short-term goals, it becomes easier for them to start picking their products. You now risk becoming a vendor again.

When you help senior-management customers to achieve their long-term business goals, you become a partner. These goals center on Column 2 measurable benefits, such as improving market share, increasing stock price, and reducing employee turnover. You then help customers recognize how your products help them to achieve short-term goals that are consistent with their long-term objectives. Now the Column 1 value of your relationship and the cost of change become greater barriers to customers who consider competitors to be mere vendors and suppliers.

Market Segments and Customers' Goals

When you understand the concept of *market segments*, you understand the goals that customers want to achieve. Market segments are groups of customers with similar goals that respond to the same offers in the same ways. Their goals are predictable. When you can predict their goals, you can duplicate your sales successes. The market segments sharing goals that your unique strengths or strongest features can achieve are your best sales opportunities. They place the highest value on your greatest strengths. How far you segment a market depends on the point at which customers' goals match up to the unique strengths of your products and your company.

Example

Salesperson Judy Wright sells laundry services to hospitals, but not just any hospitals. She knows that large hospitals and publicly funded hospitals do not make good prospects.

The former have their own laundry facilities when they have more than three hundred beds, while the latter always bid out laundry services solely on lowest prices. She realizes that *hospitals* are not a market segment because they have many varying factors. Instead, she classifies *private hospitals with fewer than three hundred beds* as a high-opportunity market segment.

The more specific the market classification, the better the chances that your target market segments respond to the same offer, the same way. Obviously, do not classify market segments to the point where their size is minuscule (niche markets) unless your profit margins on those sales are huge.

The concept of market segments further highlights the differences between goals and needs (pain). Businesses set up their organizational structure to concentrate on different market segments. Almost any company these days has groups of employees who cater to specific groups of customers with similar goals. It would not make sense for this type of structure to exist if customers bought primarily for subjective or emotional reasons (pain, needs).

Organizational Characteristics Affect Customers' Goals

Even taking into account styles, attitudes, and personalities, customers' goals are not as arbitrary as one would imagine. Two factors influence what goals customers seek and the market segments they belong to: the characteristics of their organizations and their positions. Using these two factors helps you to suggest goals that customers can relate to when you initially contact them. Your knowledge of their goals helps to solidify your status as a customer expert.

Note: Sources of information can range from Google on the Internet, www.ceo.com, annual reports, company homepages, *Wall Street Journal* Interactive, local newspapers, tradeshows, industry publications, other departments in the company, other noncompeting salespeople who sell to the same account, and so forth. Siebel ebusiness has an excellent booklet, called "Information Sources Handouts," which provides numerous ways to gather data.

In addition, a company's sales brochures tell you how it is trying to sell value or position its offerings. How a company sells value is often how it measures value. For example, if the company sells reliability to its customers, it is going to seek solutions that improve reliability for them. (For example, FedEx guarantees delivery to its customers and looks for business partners that sell solutions that do the same). Also, try to obtain the sales literature of the company's competitors to see whether you can offer solutions that help it to offset its competitors' strengths or exploit their weaknesses.

Organizational characteristics are the primary attributes that influence the way companies view themselves. They are the undisputed traits customers readily identify about themselves. These traits help establish the goals customers want to achieve. Here are a few examples:

- *The product or service the company is selling.* Does the company sell a mass-produced product or does it focus on niches? The primary goal of many car manufacturers is to *standardize components*. Their huge economies of scale motivate them to have as many models as possible share common components, which keeps their inventory and design costs down. If you sell products that standardize components, you know they "should" interest car manufacturers.

Note: The word *should* emphasizes that you start with customers' *potential* goals. Chapter 4 examines the nine circumstances of a sales opportunity that determine the customers' *actual* goals, as well as their ability (and yours) to achieve them.

- *The degree of contact that occurs between the company's employees and its customers.* Is the company isolated from the end users of its product or does it have daily contact? One of a credit card company's main goals is to *improve customer services*. Its daily contact with customers means its fortunes directly tie into how well it excels at customer service. If you sell products that *improve customer services*, you know they should interest credit card companies.

- *The operating profile of the organization.* Does the company operate on an eight-hour day, five days a week or around the clock? A main goal of a convenience store that operates on a twenty-four/seven basis is to *improve security*. If you sell products that *improve security*, you know they should interest around-the-clock convenience stores.

- *The human and dollar costs of interrupted service.* Is the company's operation of a critical nature or low urgency? One of a hospital's main goals is to *minimize downtime*. Lives are at stake if the electrical or mechanical system fails. If you sell products that *minimize downtime*, you know they should interest hospitals.

- *The image the company is cultivating.* Is it high technology or low technology? Is the company viewed as a leader or a follower? One of a sporting goods company's main goals is to maintain a *youthful and healthy image*. If you sell products that project a *youthful and healthy image*, you know they should interest sporting goods companies.

- *The company's business climate.* Is it in a high-profit, fast-growing industry or a low-profit, declining business? One of a cutting-edge computer company's goals is *managing growth and change*. If you sell products dedicated to *managing growth and change*, you know they should interest computer companies.

- *The company's tolerance for risk.* Is it willing to take chances or avoid risks? One of an insurance company's goals is to *improve safety*. If you sell products that *improve employee or policyholder safety*, you know they should interest insurance companies.

If this section is beginning to sound repetitive, that is good. The repetition of the phrase will help you to commit it to memory. By now, you are probably saying to yourself, "If companies have these organizational characteristics, then they have these goals. If those goals match up to my unique strengths, then I want to contact them. When I mention their goals, they should show interest." You have got it.

Note: Your list of market segments and organizational characteristics can vary and might be quite long, depending on your industry. Again, use your unique strengths and strongest features to determine the characteristics of the market segments that produce the customers' goals that you should focus in on.

How Your Contact's Position Affects His or Her Goals

The position of the person who is your contact at a company further narrows the goals he or she wants to achieve. The roles and responsibilities of a position determine individual goals. The director of purchasing has different goals (and sometimes conflicting ones) from those of the vice president of operations or the engineering manager. The head of finance has different goals from those of the director of maintenance or human resources or vice president of sales.

In addition, your contacts' positions also determine how their performance is measured (which helps determines their goals). For example, if a vice president of operations receives his performance review (or bonus) based on reducing downtime by 10 percent, that will be his goal.

Note: If you can't through questioning uncover the customer's goals or the person isn't sure what you mean, ask how his or her performance is measured.

The following examples demonstrate how people's positions, combined with the characteristics of their organizations, further predict their goals:

- Is a vice president of a national sales force interested in sharing customer purchasing information better?
- Is the vice president of finance for a credit card company interested in improving cash flow?
- Is the director of manufacturing interested in improving on-time deliveries?

You bet they are! Your sales go up as your ability to understand customers' goals improves. Discussions about goals provide a great starting place for your sales calls. Customers appreciate that you are focusing on their destinations (goals), not yours (products).

Note: In sales situations involving more than one decision maker in various positions, divide your written proposal into *areas of interest* sections for quick referencing. These sections reflect their different areas of expertise and their separate goals. You might need to make different types of presentations within the same organization depending on the positions of those in your audiences.

How Customers Assign Value to Their Goals

You help customers to figure out their goals. Next, you want to help customers calculate the dollar value they receive from achieving these goals. The computing tools you use in this endeavor are Systems of Evaluation (SOEs). You find out their numerical details in MP 2: Measure Potential. As you will see, more sales are won or lost at the SOE level than at the product level.

Note: SOEs or often referred to as key performance indicators (KPIs). However, SOEs focus more on calculating measurable value than do KPIs, henceforth their difference.

Example

A customer wants to purchase a new piece of manufacturing equipment to improve reliability (goal). If the salesperson of the product with the best-documented performance persuades the customer to use the SOE of *mean time between failures* to calculate reliability, he will win the sale.

Yet, if the salesperson of the product with the best predictive diagnostics convinces the customer to use the SOE of *warning time before failures occur* to calculate reliability, she will win the sale. The key lies in which SOE produces the most measurable value in dollars.

The number one requirement of SOEs is that they must accurately reflect the attainment of customers' goals. For examples, see Exhibit 3-2.

Exhibit 3-2. SOEs must reflect the attainment of c'

Customers' Goals	Systems of Evaluation to Assign Value	⌐
Minimize initial cash outlay	Initial purchase prices	Dᴗ. competᴎᴗ.
Reduce life-cycle costs	Total cost of ownership	Dollar amounts ot ᴗᵣ maintenance, and repair ᴗᴗ
Increase reliability	Number of hours lost to downtime	Number of annual downtime hours and the cost per hour

Note: Besides knowing their goals, you can often determine which SOEs customers use to calculate value by reviewing their Web sites or sales literature. The SOEs they use to sell value to their customers are the same ones they will use to measure value. For example, a computer manufacturer stresses reliability and an SOE such as "lowest defect rate per million parts" to their customers. If you show how your products improve reliability via the same SOE that the company uses, it will respond positively. Your sales approach becomes a unique strength when you help customers to identify valid SOEs that competitors have no experience with.

Systems of evaluations have two tremendous benefits that you use to outvalue the competition and earn compensation for doing so. First, they provide customers with the means to convert perceived value into measurable value. Each SOE adds a measurable benefit row and dollar amount in Column 2. If you have four SOEs, you have four rows of dollar amounts that add to your total measurable benefits. Each additional SOE helps to offset the actual and perceived dollar value of the four Column 1 items.

Second, you use SOEs that favor your unique strengths to dominate a marketplace. While either benefit is acceptable, having both is overpowering as illustrated by the following real-life example.

Example

Ray Kroc and McDonald's made billions selling what many considered to be the ultimate commodity, hamburgers. Kroc used SOEs to make the perceived value of customers' goals such as good taste, consistency, high food quality, and cleanliness of facilities all measurable. Case in point: McDonald's measured taste and consistency using identical ingredients, weights, standardized cooking methods, and uniform packaging. You knew McDonald's made its hamburgers measurably more consistent than did mom-and-pop burger joints. No surprises as to what a hamburger looked and tasted like at McDonald's.

Kroc used these SOEs to turn a so-called commodity into a product with unique strengths. He dominated the marketplace by establishing SOEs that favored McDonald's unique strengths. He highlighted the unique point-by-point checklists McDonald's used to ensure cleanliness as a unique strength of the company's.

He forced other burger joints and fast-food restaurants to compete on terms that matched up to his unique strengths. No surprise who won. The competition's only immediate defense was lowering its prices. This tactic probably explains why most independent hamburger joints went out of business. You cannot continue to use lower prices as a marketing tool without eventually losing money and diminishing quality.

Yet, systems of evaluation vary sharply in how customers calculate value. They include methods stressing lowest prices to ones emphasizing highest returns on investments. Exhibit 3-3 shows the different systems of evaluation customers use to calculate the value of diamonds.

As the McDonald's example demonstrates, SOEs put either you

Exhibit 3-3. SOEs calculate value differently.

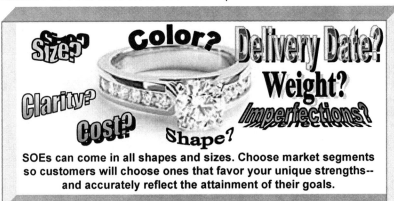

SOEs can come in all shapes and sizes. Choose market segments so customers will choose ones that favor your unique strengths-- and accurately reflect the attainment of their goals.

or competitors at advantages or disadvantages depending on whose unique strengths best match up to them. When customers use SOEs that bind their goals to your unique strengths, you outvalue competitors to win sales. You dominate the marketplace. The opposite is also true, which again reinforces the need for you to know which SOEs favor whose unique strengths.

How to Calculate the Value of SOEs

To know the customers' SOEs is one thing, to calculate their value in dollars is another. Your goal is to provide the formulas to use for the calculations and let customers plug in their numbers. If they don't know these plug-in numbers find out who does, or as an industry expert, use industry averages (if acceptable to the customer). Exhibit 3-4 illustrates this concept.

Note: When customers use systems of evaluation beyond their technical expertise, it usually indicates that an outside consultant is helping them select one. In addition, to find out which SOEs favor your unique strengths best, ask your highest-value customers what measurable benefits they received from the goals you helped them achieve and how they calculated their SOEs.

Example

Michelle Ross sells a product costing more than that of her competitors (sound familiar?) Yet, her unique strengths produce two-year paybacks. Her lower-priced competitor's product has a four-year payback. She knows that with customers who favor the goal of *largest savings* versus *lowest up-front costs*, she wins the sale.

Michelle must prove to customers that achieving the former goal over the latter provides more value to them—if they use the SOE of *total dollars saved over a four-year period*.

Note: Customers without any SOEs are tough to sell value to. Subjective or emotional factors found in Column 1 and their simplest calculations, price or delivery, become their primary SOEs for calculating value.

Exhibit 3-4. Everyday examples of SOEs.

Systems of Evaluation	Typical Customer Calculations and Formulas Used to Measure Value (in Dollar Ramifications)	Typical Unique Strengths They Favor
1. Return on investment (ROI)	Net profit divided by invested capital	Highest performance track record
2. Payback	Total savings divided by total investment	Quickest recoup of initial investment
3. Initial costs	Total purchase price	Lowest prices
4. Life-cycle costs (costs of ownership)	Total purchase price plus add in all lifetime operating costs (operating, training, parts, maintenance, repairs, utility, upgrading, etc.)	Lowest product-life operating costs
5. On-time delivery percentage	The percent of missed deliveries multiplied by the cost for a missed delivery (return costs, lost or delayed revenues, penalty costs for missed deadlines, etc.)	Computerized scheduling
6. Number of distribution centers	The percent of missed deliveries multiplied by the cost for a missed delivery (return costs, lost revenues, penalty costs for missed deadlines, interrupted production costs, etc.)	Worldwide parts depots
7. Percent of in-stock merchandise	The percent of unfulfilled orders multiplied by the cost for a lost order (average order size, lost revenue, interest charges, costs of inventory, etc.)	Highest order fulfillment rate

(continues)

Exhibit 3-4. (Continued.)

8. Costs of changes (switching out suppliers or products)	Total costs in new training, parts inventory, equipment, etc.	Highest flexibility
9. Number of product lines	Total dollar benefits of different goals customers want to achieve addressed by various solutions from the same vendor (such as transaction costs and economies of scale)	Broadest selections
10. Hours of downtime	Number of downtime hours multiplied by the average hourly cost (labor, administrative, lost revenue, etc.)	Quickest response times
11. Percent of on-time project completion dates	The bonus or penalty incurred for each day ahead/behind schedule	Comprehensive project management
12. Total profit impact	Total savings or costs reduction achieved	Highest documented savings
13. Market share impact	Profit or revenue calculations for each point increase/decrease in market share	Most competitive products
14. Cost of doing nothing	Total dollar value of unrealized benefits	Existing supplier or status quo if savings aren't measurable; the most dollar savings if they are.

The Cost of Doing Nothing

One of the most common systems of evaluation that customers use is the *cost of doing nothing*. As shown in the list in Exhibit 3-4, this SOE favors existing suppliers or status quo. The cost-of-doing-nothing SOE becomes more prevalent during economic downturns. The most effective way to overcome this SOE is to substitute one that calculates the measurable benefits from achieving suggested goals on a per diem basis. Use SOEs to help customers measure the dollar difference between what they are doing now and the goal they want to achieve. When customers realize what potential savings or revenue they are losing daily it increases their sense of urgency.

For example, your products can reduce customers' operating expenses by $300,000 annually. Instead of focusing on this annual savings amount, point out to customers that every day they lose the opportunity to save $822. Demonstrating that time is money is a powerful way to overcome the cost of doing nothing that favors existing suppliers. You might also want to point out to customers how much products and/or services their companies must sell to generate $300,000 worth of savings—if a company has a 10 percent profit margin, they must sell $3,000,000 to equal savings of $300,000.

Making Goals Measurable

With apologies to the movie *Field of Dreams*, if you help customers measure their goals, they will come. Customers and you both want to know whether customers are getting the most value possible. When you build value from their goals down, not from your features up, everyone does know. To ensure repeat business, ensure that customers achieve their goals every time they do business with you. If you always start with their goals, not your products, you will reduce the chances of unfulfilled expectations. The first time they do not achieve their goals you will remember the following sales adage: "Competitors do not win over your customers; you unwillingly lose them due to unfulfilled expectations."

Yet, if you do not make customers' goals measurable, you risk losing them. Ironically, you usually find out how customers measure the value of their goals after you lose a sale or disappoint a customer. A statement such as, "I thought you were looking for it to do this, not that," indicates you were measuring their goals differently than they were.

You also risk having customers who cannot tell that you provided more value than competitors—so they will not compensate you for doing so. Finally, without measurable goals, it is hard to guess how customers who purchased your products will judge the merit of them. You want your customers to look back on any purchase they made from you and be able to measure how it achieved their goals. When this occurs, your sales approach helps you build barriers to competition and have long-term relationships with both individual contacts and their organizations. Sales success is a simple formula: make your Column 2 professional bonds with organizations as strong as your Column 1 personal ones with individual contacts to create long-term customers. Measurable and documented goals that you helped an organization to achieve become your "value-tether" to it even if your contact leaves and is replaced by someone who favors competitors.

You make goals measurable by making the customer's benefits measurable. The benefits of goals are similar to the benefits of features. Customers assign them value by the measurable value they produce. You convert their benefits into time or money also. You know this occurs if the word *by* appears in your benefit statement followed somewhere down the line by a dollar amount. A "by" will usually turn into a "buy."

Example

"Reduce costs *by* $32,000" (measurable benefit) or "increase production capabilities *by* 18 percent to generate seventy thousand (measurable benefits) more widgets weekly." You still need to know how much each widget generates in profit or sales dollars. Therefore, convert time or percentages to dollars too.

Note: Goals without measurable benefits to new prospects are like hearsay to a jury; goals with measurable benefits are like evidence. Measurable benefits turned verbal references dependent on one customer knowing another into powerful documented dollar savings ones that only depend on the facts.

If you or customers leave out the measurable benefits of goals, they attract look-alike competitors. For instance, if customers are looking to *improve efficiency*, me-too competitors will claim that they too can improve efficiency. The only way to differentiate customers' goals is through their measurable benefits. One way to make the goal of improving efficiency measurable is to add the phrase "by reducing $100,000 of redundant production costs" to it. Now, me-too competitors must compete against this benefit's measurable benchmark of $100,000 worth of savings. (See Exhibit 3-5.)

Note: When you have products and services that provide measurable dollar savings, you are able to broaden the goals you can help customers achieve.

Example

Mark James sells the outsourcing of services to colleges and universities. Outsourcing is a service where a company hires and manages the labor force to perform jobs such as janitorial, engineering, housekeeping, and food services more cost effectively than the existing work force (although, they will often hire many of the existing employees). This company has a proven track record of reducing an institution's labor costs by hundreds of thousands of dollars.

Mark calls Dr. Roberta Brown, the president of a university, and finds out that she wants to upgrade the campus computers over the next three years. Mark tells her that he can help her to achieve that goal.

How? If Mark can save the university money on its facility services, that money can go toward the upgrading of computers. By

Exhibit 3-5. Use SOEs to make customer's goals measurable.

SOEs make the benefits of customers' broad goals measurable in financial terms to calculate the value of achieving them.

converting goals into measurable dollar benefits, Mark will be able to show Roberta how an outsourcing company helps her to upgrade computers. Think of how many new opportunities you can create when you sell measurable value.

Customers Who Equate Needs with Goals

You also deal with customers who have only specific needs and products in mind. A customer might think she is satisfying her specific needs and that buying those specific products are her goals. They are not. You know the type. "Just give me a price on what I need and I will call you if you get the job." This person is the boss and that is that. You need a lot of willpower not to throw out a price and duck—and wish her (and you) luck.

Resist the temptation. You do not want to react to her specific product requests without either of you knowing her measurable goals. The risks of unfulfilled expectations run high. What do you do?

With diplomacy, you stick to helping the customer to define her goals. Once defined, customers do not become defensive if you ask them to review how their proposed product choices achieve those goals. Leave your product recommendations out of these discussions; it is too self-serving and you lose credibility. You want the customer—on her own—to come to the same conclusion you have: *She is making the wrong purchasing decisions and her goals will prove it.*

When a customer compares her specific product needs against measurable goals, she comes to one of two conclusions. She either proves herself right and proceeds as planned or she starts looking at different alternatives. If you are in market segments where customers' goals match up to your unique strengths, they look at your alternatives. You now have a powerful force on your side; no one knowingly makes bad decisions, not even customers who prefer competitors.

Example

Harry, an extremely technical customer, walks into a computer store. True to form, he starts blurting out abbreviations such BIOS,

SDRAM, LDAP, and the like. He needs to buy a math coprocessor, a 120-MB RAM video card, and sophisticated multimedia software to upgrade his computer. The initial urge of Joan, the salesperson, is to say, "How many do you want?"

Instead, Joan wants to build long-term business relationships and repeat business. She helps her customers achieve their goals on a consistent basis. Therefore, the question she asks is: "What are you trying to accomplish with these components?" Harry cannot help but feel that Joan has his best interests (goals) at heart. Harry explains that he wants to use these components to more quickly create video productions with stereo sound. Joan advises Harry that those types of applications consume a lot of memory. She recommends purchasing 500 MB of RAM to prevent his computer from crashing.

Joan probably could have sold him those components without knowing his goals. However, in doing so, she risks that a week later a frazzled customer returns complaining how the parts she *sold* him did not "work." His computer keeps crashing because of out-of-memory errors. He demands his money back and is never seen again.

Significant differences and outcomes exist between trying to satisfy needs and helping customers achieve their goals.

Note: If Harry didn't know what he was trying to achieve (goals), Joan could have suggested some from a Market Profile sheet she developed. There are no "What do you mean, what do I mean?" questions with superstars.

Determining Which Goals You Can Achieve

The only customers' goals you pursue are the ones your products achieve. Your potential goes up as the number of your features—especially unique strengths—that could achieve their goals goes up. Although you think about specific products in this planning stage, do not mention specific products to the customers until you find out their purchasing requirements. You will examine this topic in Chapter 4.

Market Profile sheets motivate you to think about goals in ways customers in specific market segments do. You think about which goals you would want to achieve if you shared their organizational characteristics and positions. For instance, what would be your goals if you were the vice president of manufacturing for a personal computer manufacturer? One of your main goals would probably be minimizing production downtime. You then think about which unique strengths or strongest features of your products best achieve those goals. In addition, which systems of evaluation will accurately reflect the achievement of customers' goals via your unique strengths?

The following five-step evaluation can help you to fill out your Market Profile sheets accurately:

1. Review your past sales successes to see which types of customers produce the most wins.
2. Determine which organizational characteristics they have in common.
3. Classify them as market segments.
4. Evaluate the top three sales in each market segment for the goals, measurable benefits, and systems of evaluation they used.
5. Review with your two top customers in each market segment what you think their goals, measurable benefits, and SOEs are. Solicit their feedback for additions, deletions, and modifications.

Using this process, you will also end up with references that have measurable dollar savings—and customers who understand why doing business with you is a smart and well-thought-out decision.

Note: *The Science of Sales Success*'s focus is on helping customers to achieve their predictable *professional* goals. Customers' *personal* goals, like spending more time with their families or becoming financially secure, have too many intangibles which make them unpredictable. In addition, customers usually reserve discussions about their personal goals for salespeople who earned their trust by helping them to achieve their *measurable* professional goals. Again, it helps if you understand how your contacts' performance is measured, which, in essence, helps to form their goals.

Protecting Yourself Against Bust Cycles

When selecting which market segments to pursue, one final analysis—*economic sensitivity*—remains to be taken into account. Economic sensitivity is a measure of how a market segment (and the customers within it) will react to changing economic conditions. It includes the following three categories:

1. *Cyclical.* The market segment follows the general economy. If the economy is booming, so is the market segment. If the economy slows down, so does the market segment. Typically, market segments in the manufacturing sector are cyclical in nature. For example, in a strong economy, people buy new products to support growth and replace old ones rather than repair them.

2. *Countercyclical.* The market segment goes in the opposite direction to the general economy. If the economy is booming, the market segment slows down. If the economy slows down, the market segment grows. Typically, market segments in the service sector are countercyclical in nature. A weak economy means people repair products rather than replace old ones.

3. *Noncyclical.* The market segment includes companies with both manufacturing and service business units. Therefore, these market segments will redirect their investments (that is, sales opportunities) depending on the direction and condition of the economy.

The key to consistency is to make sure you balance your market segment so value-driven and profitable sales opportunities exist during all three economic conditions.

Market Profile Sheets

The Market Profile sheet analyzes individual customers in specific market segments in terms of the concepts discussed in this chapter. Use your Product Profile sheet from Chapter 2 (Exhibit 2-5) to fill in the information for the product and unique strengths feature columns. A Microsoft Word template for these sales tools is found as a downloadable file on www.measuremax.com. You need to fill out the following information:

- *Company Name.*
- *Market Segment.* The more specific you are in defining your market segments, the greater the chances that customers will express interest in the potential goals you mentioned to them on your initial sales contact. Remember the hospital example.

- *Economic Sensitivity.* Determine whether the market segment falls into the cyclical, countercyclical, or noncyclical category. Try to balance your market segments to ensure consistency of sales opportunities during all types of economic conditions.
- *Organizational Characteristics.* The more detailed these are, the more confident you can be about identifying customers' goals accurately.
- *Contact Name.* Person you are contacting or working with.
- *Position.* An individual's position coupled with the organizational characteristics determines his or her potential goals. One position can have more than one *goal category.* For example, a vice president of manufacturing's interest probably lies in the goal categories of both *operations* and *finances.*
- *Previous Market Segment Success Stories.* Run on your record of expertise in their industries.
- *Profit Levels.* What profit margins does the company generate? Find out this number via the company's Web site or annual reports, or ask during MP 2: Measure Potential.
- *Annual Sales Dollars.* Find out this number via the company's Web site or annual report, or ask during MP 2: Measure Potential.
- *Number of Employees.* Find out this number via the company's Web site or annual report, or ask during MP 2: Measure Potential.
- *Annual Growth Rate.* Find out this number via the company's Web site or annual report, or ask during MP 2: Measure Potential.
- *Current Use of Similar Products or Services in Dollar Amount.* Ask during MP 2: Measure Potential.
- *Potential Use of Similar Products or Services in Dollar Amount.* Ask during MP 2: Measure Potential.
- *General Goal Category.* General goals that interest customers.
- *Typical Goals.* Subsets within the general goal category. For example, the goal of *improves reliability* is a subset of operations; the goal of *increase return on investment* is a subset of finance.
- *Benefits of Achieving Goals.* The benefits of the goals expressed in time or money. Please note that a goal can have more than one benefit.
- *Systems of Evaluation.* The methods customers use to assign value to their goals. You win when these SOEs accurately reflect the measurable value of their goals and connect to your unique strengths.
- *Product.* The products that achieve the goals.
- *Unique Strength Features.* Review the summary on unique strengths from Chapter 2 before you classify a feature as such. Again, not every feature is a unique strength. As a reminder: Sometimes your unique

Exhibit 3-6. Market profile sheet for Positron.

Market Profile Sheet

Customer Name: Positron				Profit Levels: 30%	
Market Segment: Global computer manufacturers	Economic Sensitivity: Cyclical due to their manufacturing status			Annual Sales $: 3 Billion	
Organizational Characteristics: 7/24 operations, high-dollar down-time, critical manufacturing tolerances, on-time deliveries and inventory levels critical, sensitive to competitors, receptive to state-of-the-art-technologies, revenues of $3 billion, 20,000 employees				# Of Employees: 20,000	
				Annual Growth Rate: 28%	
Contact Name: Olivia Ontime		Position: VP of manufacturing		Current Use Of Similar Products or Services in $: 2 million	
				Potential Use Of Similar Products or Services in $: 3 million	
Previous Success Stories: Advanced Computer Co., Star Computers, PC Power Ltd., and Computer Giant Inc.					
General Goal Category (broad groupings)	Typical Goals (more specific by position)	Benefits of Achieving Goals (in time or money; insert an "I" for internal benefits, an "E" for external ones, or a "B" for both)	Systems of Evaluation (calculations to determine if goal is achieved)	Products	Unique Strengths or Features with Their Benefits (features are in *italics*; check marks denote a unique strength)
	Reduce downtime	Prevent production stoppages (B) and lost revenues (I)	Hours of downtime	*Predicto Services*	*Variance Alerts* prevent unscheduled breakdowns
					✓ *Tolerance Checks* prevent unscheduled breakdowns

(continues)

Exhibit 3-6. (Continued.)

Operations				
Increase productivity	Lowers manufacturing costs (I) and product costs to distributors (E)	Man-hours used	ProdoGain	✓ Single-Operator Controls eliminate need for current two operators
	Increases revenues (I)	Amount of production capacity	ProdoGain	✓ 200-Unit Capacity increases capacity by 15%
Reduce operating expenses	Eliminates budget deficits (I)	Amount of unallocated expenses	Predicto Services	Variance Alerts prevent major equipment failures
	Frees up money for equipment upgrades (I)	Dollar value of repair costs	ProdoGain	5-Year Warranty eliminates repair parts costs
Administrative				
Ensure compliance with laws and codes	Protects company against fines or forced shut downs (I)	Amount of code violations and fines	The CodeCheck Program	✓ Computerize Program analyzes operations for potential violations

Top Two Competitors	Competitive Unique Strengths
1. PricePoint Services	Low price
2. FastShip Technology	Fastest delivery

strengths occur at the organizational level (location of distribution centers, stocking levels, warranty policies, technical support, payment terms, and the like) and not at the product levels. If you do not have any unique strengths, try to redefine your market segments, packaging (Chapter 2), or use your strongest features and denote it as such.

Note: You can still win sales without unique strengths as long as you show how your products produce *measurable* benefits from achieving customers' goals better than competitors.

- *Top Two Competitors.* List your top two competitors in this market segment.
- *Competitive Unique Strengths.* List your top two competitors' unique strengths.

Note: If more than one position is involved with the sale, you would create a new Market Profile sheet to reflect that position's goals.

The Market Profile sheet in Exhibit 3-6 on the previous spread builds on the Product Profile sheet Steven Smartsell used in Chapter 2. His Market Profile sheet is for Positron, a computer manufacturer, and its vice president of manufacturing, Olivia Ontime.

Note: When you create a target list of customers you want to pursue, start from the bottom of the list, not the top. With the bottom-up approach, you'll have little to lose (there's only upside), you'll hear every customer concern in the world, you won't be practicing on your best prospects, and you'll be prepared for a good opportunity when you see one.

Strength Through Knowledge

Market Profile sheets help to make your sales become planned events rather than random occurrences. When you review their wealth of information before contacting customers, all your questions have one target: making customers' goals measurable. Then, you see whether you can help customers to achieve them.

Yet, one more issue remains in your pursuit of providing customers with more value than competitors and getting compensated for it. You need to know if the *customers* can achieve their goals, let alone you. Chapter 4 can help you in this endeavor.

SUMMARY

- Focus on the value of goals, not on the pain of needs.
- Needs are product focused, goals are customer focused.
- Goals provide opportunities to create sales where no evident pain exists.
- Knowing customers' goals when they do not will position you as being a customer expert.
- You make the progression from needs to goals by knowing:
  - How market segments choose customers and goals
  - How customers calculate the value of achieving their goals
  - How customers make goals measurable
  - How customers achieve those goals via your unique strengths
- Market segments are groups of customers who share the same organizational characteristics and goals. Know your competitors' strongest market segments so that you can avoid them whenever possible.
- Organizational characteristics and the position of the person involved with the purchasing decision determine a customer's goal.
- Customers' professional goals reflect their personal goals.
- Systems of evaluation (SOEs) are the methods customers use to assign value to goals.
- If you establish SOEs that accurately assign value to the customers' goals and match them up to your unique strengths, you dominate those market segments.
- You use SOEs to convert perceived value into measurable value.
- You make goals measurable by making the customer's benefits measurable.
- Measurable goals empower you to fulfill customers' expectations by building your products from their goals down, not from your features up.
- You want to motivate customers to prioritize goals that are realistic for their circumstances, have a self-imposed sense of urgency to achieve, and are advantageous to your unique strengths.
- Market Profile sheets highlight which customers share goals that place the most value on your unique strengths—and on those of competitors.

Chapter Four

Tests of Reasonableness

Your sales opportunities look great. You have customers expressing interest in achieving goals that might connect to your unique strengths. Yet, one question looms: Do customers have the capability and resources to achieve their goals? You need to know the answer to this question before you are able to consider whether your products can help them to achieve their goals.

This chapter empowers both you and customers to perform *tests of reasonableness* on each other's ability to achieve their goals by explaining:

- How to motivate customers to share purchasing information
- How purchasing requirements revolve around customers' measurable goals
- How nine purchasing requirements (filters) influence every sales opportunity—whether you are aware of them or not
- How the three types of customers share information differently

The End of Qualifying As You Know It

Past sales training taught you the importance of qualifying your customers on the first sales call. You want to "discover" (using the more popular and softer term for the harsher-sounding "qualify") the answers to four questions. You usually start with the first question, and then ask the other three in any order that pops up:

1. Do they have a need to buy your products?
2. Do they have the money to buy your products?
3. Do they have the authority to buy your products?
4. How soon do they want to buy your products?

Finding the answers to these questions makes perfect sense. Neither customers nor you want to waste time and effort on opportunities that do not pan out. Yet, one slight problem exists with this traditional view of qualifying. You should not qualify customers first; they should qualify themselves first—but not about whether they can buy your products (notice how the four qualifying questions end).

Let customers qualify themselves on two points. First, on whether they chose the correct goals; and second, on whether they have the ability to achieve them. Once they gather enough facts to confirm both, you qualify (but not in front of them) any potential product selections by using the same information. You do this step before you mention any *specific* products to customers. When customers qualify themselves first, they discover new things. They discover that you can help them to make wise purchasing decisions, which fulfill measurable expectations. You will discover how customers reward you for providing this service.

As a customer expert, therefore, your initial responsibility is to help guide customers through this self-qualifying process.

Note: If you find that you are disqualifying more than qualifying customers on initial contacts, rethink your choices of whom to call on. You are probably in market segments where customers' goals do not connect to your unique strengths.

Motivate Customers to Share Information

When customers qualify themselves, you ask them to share information. Sometimes, they consider this information confidential. For instance, customers often consider topics such as funding and their roles in the decision-making process to be private information. A customer's biggest disincentive to share information is the fear that it weakens his or her negotiating position. It does when you mention specific products before customers state their goals.

Customers know how the game works. They quickly realize that any information they supply you with always ends up helping you to position your products as the right choice for them. You further diminish their faith in you when you offer specific products as remedies to their problems with little or no knowledge of their goals. It is time to change the rules to benefit both you and customers.

Trust replaces tension when you let customers know that you too share their destinations. Customers gain more control, not less, when *your* questions seek to make *their* goals more measurable. As specifics about their goals emerge, their resistance to share information about their purchasing considerations (referred to as filters) decreases. Also, the more transparent it is to customers how goals and filters affect their purchasing decisions, the more they will feel that they have been treated fairly and the more willingly they will share information. (Dr. Martin G. Groder discusses the concept of transparency in his book *Business Games: How to Recognize the Players and Deal with Them.*[1])

Contrary to past selling philosophy, you give up manipulation so that you and customers gain control. Otherwise, you end up with sales calls running out of control on emotions and chance rather than on clear thinking and planning. You do not wrestle with customers in order to manipulate details to fit your products. Instead, you share control with customers to ensure that your combined focus is on achieving their goals. However, this control is different and positive. It is a version of management by objective (MBO) followed by you and your customers. Where do they want to end up (their goals)? Moreover, are you able to help them get there?

Customers view requests for information not as attempts to jockey products but rather as a means to better define what it takes to achieve their goals. They have no reason to conceal information. You have not mentioned any specific products or services. At the predetermined perfect time, you will—when "yes" answers are foregone conclusions.

Once customers' goals are firm, they know that disclosing the specifics of their filters also makes good business sense. They do not want to try hitting moving targets either. The more detailed the information, the more it eliminates uncertainty about their goals. These details put them and you in better control over whether they can achieve their goals. You know the requirements your products must satisfy. Customers realize that the more information they provide about their goals, the more requirements that any yet-to-be-specified products must meet.

You are now both in a position to determine whether customers can achieve their goals and whether you can help them in their pursuit. You both decide whether further efforts will be time well spent.

Therefore, start your sales call by focusing on customers' goals, not specific products, so that customers have no reason to conceal information. When customers know their *measurable* goals, they feel in full control—and so do you.

Example

Ellen Conley sells various types of high-tech telephone systems. Mike Wells, the customer service manager of a large mail-order house, asks Ellen to make a presentation about some of her company's telephone systems. He tells her that he wants to reduce customers' wait times before they speak to a representative.

At the beginning of the sales call, Ellen confirms that Mike's interest lies in reducing waiting time. Ellen, like most product-focused salespeople, asks Mike what price ranges he is looking at so that she can know what products to present. Ellen also asks Mike when he would need a new system to be functional. Ellen, again like most product-focused salespeople, is working backward. She is allowing price and delivery to become the systems of evaluation (SOEs) that determine the product selection, not Mike's measurable goals.

Mike is hesitant about telling Ellen exact amounts or dates. He does not like transferring control over which products he can choose from to a salesperson he hardly knows. Tension mounts as Ellen and Mike enter the brinkmanship selling mode. They both jockey for control over when details about prices, budgets, and deadlines surface. Let the dueling begin.

Ellen can motivate Mike to share details by making his goals measurable. For instance, she could ask Mike about the financial impact of reducing wait time. She might end up with an SOE using sales dollar lost per minute of wait time to justify price, not just a budget figure. Her questions will now reference Mike's deadlines and budgets to his goals rather than to her products. The key point is to understand the customer's measurable goals before trying to flush the person out with product presentations.

Filters Must Measure Up

You probably can list dozens of circumstances that influence your and your customers' ability to achieve their goals. So, which ones do you choose to consider and which ones do you toss out? Again, you resort to the powerful business axiom: "You can only manage what you can measure." When you start reevaluating the circumstances on your list in terms of whether you can measure their effect, it starts shrinking dramatically.

Nine purchasing considerations or filters pass this test of measurability. These so-called filters earn their name because they filter out what goals (if any) customers can achieve. They also filter out what products (if any) can achieve those goals. Filters provide you with information about the unique circumstances of each customer and the constraints under which he or she operates in making purchasing decisions. Without measurable goals and filters, it becomes anyone's guess whether customers or you can achieve their goals.

It is essential to ensure that customers' goals are not merely wish lists. Although you can measure customers' filters, like goals, they usually do not start out seeming measurable. You need to convert them from broad concepts to measurable ones. Chapter 5 discusses in detail the mechanics and techniques behind making goals and filters measurable through *active listening and questioning*. Once measurable, these nine filters enable you and customers to conduct tests of reasonableness to determine whether their goals are achievable. These tests then determine if sales opportunities are worth further investments of time, energy, and resources. (When they are not worthwhile because sales opportunities will be price or delivery driven, or customers' goals are not achievable, then nothing ventured is everything gained.)

Note: By agreeing to discuss the details of their filters, customers are expressing a desire to find out whether they can achieve their goals. They are acknowledging that the possibility of achieving their goals is worth the additional effort to sweat the details of their filters.

Prerequisites and Influencers

It is easier to understand filters by dividing them into two categories: prerequisites and influencers. *Prerequisites* are exactly what their name implies. Customers and you *must* satisfy these filters to achieve their goals through your products. No leeway exists. Consider them purchasing constraints or "hard" filters. You can probably do an excellent job of finding out three of the four prerequisites. Yet, as you will see, the fourth one is the key to the sale.

Influencers, as their name implies, influence the customers' and your ability to achieve their goals. Customers might or might not consider them when deciding to pursue goals or buy your products. While they are measurable and motivate customers to act on their goals and your products, these five filters are not requirements of the sale. View them as peripheral issues or "soft" filters. You can probably do a great job finding out four of the five influencers. However, the fifth one affects the outcome of sales almost as much as prerequisites do.

Note: Filters are to goals as features are to benefits. Always think of them together. Every filter links back to the customer's goals to measure its effect. In addition, whether you find them out or not, filters work behind the scenes to affect the outcome of every sales opportunity that you encounter.

A Quick Snapshot of the Nine Filters

The order in which filters surface changes on every sales call based on customer responses. When they surface is not important (as long as it occurs before you mention specific products). What is important is that you make them measurable when they do surface—and that you find out as many of the nine as possible.

In the following list, the letter *P* stands for "prerequisite" and the letter *I* stands for "influencer." The nine filters are as follows:

1. *Goal Motivation (I).* Why does the customer want to achieve his goals?
2. *Current Situation (I).* What is the customer presently doing to attempt to achieve his goals?
3. *Plans (I).* What does the customer want to do in the future to achieve his goals?
4. *Alternatives (I).* What courses of actions, besides using your products, does the customer have to achieve his goals?
5. *Decision Makers (P).* Who are the people involved with making the purchasing decision on achieving these goals?
6. *Complete, Start, Budget, and Decision Dates (P).* What is the customer's time frame to complete, start, budget for, and decide on these goals?
7. *Funding (P).* How will the customer pay to achieve these goals?
8. *Keys to Previous Successes/Failures (I).* What past projects were successful or unsuccessful in achieving similar goals and why?
9. *Attainment Measurement (P).* How will the customer measure whether his or her goals were attained?

Note: All the filters end with a reference to goals. Your questions about filters should reference their goals also as you will see in Chapter 5.

Do not think of this list as a set-in-stone sequence. Salespeople often find it easier to start with the *influencers* to build credibility. Once customers realize you are seeking information to help them better understand their ability to achieve their goals, details of the *prerequisites* flow freely.

Once you know these filters, you and customers determine:

- Whether their goals are attainable.
- If your products achieve their goals.
- What would need to change—goals, filters, or the product—to make it all work?

Think of filters as a sieve. The customers' goals go into the top of the sieve. The filters then act as strainers. By the time you and customers come out the bottom of the sieve, only the goals customers can achieve and the products you can offer remain. (See Exhibit 4-1.)

Exhibit 4-1. Filters are like sieves.

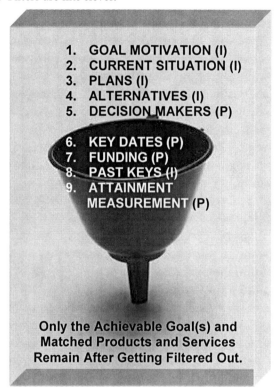

1. GOAL MOTIVATION (I)
2. CURRENT SITUATION (I)
3. PLANS (I)
4. ALTERNATIVES (I)
5. DECISION MAKERS (P)

6. KEY DATES (P)
7. FUNDING (P)
8. PAST KEYS (I)
9. ATTAINMENT MEASUREMENT (P)

Only the Achievable Goal(s) and Matched Products and Services Remain After Getting Filtered Out.

Customers Come in Three Flavors

The three types of customers will not surprise you; their classifications are almost self-explanatory. Whether a customer is *positive*, *neutral*, or *negative* influences his or her willingness to share specifics of goals and filters.

Positive Customers

They are your long-term and loyal customers with whom you practice relationship selling. As long as positive customers cannot measure value, they always choose their trusted and existing supplier—you. Therefore, competitors who rely on products with perceived value have an uphill battle to make positive customers switch to them. When they do not compete on measurable value, they face an undesirable prospect. Competitors either buy sales by offering the lowest prices or are fortunate enough to meet crucial delivery dates. Understandably, competitors usually do not want to bother with your positive customers; they figure there must be easier sales opportunities out there (more on this shortly).

Note: With positive customers, the cost of change can become a more formidable barrier to competitors if you attach measurable dollar amounts to these costs.

Your strongest support from positive customers occurs when your unique strengths achieve their goals and produce measurable benefits. Therefore, ensure that they know how your company helps them to achieve their goals measurably better than anyone else does. Again, measurable value builds barriers to competition and ensures that you exceed customers' expectations. Remember, "Competitors do not win over your customers, you unwillingly lose them due to unfulfilled expectations."

Note: A good indicator of whether your customers fit the positive category is their willingness to write reference letters. These endorsements highlight the goals—and measurable benefits—you help them achieve. Use them with other potential customers in the same market segments. Provide them a sample reference letter to save them time and effort. In addition, nothing is worse than reference letters with grammatical and spelling errors, typos, and a failure to point out your unique strengths or documented savings. Treat hesitant reference letter writers as caution signs. They might not yet qualify as positive customers.

Neutral Customers

As their name implies, these customers do not prefer a specific company's products and services. They are fair game for every salesperson, so they provide the largest number of sales opportunities. Yet, they are a neglected group because they have the most unknowns, such as how they select suppliers other than on a seemingly random basis. When you deal with unknowns, selling efforts increase although your prospects for success might not.

You usually wait for neutral customers to contact you first. At least you know they are serious about buying something—maybe even from you. You use the courtship selling mode with them. Your objective is to move them to the positive category or at least stop them from sliding into the negative category. If you can show them how the measurable value of your unique strengths matches up to their goals, you will achieve your objective. Competitors are planning to do the same thing, but they do not consciously think in terms of measurable value; you do. Thus, they do not stand a chance in the battle for the neutrals.

Negative Customers

They are long-term and loyal customers—of competitors. You use brinkmanship selling with them. With them, you always lose the battle of perceived value. They select competitors' products with perceived value over your products with perceived value every time (so that is why you lost that last sale). Therefore, without measurable value, you have an uphill battle (lowest prices or meeting crucial deliveries) to make negative customers choose your products. Otherwise, wait for competitors to lose them. The "create-and-wait" strategy described later in this chapter helps you in this endeavor.

Now, let us examine the details of the nine filters.

Goal Motivation (Influencer)

The greater the measurable benefits of their goals (or how their performance is evaluated), the stronger is the motivation for customers to act quickly. Often, some compelling event occurs that heightens customers' motivation to achieve a goal. For instance, a drop in a company's market share by 10 percent increases its motivation to achieve the goal of improving marketing and selling efforts. Uncover the event, and you know the motivation—and how they measure it. For example, what does 10 percent equal in dollars lost?

Note: A good question to ask customers to uncover goal motivation is, "What has prompted you to want to achieve that goal (fill in the blank) at this time?"

Moreover, introducing new goals with measurable benefits motivates customers to move out of their status quo. You do not need to wait for a negative event to occur for them to take action. To create demand you use goals that customers were not even aware were achievable. You help them calculate what the cost of doing nothing equals in dollars. Additionally, when finding out goal motivation, you often uncover the next filter of *current situation.*

Current Situation (Influencer)

Customers' current situations influence the goals they want to achieve. They calculate the value of achieving proposed goals by comparing it with what value they receive from what they are presently doing to achieve those goals. Again, the greater the difference between them, the stronger is the goal motivation. Measurable value always makes it easier to calculate these differences, and it motivates customers to act more quickly.

Example

Billy Thomas, a plant manager, has a goal to reduce defects to 1 per 1,000 units manufactured. His current quality control program has a defect rate of 3 per 1,000. Linda Hart sells high-capacity production equipment. If Linda knew what an individual defect cost, she could determine whether Billy has a strong motivation to pursue this defect-reduction goal.

Plans (Influencer)

The courses of action customers consider in achieving their goals can provide you with valuable insight. They illustrate how much thought and investment customers are giving to achieving their goals. How much influence you exert depends on their commitment to these plans. The more highly developed the plans, the less you can influence them. You influence their plans by introducing new systems of evaluation (SOEs) that more accurately measure their goals.

Example

Billy plans to add a new permanent shift to *increase production by 30 percent* (goal) rather than buying new production equipment. Linda asks Billy how he decided between those two choices. He explains that when he calculated the labor costs—including fringe benefits, insurance, and overtime (SOEs)—compared with purchasing equipment, it made more financial sense. Linda shows Billy that if he includes training and turnover costs (additional SOEs), adding a shift might not be the most cost-effective way to increase production. In addition, leasing rather than buying new equipment to create positive cash flow (a new SOE) might be a more profitable course of action.

Plans consist of the broad methods customers are considering to achieve their goals. When these plans have specific products attached to them, you are dealing with the next filter of *alternatives*.

Alternatives (Influencer)

Customers might be considering specific products from your competitors to achieve their goals. This filter differs from *plans* because competition exists. It also means competitors are further along in sales opportunities than you are. These proposed products influence the goals customers want to achieve. As discussed in Chapter 3, customers often consider their goal to be the purchase of specific products.

Two reasons prompted the use of the word *alternatives* instead of the word *competition*:

1. *When you think of competition, you naturally think of competitors in only your industry.* Yet, customers often consider alternatives outside your industry. Many industries, not only yours, are trying to achieve customers' goals better than you can and win whatever money is available. When you reference this filter to goals ("What other ways are you looking to improve reliability?") and not to specific products, you will discover if any nontraditional competitors exist.

Example

Walter Jones sells air-conditioning equipment. Tara Stein, the operations manager of a hotel/casino, explains that there is a big push to improve profits. Tara is positive she can reduce electrical costs to improve profits. She tells Walter she is ready to buy his equipment because it provides a two-year payback, which is eight months faster than any other air-conditioning company.

A week later, much to his surprise, Walter learns that he lost the sale. Why? The facility manager of the casino used the funds for a new air-conditioning system to purchase four slot machines that provide a six-month payback. Walter did not lose the sale to any of his usual competitors. He and Tara lost her budget money to a slot machine. Join the crowd.

What could Walter have done differently? He should have asked Tara if the other departments in the casino were also examining ways to improve profits. Once he found out what they were, Walter could have asked her how the casino would fund the different initiatives. If Tara told him on a corporate rather than on a departmental level, he would have known that he was competing against nontraditional competitors vying for limited funding. He could have used SOEs that also included costs such as downtime and guests who did not return because of poor climate control in their rooms or gambling areas. These SOEs would have added to his electrical savings, further lowering his payback. In addition, leasing might have made positive cash flow another key SOE that favored his products.

2. *When customers' measurable goals match up to your unique strengths, you can outvalue anyone.* Therefore, if you define your market segment correctly, your only competition is whether you can help customers prioritize and justify achieving their goals. Take great satisfaction when the competitors refer to you as the "competition." Do not let customers think you consider other companies as competition.

Example

Rich wants to buy a sports car. He goes to a Chevy dealership to look at Corvettes. Rich is not certain what he wants. Inevitably, Marty, the salesperson, in trying to flush out Rich's preferences, asks, "What other cars have you been considering?" Rich asks Marty which ones he thinks are similar. He says, "BMWs or Porsches." Rich responds, "Thanks for the tip. I will get back to you after I check them out."

What could Marty have done differently? Marty should not have used car (product) selections to uncover Rich's preferences. Marty should have reassured Rich that most people, with so many choices, are not sure which car they want.

However, ranking what is most important to them (goals) about a sports car helps narrow their choices. For instance, is it comfort, image, efficiency, or costs? Marty further tells Rich that if he understands a little more about his background (driving habits, occupation, past cars, family status, and the like) he can provide him with the reasons why other people in his situation (market segment) selected their sports cars.

Avoiding the "What Do They Do for You?" Trap

When you find out about customers' alternatives, do not end up in wars over features or price. If customers compare your features with competitors' features, their goals get lost in the shuffle. When customers do not evaluate features of products on how they achieve their goals, they are less likely to change their current supplier. When customers consider products to be commodities, comparing the number of features becomes their system of evaluation.

Example

Rebecca Hoffman sells accounting services. Dennis Ketchum, a neutral customer, tells her that he is using XYZ Company to do his accounting services. Rebecca resists the urge to ask Dennis the product-focused question: "What do they do for you?"

Instead, she asks: "What do you see as the major goals *you* want to accomplish with an accounting service?" This question is customer oriented not product focused, and it is one that Dennis has never heard. As expected, he does not know what she means by "goals" and looks like he is trying out a new pair of eyes. No problem. Before their meeting, Rebecca reviewed the Market Profile sheet for this type of customer, and she is ready to suggest pertinent goals, such as ensuring tax record-keeping compliance or providing access to lending institutions.

> Which type of question do your customers hear more often: "What do they do for you?" or "What are you trying to accomplish?"

You want customers to use goals, filters, and measurable value as their yardsticks to compare products. If possible, your proposals should look like a modified Market Profile sheet by listing how their specific goals and measurable benefits connect to your features and benefits. Customers can use this list to check off how many of their goals you achieve versus competitors and the value of each one. You vividly illustrate to customers how your products achieve their goals. You learn how to create these checklists in Chapter 7.

Again, if you choose market segments correctly, your unique strengths win the sales. In the interim, you can hope that competitors focus on your products and try to figure out how their features compare with yours. Let them suffer the fate of ignoring customers' goals.

Handling Customers Satisfied with Their Existing Supplier

Without a doubt, you will contact satisfied negative or neutral customers. They feel their current suppliers (competitors) do a good job of achieving their goals. While subsequent chapters show how to convert them to positive customers, sometimes, regardless of what you offer, customers are not ready to make changes. You cannot move them forward in the sales process. In these situations, use the create-and-wait strategy. Slowly create opportunities and then wait for the right time to seize them. Think of this strategy as a means of last resort or your best walk-away position. The strategy works as follows:

- If possible, walk away from these potential sales opportunities only after learning their goals (measurable ones, if possible), not what they like about their current suppliers.
- Position yourself as a customer expert, a conduit of industry information. Offer to keep them updated about innovations and trends relevant to achieving their goals. Send them any new articles on systems of evaluation that reflect the goals they are seeking to achieve and favor your unique strengths. Do not send sales litera-

ture. Do keyword searches and look for articles on the Internet that are relevant to their market segments and goals.

- Find out if the company has a Web site. If so, visit the company's news sections monthly to see whether it is making any changes that might favor your products. Research the company's products and services, stated corporate goals, financial performance, acquisitions, changes in personnel, and the like for potential opportunities. Understand how the company sells value to its customers, so that you can highlight similar value to the company, if possible. Check employment listings to see whether its hiring requirements might offer you sales opportunities. Who knows? You might find your completely satisfied contact has left his or her position. (New hires are excellent sales opportunities. Companies give them more latitude during their honeymoon stage; and new hires are more open to change. The fact that they changed jobs proves it.)

- Ask your satisfied customers for the best way to correspond with them. Send letters, faxes, or, preferably, e-mails, with telephone follow-ups every three to six months. If possible, set up your reminders electronically in software programs like Outlook. Ask your positive customers in the same market segments whether they know these satisfied customers. If they do, confirm that you can use their names in your correspondence.

- Ask positive customers whether they see these "create and waits" at trade or association meetings. If they do, find out whether they would mention how you achieve the same or similar goals for them. A word of warning: Ensure that your products are measurably better than those of their current suppliers. Otherwise, this tactic could backfire on you. Your goal is to have positive customers win over negative customers—not the other way around.

- After a few months, offer "create and waits" the opportunity to attend training seminars relevant to their goals. Again, proceed with caution for the reasons mentioned in the previous step. In addition, start sending case studies on your company's successes in their market segments.

- Try this strategy for one year (hopefully less). If there are no sales, decide whether it is worthwhile to go one position higher (more on this strategy in the next filter). However, if you have the patience, continue to wait for stumbles by existing suppliers. Just make sure the company considers you to be its second choice. Check periodically so that you can be the first one on the scene if the contact leaves his or her position or company.

Note: The create-and-wait strategy also works with customers who find their current methods of achieving their goals (filter of *current situation*) satisfactory.

Gatekeepers, Advocates, and the Final Decision Maker (Prerequisite)

Three people stand between you and a successful sale: the customer's *gatekeeper, advocate,* and *final decision maker (FDM)*. In smaller, decentralized, and less-bureaucratic companies, the same person might assume two or three of these roles. Sometimes, people pretend to assume roles they do not really play. Your challenge is to find out what role each person *really* plays. You need to know, not assume, who gives the final yes to buy your products.

Note: Most sales theories break contacts into two groups, the *C* level and the *D* level. The *C* level comprises the chief executive officer (CEO), chief operating officer (COO), chief financial officer (CFO), chief information/technology officer, and so forth. The *D* level is composed of directors and heads of departments such as operations, finance, engineering, accounting, and customer service. Ensure that you understand both *C* and *D* level goals to gain support throughout the organization.

The roles, in order of their ability to issue purchase orders if they are three different people, are as follows.

Gatekeepers

Gatekeepers play an interesting role. They either open or close the gates on your efforts to get to the advocates or final decision makers. They can say an initial no to your pursuing sales opportunities but not a final yes to purchasing your products. Yet, if they feel you take their goals seriously, gatekeepers provide invaluable information. They know what goals interest the advocates and FDMs most—and details of the filters. They can also tell you what the best way is to build rapport with them.

Gatekeepers' areas of expertise are mostly technical or operational in nature. Their goals often look more like requirements or specifications. Purchasing agents use gatekeepers to help them insert technical language into requests for proposals (RFPs). Advocates and FDMs view gatekeepers as inside consultants. If your products fall within their field of expertise, your products must satisfy their technical requirements. Because of their technical nature, gatekeepers tend to discuss specific products and features rather than broad goals.

Companies often use outside consultants as external gatekeepers. They provide guidance on how best to achieve their goals. Like gatekeepers, they too can give you an initial no but not a final yes. The role of consultants surfaces when you discuss the filters of *plans* or *alternatives*. When gatekeepers show uncertainty about their goals or filters, do not be surprised if outside consultants appear. Companies hire consultants to help them clarify their goals, make them measurable, and eliminate uncertainty.

Advocates

Advocates receive the most benefit from any proposed goals. They are responsible for making sure your products achieve *their* goals. Advocates become your internal salesperson because they have the most at stake. They become your coach—a coach who wants you to win. They sell the benefits of their goals—and your products—within their organization without you being there. They know what it takes to get the FDM to say yes. Often, the advocate's recommendation is all it takes to get orders. The FDM's approval is merely a rubber stamp.

Sometimes, an advocate will tell you that he or she doesn't need you to make a presentation. The advocate wants to handle it on his or her own. This situation often occurs because the advocate is not sure what you will say in front of his or her boss. Ask your advocate if there are any topics he or she doesn't want you to bring out at a meeting with the boss or others. You will continue to build trust as a confidant with this approach.

You also need to point out to the advocate that if you aren't at the meeting, any unanswered questions/concerns can take on a life of their own and jeopardize the goals he or she wants to achieve if these questions are not addressed promptly. Offer to make your presentation and then leave so the advocate and his or her boss can discuss any concerns without you there. However, agree to wait outside (and out of earshot) until they summon you when they have completed their internal discussions. Answer all concerns at that moment or set up a return meeting if you need to review these concerns with your sales team.

Everyone wins with this approach. You present (after all, no one can make a presentation better than you—or they should be working for your company as a salesperson), the customer gets to discuss matters in private, and you address any concerns immediately, so the advocates and your goals are not at risk.

Their role becomes critical to your success if you cannot meet with the FDM. Now, you need the advocate to sell your formal proposals to them. If you format your proposals properly, they will guide advocates in their selling efforts. By highlighting goals, measurable benefits, SOEs, and unique strengths in your proposals, advocates sell measurable value the same way you do.

Note: Ask your initial contacts to draw an organizational chart to help identify their role in the company. Ask them to draw their direct subordinate and supervisor boxes. Ask them also to draw any dotted line boxes (staff positions). Find out how these positions (people) interact with them with respect to purchasing decisions and the amount of sway (political influence) they have.

The Final Decision Makers

The saying, "The buck stops here," definitely applies to FDMs. They release or allocate money to achieve any proposed goals. They also give the final approvals on the measurable specifics of the four prerequisites. If they choose to delegate their responsibilities, they decide who becomes the anointed FDM. Sometimes, they skip the advocate and appoint the gatekeeper as the FDM. This is yet another reason not to ignore the goals and filters of gatekeepers.

Note: Consider these two requirements as the acid test for the FDM: They must be able to (1) release funds and (2) approve the SOEs used to calculate the value derived from achieving specific goals.

Locating the Final Decision Makers

You try to locate FDMs by using your customer knowledge, experience, and educated guesses. You can also locate FDMs by reviewing sales opportunities you lost and won in similar-size organizations and market segments. Ask yourself, "What positions made the final decisions involving those sales?"

Once you review your answers, factor in one more aspect to complete your evaluation. Are you contacting positive, neutral, or negative customers? (See Exhibit 4-2.) Using your answers as reference points, you would:

- For positive customers, start at the same contact level.
- For neutral customers where you had successes, start at the same level. Begin one level higher where you lost sales.
- For negative customers, start one level higher than the position of your positive customers.

Exhibit 4-2. Customers are positive, negative, or neutral.

Type Of Customers	Past Contact Levels	Revised Contact Levels as Compared to Positive Customers
Positive	Position X	Same level
Neutral	Position Y	Same (successful) or one level higher (unsuccessful)
Negative	Position Z	One level higher

Top-Down Often Beats Bottom-Up Selling

Many public figures (Arthur Clarke, Mark Twain, and Henry Kissinger) have commented that debates among academics become vicious because so little is at stake. In the debate over where you begin your sales calls, a lot is at stake. If you start your sales calls with the gatekeeper or the advocates, he or she might block you from the FDM. If you start with the FDM, he or she might redirect you to gatekeepers or advocates who feel you went over their heads. So, where do you start? Again, it depends on whether sales opportunities involve positive, neutral, or negative customers. However, often top-down selling means starting with C-level positions: chief executive officer (CEO), chief operating officer (COO), and chief financial officer (CFO). Make sure you know their goals, industry trends, company market position, and so forth. These chiefs will demand that you do before you meet with them.

How Much Sway?

When dealing with a gatekeeper, advocate, or final decision maker, you want to evaluate his or her influence or sway on the purchasing decision. For comparison purposes, assign sway a 1, 2, or 3 value as follows:

1. Can't define measurable benefits gained from achieving his or her goals
2. Defines measurable benefits of goals and systems of evaluations used to calculate benefits
3. Defines measurable benefits, SOEs, and releases funding

You should question why you worked up a proposal if your contact doesn't qualify as at least a 2 in the sway category.

Contacting Neutral or Negative Customers

Start at the highest position that would receive the most financial benefit from your product. That is probably the FDM. The higher up the organizational chart you go on your initial contact, the more receptive these positions are to change. Their perspectives are more concerned with the so-called big picture. They do not think in terms of specific products, but rather measurable results. Results-oriented individuals with broad goals are excellent candidates for you. They reward sales professionals for converting their general goals into measurable value and benefits.

Conversely, the lower you start on the organizational chart, the more resistant individuals are to change. Their goals and responsibilities are narrower. They think more in terms of specific products than broad goals. They equate measurable value with lowest prices or fastest deliveries. Yet, a common sales mistake is to start with negative or neutral customers at the same level (position) you do with your positive customers. While you are more familiar with these positions, they are not your best place to start. Fortunately, competitors fall into the same trap with whom they should contact first. First one out of the trap wins.

Contacting Positive Customers

Continue to work with the decision-making roles that make sales happen. If the person is not the FDM, use the one up, one down strategy. Encourage your contacts to set up meetings at least once a year with the FDM ("one up"). Make sure that if your contact leaves, the FDM knows how you provide value for the company and will pass the word on to your contact's replacement, making it easier for you to maintain the company as a positive customer.

In addition, meet with your contacts' subordinates ("one down"). If your contact leaves, a subordinate might be promoted to fill the vacancy. It benefits you for the person to know the goals you achieved for his or her company. Past goals that produced *measurable* value are your best assurances that companies, not just contacts, remain positive ones.

Note: Most salespeople who have a history of sales successes dealing with gatekeepers or advocates rarely meet with the FDM. They do not feel they have any reason to meet other than for public relations. Again, this presents you with excellent sales opportunities to dislodge competitors. Nothing beats the surprised look on competitors' faces when they find out they lost sales to you—and they did not even know you or their contacts' bosses existed.

Contacting Gatekeepers or Advocates at the FDM's Request

Often, FDMs require you to obtain the approval of advocates or gatekeepers before they enter the purchasing process. You use the FDM's interest to help raise the interest level of advocates or gatekeepers when you meet them. When contacting advocates or gatekeepers, even at the FDM's request, keep your focus on their goals and filters first. You earn the support of gatekeepers and advocates when you help them to achieve their goals. They might not be the same as the FDM's goals, but they must be met. Otherwise, you will not make it back to the FDM. A good sign of their support is when gatekeepers or advocates encourage you to meet with the FDM after your meetings.

Note: Most bruised egos occur with uninterested or hostile gatekeepers or advocates when you contact the FDM after making initial contacts with them. With neutral and negative customers, you might as well start where you need to end up—with the FDM. Finally, let FDMs or advocates—not you—confer authority, responsibility, and importance on people and positions.

However, gatekeepers and advocates will be pleasantly surprised when you tell them that you discuss only broad goals, systems of evaluation, and measurable benefits with their bosses, not specific products. After all, that is *their* job.

Get the Top Five Buzzing

If you still are not sure whom to contact, use a top-five approach. Go to a prospect's Web site or call the receptionist and find out the names of the top-five positions or *C* levels that would most likely benefit from goals achieved by your unique strengths. Send the same letter to each one outlining potential goals, measurable benefit, and systems of evaluation. Include references from similar companies by positions. Put a cc on the bottom of the letter with the names of the other people you sent it to. Put in the letter to the top position the date on which you plan to make a follow-up call (two weeks from the delivery date). In the other letter, reference the date of your follow-up call.

Your goal is to create an internal buzz ("Hey, did you see that letter from . . . ?") Call the highest position first and see what happens. Work your way down the list (if need be) but always refer to the letter and the others to whom it was sent when you start your follow-up telephone calls. At worst, they know you did your homework and have an understanding of their industry.

Note: Without measurable details, it is difficult to distinguish between decision makers' roles. Verifying vague and general information will not cause any differences between decision makers to surface. The more details you receive, the more you can determine a decision maker's authority and influence.

Complete, Start, Budget, and Decision Dates (Prerequisites)

Each of these four dates provides you with insight into a customer's sense of urgency to achieve his or her goals. You should ask the dates in the following chronological order for these reasons:

1. *Complete dates are when customers want to finish achieving their goals.* Once you know the customer's targeted completion date, ask him or her when to begin.
2. *Start dates are when they want to begin the process of achieving their*

goals. Again, no firm start or complete dates means customers have not assigned a cost to doing nothing. Their goal motivation is definitely low. Yet, you are now in a position to ask the customer whether he or she wants to start on this date and what date the budget needs to be approved by to accomplish this deadline.

3. *Budget dates are when money becomes available to accomplish these goals.* If customers have not budgeted money yet, it means they do not consider these goals priorities. They have not assigned a dollar figure to doing nothing. Focus your selling efforts on helping them to calculate these lost opportunity costs. For instance, if they set a goal that could save them $1,000 per day in labor costs, then every day they do not achieve this goal is costing them, in effect, $1,000. When the customer's complete, start, and budget dates are known, ask him or her when a decision needs to be made.

4. *Decision dates are when customers decide whether to achieve a goal.* The date when customers want your proposals is not always a sign of their sense of urgency—or when they will make a decision. One thing often has no correlation to the other. You, and especially your sales support team, discover this difference when you push everything aside and tie up everyone's time to get customers full-blown proposals by their so-called must-have dates. The reward for your efforts is that customers tell you thank-you, as they use your numbers to put into next year's budget (maybe).

Note: Make sure customers agree on a signature or decision date that enables you to meet their completion dates. This date is extremely important if you work with long lead-time products or you contract outside services. Customers understand you cannot commit resources to these start and completion dates without written purchase orders.

Funding (Prerequisite)

The amount of money the customer has allocated to achieving goals raises five questions:

1. Has the customer set aside money to achieve these goals? Like budget dates, it illustrates the customer's sense of urgency.
2. Can the amount of money set aside achieve the customer's goals? You need to decide whether the customer has filet mignon taste with a hot dog wallet. Also, the larger the amount, the greater the

chance is that the gatekeepers, advocates, and FDMs are separate people.

3. Who allocated the funding? This information points you in the direction of the FDM.

4. How did the customer arrive at the dollar figure to budget? Find out if the customer has specific products in mind. Did competitors supply the product selections or furnish a budget number? This information tells you whether to consider a customer to be neutral or negative.

5. Is the money to fund the goals coming out of an operating budget or is it a capital investment? Goals funded from an approved operating budget lower decision-making levels while capital investment raises decision-making levels. Operating budget funding can turn gatekeepers or advocates into FDMs. This can either help (if you are trying to protect positive customers) or hinder (if you are trying to win over negative ones).

In addition, operating budgets speed up sales. If customers move funding for a goal from a capital investment to an operating budget, you shorten the time frame. They do not need to request funds or seek approvals; they already have both. Your pricing strategy and how you structure the payment schedule influence whether it is a capital investment or an operating budget expense. For example, you might spread payments over two fiscal years for a positive customer to fund a sale out of an operating budget. These payment terms lower the approval level, thereby allowing the advocate or gatekeeper to make the decision.

Keys to Previous Successes/Failures (Influencer)

Customers and you review the reasons why they pursued or abandoned projects with similar goals in the past. This analysis provides both of you with reality checks on whether their goals are achievable and the extent of their interest levels. You should not focus on why they did or did not buy a product or you will end up in the "What did they do for you?" trap. If they deem goals worthwhile, they want to make sure they repeat their formulas for successes while avoiding the mistakes of the past.

This filter also tells you which role you are working with. Gatekeepers usually do not know why previous attempts to achieve specific goals failed; advocates and FDMs do. Information on failed attempts also furnishes you with the type of cost justifications and measurable benefits customers need to say yes.

Attainment Measurement (Prerequisite)

For both customers and you, this filter is the single most important piece of information you need to have. It is how you and customers know how they measure the attainment of their goals. You have discussed with customers many details concerning the previous eight filters. You combine and summarize the decision makers' prerequisites of dates and funds with their SOEs and measurable benefits. This summary forms the attainment measurement (often referred to in sales vernacular by using the more general term *critical success factors*) and sets the conditions for achieving their goals. This summary also provides customers with the opportunity to confirm (or add any missing ones) that all the requirements that need to be satisfied for achieving their goals have been identified.

Sounds familiar? The attainment measurement encompasses Column 1 and Column 2. Again, by packaging the measurable benefits with price and delivery, you can offset lower competitive prices or value-justify your own price when there is no competition. You also use the measurable benefits to offset competitors' quicker delivery dates, existing relationships, or costs of change. For instance, if your product takes longer to deliver, you will need to show customers (if possible) that even with the delay, your products will produce more measurable benefits than competitors over a six- or twelve-month period.

Example

The goal of Ralph Cortez, the vice president of production, is to increase manufacturing capacity by 25 percent. Alan Robbins sells high-capacity production equipment and has found out the following data to help Ralph define his attainment measurement:

- A 25 percent increase means going from 2,000 to 2,500 units per hour.
- Ralph uses units per hour as his SOE. Production runs 5,000 hours annually.
- Each unit generates $.04 per hour of profit.
- The completion date is October.
- Funding is $50,000.
- Measurable benefits are $20 per hour (500 more units x $.04).

Mark summarizes Ralph's attainment measurement as the advocate/FDM as follows:

Alan: So, Ralph. We went over a lot of details about increasing capacity to 2,500 units per hour (goal and SOE). You want to be up and running by October (completion date), and not spend more than $50,000 (funding). This productivity gain would produce $20 more per hour, or about $100,000 annually (measurable benefit). Is there anything else?

Ralph: We also want at least an eighteen-month payback.

Alan: In addition to the other requirements you stated, with an eighteen-month payback, would you feel you achieved your goal of increasing capacity by 25 percent?

Ralph: Absolutely!

Alan: I'll review your situation with my engineering group and we'll see what we can come up with.

Ralph and Mark now both know what it will take to achieve Ralph's goal of increasing capacity by 25 percent. You will also use attainment measurements to know what your products need to do to earn the sale.

Note: Often, attainment measurements surface when you make customers' goals measurable. For instance, in the previous example, you could find out much of the attainment measurement details by simply asking Ralph, "How would you know if you increased productivity by 25 percent?" Again, you need to start with customers' goals.

Attainment measurements eliminate the "I hope this solves our problems or achieves our objectives" concerns for customers. They also eliminate the "I hope my products meet their requirements" concerns for you. The risk of being disappointed or not meeting each other's expectations are gone. When you satisfy a customer's attainment measurements, you never have to say you are sorry. They earn you repeat business and long-term, loyal customers.

Attainment measurements resemble "trial closes" that *customers* do on themselves. A *major* difference exists between a customer's trial closes and a salesperson's. Customers are not agreeing to buy specific products if certain conditions are met. They are agreeing that specific goals are worth achieving if they can satisfy the conditions of their attainment measurements. Chapter 6 covers this topic.

Why Guess?

Whether they are prerequisites or influencers, filters are as important as goals. You cannot have one without the other. They allow you and customers to determine whether they can achieve their goals—and if you can help them in their pursuits. With filters, like goals, the devil is in the details.

Chapter 5 explains how active listening and questioning motivate customers to supply the details. It will become apparent to customers how these details serve their self-interests.

SUMMARY

- You want customers to qualify themselves first on whether they chose the right goals and have the ability to achieve them.
- You qualify your own products on their ability to achieve customers' goals before you mention any specific ones to customers.
- If you find yourself disqualifying customers more than qualifying them, you should review how you defined market segments.
- Starting sales calls with a focus on making customers' goals measurable puts them in control and motivates them to share information with you.
- Filters allow both customers and you to perform a *test of reasonableness* on whether you both achieve their goals.

- Filters fall into two categories: *prerequisites* and *influencers.* The four prerequisites must be satisfied for sales to occur. The five influencers can sway customers' purchasing decisions and the goals they seek to achieve.
- The filters are as follows:
  - Goal motivation (I)
  - Current situation (I)
  - Plans (I)
  - Alternatives (I)
  - Decision makers (P)
  - Complete, start, budget, and decision dates (P)
  - Funding (P)
  - Past keys (I)
  - Attainment measurement (P)
- A customer's positive, neutral, or negative status determines its willingness to share information about filters—unless you make goals measurable.
- Use the create-and-wait strategy to win over satisfied negative customers.
- Locate the FDM by looking at the contact positions in similar-size organizations and market segments in which you have successes and failures. Adjust your contact level according to whether they are positive, neutral, or negative customers.
- Moving funding from a capital investment to an operating budget expense lowers the decision-making level and shortens the sales cycle.
- Attainment measurement is the most-important filter for both customers and you because it determines whether they can achieve goals via your products.
- A person qualifies as the FDM if he or she determines the specifics of the four prerequisites and releases or allocates funds.
- Make sure you focus on the goals customers want to achieve, not on how they are using features of competitors' products.

Notes

1. Martin G. Groder, *Business Games: How to Recognize the Players and Deal with Them* (New York: Boardroom Classics, 1980).

Chapter Five

Every Question Counts

The devil is in the details. You and customers both need to know the specifics of their Goals, Filters, Measurable benefits, and Systems of evaluations (SOEs). The mnemonics (memory aids used to help you remember these four items) for them: **Go For Measurable Specifics** (GFMS). When you quantify their details, you know exactly what customers are trying to achieve. You also know whether your products achieve those goals.

You use your listening and questioning skills to accomplish this task. Your mastery of these skills is vital because the difference between a successful and a wasted sales call is extremely subtle. Forgetting to ask only one or two questions to quantify a customer's comments can make a large difference. You know you missed a question when you say, "If I had known that, I would have . . . (fill in your own blank)" after you lost the sale or disappointed a customer.

Yet, questions are like limited natural resources. You can only ask so many questions before you exceed a customer's grilling threshold. Grilled customers fight back with curt answers such as "Yeah," "Nope," and "Okay." Therefore, make every question count. This chapter shows how to make every one count by explaining:

- How to get customers to consider you an expert because of the questions you ask
- How your active listening and active questioning skills motivate customers to provide measurable answers
- How your customers use three types of answers to share information—and how only one of them counts
- How the four key questioning techniques work to transform vague responses into crystal-clear statements

Business Questions, Not Product Statements, Demonstrate Expertise

You let customers know how well you understand their business by the questions you ask. When you recite large amounts of technical facts about your products, you reflect only how well you understand your products. Nevertheless, a common myth prevails among salespeople that product experts are customer experts.

It is easy to understand the roots of this myth. If your sales training was typical, it mainly involved learning features and benefits. There is one slight problem: Your customers do not have features and benefits; they only have goals and filters. Conflict and inefficiency result when salespeople focus only on their products. When you do as you were trained, it is easy to understand why your customers justifiably feel that their interests sometimes come second.

Your product expertise is a given; how you use this knowledge as a building block to be a customer expert is not. You need to know your products inside and out so that you no longer think about them. This frees you up to concentrate on the customers. The appropriate time for you to discuss products will arrive; however, it is not immediately after you introduce yourself.

Example

Barry Olsen, head of purchasing, contacts two competing salespeople to find out who can best help him reduce inventory costs. Barry starts the meeting with the first salesperson, Joan Harkins, by asking her to explain how her products reduce inventory costs. "What an excellent opportunity," Joan thinks. She responds with a ten-minute-long scripted pitch monologue. On automatic pilot, Joan describes how her products will accomplish the goal through one high-tech feature after another. When she finally asks some questions, they all focus on whether Barry sees how her products would be able to reduce inventory costs (whatever that means). Barry tells Joan that he needs time to absorb all the information. He politely omits that he needs time to recover from boredom.

The second salesperson, Lynn Smyth, starts the meeting much differently. Before explaining how her products reduce inventory costs, she asks one of those questions that makes the difference between success and failure. Lynn asks Barry how he calculates inventory costs. Barry either (1) explains his methods or (2) asks Lynn what she means. Either response produces a desirable outcome.

With the first response, Barry explains his cost calculations. Lynn then determines which of her products (if any) would achieve his goals beyond any doubt. She also asks Barry whether he feels his current calculations capture all relevant costs. Lynn wants to make sure she fully understands how Barry measures inventory costs.

With the second response, Lynn responds to Barry's question about what she means by "calculating inventory costs." This question allows Lynn to explain new methods—that is, systems of evaluation—Barry's peers in the industry use to calculate inventory costs. She then details them and asks Barry if these methods are relevant to his inventory-reduction goals.

Of course, it would be purely coincidental if these SOEs accurately reflected the attainment of Barry's goals and matched up to the unique strengths of Lynn's products. Again, nothing prepares Lynn better than having a Market Profile sheet specific to Barry's industry that she can review before meeting with him. This preparation ensures that you, like Lynn, will not ask a question that you cannot answer.

Which salesperson do you think Barry or any other customer will consider more of an expert? Which one do you think is more of an expert?

Fortunately, you can easily break the product feature habit. Just concentrate on questioning customers about their goals. Announce to the customers your focus on understanding their goals. Make it the stated purpose of your first in-person meetings. Customers find it refreshing to discuss their goals, because it does not happen that often.

Note: For good measure, leave your glossy product literature in the car. Save your brochures for a time when you understand your customer's goals and filters. Do not use them before then. (General capabilities brochures and industry-specific case studies are acceptable and useful.)

Customers trust salespeople who are customer experts. They know customer experts build solutions from their goals down, not from your products' features up. Your questions about their goals and filters let customers know that you put their interests first. When you make customers' goals and filters measurable, you sell on value, not price, and exceed customers' expectations. Everyone wins—if you use active listening and questioning skills. (See Exhibit 5-1.)

Exhibit 5-1. Become a customer expert.

Goals and Filters

Systems of Evaluations

Measurable Benefits

A Product Expert Does Not Equal a Customer Expert

Active Listening

Great questioners know how to be active listeners. You and your customers should be completely engaged in what each other is saying, with no distractions. You let each other know you received and understood one another's messages. How relevant your responses are to customers' previous comments show how much active listening has occurred. This approach reinforces your interest in their thoughts, feelings, and perspectives. When customers are reassured that you want to understand exactly what they mean by obtaining measurable details, they keep talking.

Sometimes, salespeople keep talking even when no one is listening. They and customers never reach any quantifiable conclusions. Uninterested parties become more restless by the minute. "Active annoyance" best describes this situation. Salespeople who are guilty of this offense usually start their product pitches immediately after saying hello. If you let customers discuss their goals and filters first, it serves everyone's best interests.

Active listening also takes advantage of nature. While the average speaker only transmits 150 to 200 words per minute, an attentive and active listener receives words at twice that rate, in the range of 300 to 400 words per minute. This is why you become impatient and want a ten-minute speech to end in five minutes. You have twice as much time as you need to listen. This extra time provides you and customers with three choices: advocating, assuming, or anticipating. Only one of these choices produces benefits.

Advocating

Salespeople anxiously wait to pounce on the first opportunity that will give them a chance to advocate why their products are the perfect fit for the customer. They are listening only for details concerning pain, deadlines, budgets, and decision makers. If an opportunity does not present itself, they will force product discussions into the conversations. Out of nowhere comes questions such as "So, John, are you familiar with our products?" These questions usually have nothing to do with what the customer was saying. The salesperson needs not be overly concerned because John is not listening either. He too gave up trying to figure out the business value to him of the salesperson's questions.

When discussions finally arise that might uncover goals, measurable benefits, and SOEs, these salespeople have trouble delving into them. They do not have enough business knowledge to formulate questions to expand on the customer's comments. Therefore, they avoid the awkward position of asking a question they cannot answer either. For instance, it would be difficult for a salesperson to ask a customer, "In what ways are you evaluating the return on improving security?" Without knowledge of SOEs, such as dollar per break-in or the costs of false alarms, salespeople can find themselves scrambling if the customer asks, "What do you mean?"

These salespeople squander their extra listening time by formulating product-focused questions rather than customer-focused ones. Yet, they have only their questions to blame. Their questions set the agenda for what topics customers discuss or do not discuss. The drawbacks to this choice are obvious. Everyone takes a huge risk (unfilled expectations or lost sales) when salespeople offer products without knowing how to achieve the measurable benefits of the customer's goals within their filters. Advocating forces salespeople into their second choice, which is assuming.

Assuming

In selling, as in everyday life, assumptions can create problems for those who are not psychic. Assuming works on a simple principle that salespeople know how customers plan on completing their sentences better than they do. Therefore, to save them time and effort, salespeople complete their customers sentences for them on the slightest pause or breath. As product-trained salespeople, they naturally assume their products interest customers. So naturally, they end customers' sentences with references to products—a sure-fire way to tick off customers.

While listening to product monologues, customers also use bonus time to realize their assumptions were correct. Many salespeople only want to discuss their products to gauge the customer's interest in buying them. Therefore, customers keep their answers vague. Fortunately, it is easy for salespeople to give assuming the boot. You just replace assuming with the most powerful tool of active listening, which is anticipating. You replace a product focus with a customer focus.

Anticipating

Anticipating takes advantage of your faster listening capabilities. During half the time when customers are speaking, you can be thinking strategically. Take this bonus time to think about how measurable the information customers are supplying is. Measurable information concerning what? You answered correctly; it is their Goals, Filters, Measurable benefits, and Systems of evaluations (GFMS).

When you anticipate, you listen for verbal clues to what GFMS customers will discuss next. Use these clues to formulate your follow-up questions. Clues usually involve different aspects of goals and filters. They can range from financial matters to the roles of individuals to various time frames to their sense of urgency to the validity of their goals. These clues help you and customers measure each other's potential to achieve their goals.

For instance, if your customers consistently refer to finances in their comments, terms such as *budgets, operating expenses,* and *paybacks* pop up. These clues suggest your next question should seek out details about the filter of funding or cost justifications. Often customers imply that a sense of urgency exists. Terms such as *tight schedules, delivery dates, order processing requirements,* and *immediate attention* will surface. These clues indicate that your next question should seek out details about the filters of budget, start, decision, or completion dates.

Active Questioning

Your questions can lead you down only one of two paths. The first is a high-return, fast-paced path. It uncovers unknowns of customers' goals, filters, measurable benefits, and SOEs. The second is a low-return, slow-motion path. It seeks answers to how much customers know about the features and benefits of your products. The principles behind active questioning help you to stay on the first path and avoid the second. (See Exhibit 5-2.)

The Strategy Behind Active Questioning

Active questioning is really an old saying in disguise. Seek to understand before you seek to be understood. Make sure you understand how customers' specific comments affect their ability to achieve their goals before responding to them. Often, you and customers find out they do not. The fundamental strategy behind active ques-

Exhibit 5-2. You choose where your questions lead you.

Questions Only Take You One of Two Places

Systems of Evaluation

OR

Products

Goals and Filters

Measurable Benefits

It's Your Choice!

tioning is the Safety Zone concept. It empowers you to **Go For Measurable Specifics** (goals, filters, measurable benefits, and systems of evaluations) so customers view you as an industry expert.

Safety Zone

Customers want to share information because it makes good business sense to do so. When you ask questions that customers would want to ask themselves, it decreases uncertainty and the risks of wasted efforts and unfulfilled goals for them, too. However, for customers, disclosing information must be *risk-free* and not weaken their negotiating position while strengthening yours. As Chapter 3 demonstrated, only one place exists where customers know they are risk free and in control—their measurable goals. Customers know that without their consent, their well-defined destinations are not easily changed. They relax because they are in control. Therefore, relate your questions to their goals. The more measurable the goals, the bigger you make the Safety Zones. Like heat-seeking missiles, let your goal-seeking questions fire away. No one will get hurt—other than competitors and time robbers.

Note: You must make a decision before you conduct a sales call. You must decide whether you are there to gather measurable details or product posture at the first opportunity. If you try to do both, you lose credibility as being customer focused rather than product focused. Once that happens, customers will no longer share details about their goals and filters for the reasons stated above.

The Power of How's Zat?

The Safety Zone strategy revolves around the most powerful words in your sales vocabulary: How's Zat? You use them to understand *"How does that* customer's response affect his or her goals?" The phonetic term *How's Zat?* also includes how, why, and all the other forms of the open-ended questions discussed later in this chapter. Use them as the first words to start a follow-up question to reference customers' responses on how they think their comments affect their ability to achieve goals.

Example

Vince Higgins, the president of a small recruiting company, tells salesperson Paul Leonard, who sells a prospecting training program, that his goal is to increase his salespeople's efficiency. Vince then tells Paul that he sends his staff to a competitor's training program once a year. Just what Paul wanted to hear, right? No problem. Paul uses the Safety Zone and How's Zat? strategies to understand how Vince's comment affects his ability to achieve his goal. He does so without falling into the "what do they do for you?" trap.

Vince: I send my staff to the Got-There-First training program. (This is a specific comment concerning the filters of *current situation* and *alternative.*)

Paul: How do you feel training programs in general help you improve efficiency?

Paul's question motivates Vince to think about how training programs in general (not competitors' specific ones) relate to his goal and safety zone of improving efficiency.

The Tactics Behind Active Questioning

You know all the tactics. For the most part, they are common sense. Nevertheless, often during sales calls, a product focus makes salespeople forget these tactics, so these reminders should prove helpful.

Follow the Customer's Lead

Customers want to take the lead in discussions. It gives them a further sense of control. Let them lead, while you address the topics they bring up. Their responses tell you which questions to ask next. You know exactly what to ask, without guesswork or fishing expeditions.

Your follow-up questions should seek to make crystal clear their goals, filters, measurable benefits, and SOEs. Again, obtaining measurable specifics is the only concrete way to understand how customers define value and how your products generate value. In addition, fighting for control does not make you more productive or successful; so why waste your time. As mentioned before, following their lead lets customers know you are receiving and understanding their messages. The reward is that customers supply plenty of details.

Finally, when you follow the customer's lead, your questions motivate the customer to pull you to the next goal or filter. You are not the first one to bring up a new goal or filter, the customer is. Again, his or her sense of control benefits you.

Example

Customer: I need to get approval on any purchase over $50,000. (Customer discloses filter of *funding* specifics.)

Salesperson: Who needs to approve a purchase over that amount? (Answer about *funding* filter leads into *decision maker's* filter.)

Ask Specific but Open-Ended Questions

Give customers the opportunity to tell you everything they know—at least, everything they know about their goals, filters, measurable benefits, and SOEs. Open-ended questions accomplish that for you. They let customers tell you a lot of things you do not know. Open-ended questions start with words such as *who, what, why, when, where,* and *how.* One word of caution: An open-ended question that does not reference a goal or filter could spell trouble. In the mouths of long-winded customers, they could end up as lengthy monologues about nothing (like most *Seinfeld* episodes). Avoid questions that are no more specific than "How do you feel about life in general?" However, do not take the other extreme and box customers in either.

Yes-or-no questions box in customers and force them to select their answers from limited choices, so they only provide limited information. Customers do not have much incentive to add information. For instance, yes-or-no questions usually result in only yes or no answers. These questions also require playing a game of hit or miss to everyone's discomfort.

They can sound more like guesses or stabs in the dark than questions. "Can you see where you can save money?" "No." "Well, how about saving time?" "No." You will find that getting three consecutive no answers is usually fatal to the sales call. Your sales call just went from collaborative to confrontational as you hope your next question brings a positive response. Customers who ask, "What *part* of 'no' did you not understand?" probably should not be considered ideal prospects. A no answer causes a fight for control over where the sales call goes next. Do you now see why customers view these questions as controlling? Just answer yes or no.

Note: They do have their purpose. You use a yes-or-no question to confirm how customers measure their goals or filters.

Example of Using a Yes-or-No Question

Salesperson: Larry, is improving cash flow important to you?

Customer: No (You now have to throw out another yes-or-no question and hope you do not end up with another no. Otherwise, it is two down, one to go.)

Example of Using an Open-Ended Question

Salesperson: Larry, as head of accounting of a hospital, what are some of your most important priorities? (The answer helps the salesperson learn about how the customer's position affects his goals.)

Note: In the previous example, the salesperson would review a Market Profile sheet, so he would know what priorities (goals) accounting managers of hospitals have if Larry did not know what the salesperson meant by "priorities."

No Loose Ends

You keep building momentum in your sales calls by ensuring that each goal or filter is measurable before pursuing the next one. When you need to return to previously discussed goals and filters to gather missed measurements, it slows your forward progress. It is like stopping at a gas station and only filling up the tank halfway to save time. Eventually you are going to waste more time having to stop twice as often. Making sure you have a full tank of measurable goals and filters speeds up your progress in determining if customers' goals are achievable.

Example

Customer: Our target is to reduce our current inventory by $800,000.

Salesperson: So, is your goal to lower your current inventory from $2,500,000 to $1,700,000? (Uses a yes-or-no question to confirm how the customer measures goals or filters.)

Customer: Yes

Salesperson: What other inventory goals have you set? (Salesperson starts pursuing other goals now that the inventory goal is measurable.)

Note: As outlined in "Ask Specific but Open-Ended Questions," make sure you have accurate and measurable information—before you ask customers to commit to yes-or-no answers. In addition, you build momentum by linking customers' measurable answers to the next filter or goal that you seek specifics on. The two case studies in Chapter 6 examine "linking" in detail.

Don't Shoot Yourself

If someone shoots at you and misses, you do not hand him more bullets when he runs out. Yet, when you agree with negative statements made by customers, that is exactly what you are doing. The only difference is that one kills people; the other kills sales calls. Do not tell customers you too think something is a negative until both parties understand how it affects achieving the customers' goals. Then, if you are unable to help them achieve their goals, let them know why, and do so before they let you know why. Hitting issues head-on is another way you turn negatives into positives and build credibility and trust with customers.

Example of Confirming a Negative

Customer: Jackie, your price seems expensive.

Salesperson: Tom, why do you think we're expensive? (Nothing like asking your customers to enumerate the reasons why they think your product is *expensive*, which most people consider a negative term.)

Customer: Your price is $5,000 more than your competitors.

Example of Not Confirming a Negative

Customer: Jackie, your price seems expensive.

Salesperson: Tom, how are you evaluating price? (The salesperson does not agree her product is expensive, but instead puts the focus on how Tom evaluates price. With either question Jackie has a platform to bring up other value considerations (SOEs) involved with *evaluating price,* such as life-cycle costs. However, Jackie will not be implying that she too thinks her price is expensive with her "evaluating price" question.)

Think Positively

When you make assumptions, you usually make negative ones. Most of us learn early in life to assume the worst: "I bet he wants me to lower my price." If you are going to make assumptions, you can just as easily make positive ones: "I bet he wants me to cost-justify the price." Assumptions do not require proof, so make them benefit you and assume your customers prove you right, not wrong.

Example of a Negative Assumption

Salesperson: Mary, you mentioned before that sometimes you have to go out for public bids. Will this have to go out to public bid? (He assumes the worst using a closed-ended question, rather than assuming he could negotiate the sale.)

Customer: Yes. (Boxed-in customer gets the chance to agree with a negative assumption.)

Example of a Positive Assumption

Salesperson: Mary, you mentioned before that sometimes you have to go out for public bids. What is involved with bypassing the bid process to make sure you achieve your goal of increased efficiency? (The salesperson makes a positive assumption and references her goal or safety zone.)

No Echoes

Depending on who is counting, the English language has more than 3 million words. These words provide a plethora of choices to show off your originality. In addition, when you rephrase—and do not merely parrot customers' responses—it shows you have thought about what they said. That fact alone encourages customers to continue to share information. Rephrasing is easy if you use the Safety Zone strategy and rephrase their comments in terms of how they affect their goals.

Example of Echoing

Customer: Our computer system never works properly.

Salesperson: What makes you think your computer system never works properly? (A good question, but it is a little light on originality.)

Example of Rephrasing

Customer: Our computer system never works properly.

Salesperson: What makes you think your computer system is less than adequate?

Beyond Fluff

How do you know a measurable answer from an immeasurable one? Measurable answers let you and customers quantify their stated goals; immeasurable answers do not. The way for you to receive measurable answers is to motivate customers to progress through their three-tier response levels.

These levels consist of *vague, clearer,* and *measurable.* Customers' responses usually stop at vague because your questions stop there. Hope springs eternal—and like most salespeople, you want to sell something—so you look for any glimmer of hope. Typically, if a salesperson feels a customer's initial vague responses might provide opportunities for sales, he or she stops seeking more details. In essence, salespeople mistakenly encourage customers to stop at vague responses, except on matters of funding, deadlines, and decision-making details.

Salespeople tend to equate the absence of a concrete no response to the presence of a vague yes. They do not want to jeopardize these opportunities by finding out more specifics that might not be favorable to a successful sale. They use the strategy of "If I do not bring it up, maybe they will not bring it up." Typically, they do not find out about an unattainable goal or filter until the umpteenth call, after everyone has wasted time and money.

Remind yourself of the golden rule of soaring sales and booming productivity: Sales opportunities are not created equally. Measurable answers help you choose the opportunities where your unique strengths or strongest features connect to the customers' goals. While vague and clearer answers provide you with some successes, measurable answers provide you with many successes.

Customers will provide measurable answers if the right questions are asked, but they do not usually volunteer them. All you need to do is ask the right questions, gather those measurable goals and filters, weigh their impact on providing value-packed solutions, and reap the rewards.

Note: Let customers know that your questioning follows a predictable pattern. It always focuses on making the cost-benefit analysis of their purchasing considerations (goals and filters) measurable in dollars. No moving targets, unmanaged expectations, or uninformed decisions when everyone uses objective rather than subjective information.

The *vague-clearer-measurable* questioning follows this three-tier pattern:

1. To first find out a filter or goal, you ask some version of "What does that involve?" as in "What are your plans?"
2. To make the customers' vague responses clearer, you ask some version of "How does that affect you?"
3. Then, to make the customers' clearer responses measurable, you ask some version of "How much does that cost and save?" or "What are those details?"

The two case studies in Chapter 6 explore this questioning process in detail as it pertains to filters.

Equally powerful, *you can eliminate competition* when you make customers' responses measurable, as the following example illustrates.

Example

Watch how the salesperson's three questions keep helping the customer to think in measurable terms—and eliminate competition at the same time.

Salesperson: What is your top priority (goal)?

Vague Customer Response: I want to improve operations. (Obviously, many products and competitors can help customers to improve operations. What do you think she has in mind? No one knows until she accepts or rejects his products)

Salesperson: What does that involve? (Salesperson seeks more details and encourages the customer to provide them by working off her last response.)

Clearer Customer Response: I want to improve operations by reducing administrative tasks. (Now, fewer products and competitors can achieve this objective. Yet, what products to offer is still anyone's guess.)

Salesperson: What dollar savings are you shooting for? (Salesperson seeks financial details and requests the customer to share more details.)

Measurable Customer Response: We spend $1,800,000 on administrative tasks annually. They want to reduce them by 10 percent. (Now, very few products or competitors can save $180,000 on administrative costs to improve operations. If you choose your market segments carefully, only you can connect a unique strength to a confirmed measurable benefit of a goal.)

Note: In market segments where you have no unique strengths, if your product can achieve customers' goals, so can some of your competitors' products. The significant advantage you gain through this questioning process is that you are making their goals measurable while competitors are not. Customers view you as their business and industry (market segment) expert. You help customers enhance how they buy when you arm them with facts that empower them to make well-thought-out decisions. Your sales approach becomes your competitive advantage in these product-neutral situations. You can win the sale by connecting your features to the customer's *measurable* benefits better than competitors can.

The Power of the Four Types of Questions

Your most powerful selling tools involve four types of questions: dialoguing, qualifying, clarifying, and verifying. The last three make customers' responses progress from vague to clearer to measurable. You end up exactly where you and your customers need to be—with measurable goals and filters.

Dialoguing

You use dialoguing to break the ice and make everyone feel comfortable without falling in the water. "How do you like this cold weather?" Dialoguing creates comfort levels or rapport between you and customers. These exchanges do not include discussions about goals, filters, products, and services. Use dialoguing to establish common ground. You also know by now not to be the four thousandth salesperson to ask about the picture of a sailboat hanging on a customer's wall.

The use of open-ended questions encourages unguarded conversation and humor. It also gives a sense of each other's mannerisms and personalities. This verbal insight assists you in determining what sort of formality, pace, and levity to use in the sales calls. If customers only laugh when you say good-bye, you might reconsider how well you read their comments.

Do not merely listen for clues to their styles; *look* for them, too. Even without a degree in psychology, you might notice certain visual clues. Customers stealing glances at their watches might suggest either impatience or self-importance. Answering telephones as they motion you to stay where you are, and then talking for twenty minutes might suggest two things; okay three if you count rudeness. They either consider themselves very important or you not very important. Your focus on their goals and filters will make them feel important—and let them know you are important to their efforts in achieving them.

Listen for verbal clues, too. "I have a hectic schedule" leaves nothing for the imagination. So does the all-time favorite, "What's on your mind?" These subtle hints also reflect their degree of patience, sense of self-importance, and level of attentiveness. Be ready to shift from dialoguing to qualifying at a moment's notice. Dialoguing consists of open-ended questions. These, as mentioned before in the How's Zat? section, start with *who, what, why, when, where,* and *how.* Avoid seeking yes-or-no answers when trying to drum up conversation. A word of caution: Do not forget how a "no" answer can be a conversation-killer.

Qualifying

Qualifying is the first questioning process you learn how to use. You probably define the word *qualifying* as what you do on the first call to find out whether you can sell customers something. Qualifying can mean nearly anything. Is it finding out their level of pain?

Is it uncovering their sense of urgency? Is it reinforcing how well they like you? Is it discovering they have money? You know better.

You know qualifying means not wasting anyone's time. Therefore, qualifying starts with helping customers to gather information about their goals, filters, measurable benefits, and systems of evaluations. You first qualify customers on their ability to achieve their goals, not buy your products. Qualifying questions are open-ended. As expected, your first line of questioning most often results in vague responses. Qualifying questions, like dialoguing questions, never seek yes or no answers. The reward for saving those yes or no questions until the end is worth it.

Example

Customer: We want to improve our productivity.

Salesperson: What will that involve? (This qualifying question seeks details on what the goal of improving productivity means.)

Okay, be honest. Were you not tempted to say, "We can help you improve productivity with _____ (fill in the product or feature)?"

Clarifying

While qualifying points you in the right direction, clarifying helps you make sure you are on the right track. Typically, you use this questioning process on the second in-person sales call when you realize there are still a lot of unknowns left over from the first call. When you follow your qualifying questions with clarifying questions, you save time and reduce wasted efforts. Customers' measurable answers help them and you decide whether it makes sense for a third sales call.

Your clarifying questions turn vague responses into measurable responses. They become more measurable in terms of time or money. Clarified answers define customers' goals and filters and how they measure value. Your clarifying questions also are open-ended and do not seek yes or no answers. Clarifying means never having to say you are sorry for unfulfilled goals, wasted time, or money.

Example

Customer: I want to reduce the number of defects to improve productivity.

Salesperson: What do defect costs run annually? (Clarifying question to make the costs of defects measurable)

Customer: Defects cost us about $250,000 a year.

Salesperson: What sort of savings are you looking to achieve? (Second clarifying question to make their savings measurable)

Verifying

Verifying is the questioning process that uses yes-or-no questions. If you qualified and clarified properly, you should end up with yes answers. Chapter 8 explains how to handle "no" answers. Verifying confirms there are full agreements on the specifics of goals and filters. Verifying requires the use of yes-or-no questions that confirm you and the customers both understand their measurable points the same way. (See Exhibit 5-3.)

Exhibit 5-3. Verify customers' responses.

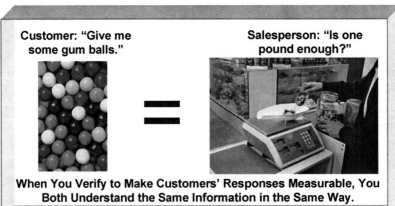

Customer: "Give me some gum balls."   Salesperson: "Is one pound enough?"

When You Verify to Make Customers' Responses Measurable, You Both Understand the Same Information in the Same Way.

Example

Customer: We feel we can reduce $250,000 of defects by 30 percent.

Salesperson: So, your goal is to decrease defect costs by $75,000? (Verifies the cost savings target)

Customer: That's right.

Tuned In

Constantly ask yourself, "Do your questions clarify customers' and your ability to achieve their goals?" Anything but a yes answer serves no business purpose. Your listening and questioning skills are invaluable tools in making sure you get to yes answers. The next two chapters explain how they make sure you conduct every step of the four selling phases in the most productive manner that fits your style. Most important, they will help you exceed the *measurable* expectations of customers.

Satisfied customers, high-value sales, and long-term relationships—all because you question how you listen and you listen to how you question.

SUMMARY

- The difference between success and failure is usually only a matter of one or two questions that you did not ask or that you asked incorrectly.
- Your active listening encourages customers to disclose information; your follow-up responses tell them that you are receiving their messages.
- Use your extra listening time to look for visual and verbal clues to anticipate (not assume or advocate a product) a customer's response.
- Your questions will take you down only one of two paths. You either find out unknowns about customers' goals, filters, measurable benefits, and systems of evaluations (Go For Measurable Specifics) or confirm what you already know about your products, their features,

and their benefits. Customer experts do the former; product experts do the latter.

- The Safety Zone strategy references all questions concerning filters back to the customers' goals. Customers understand why you ask questions when you reference their goals or filters. Other topics you might explore have only limited business value.

- Any question that starts with a version of How's Zat? to understand how the customer's comment affects his or her ability to achieve goals means you are using the Safety Zone strategy.

- How's Zat? tactics include the following:

  - *Follow the Customers' Lead.* Relate all clarifying questions to customers' last responses on how they affect their goals and filters.

  - *Ask Specific but Open-Ended Questions.* Do not use yes-or-no questions unless you need to verify a point.

  - *No Loose Ends.* Verify that a goal or filter is measurable before pursuing another.

  - *Don't Shoot Yourself.* Never confirm a negative statement.

  - *Think Positively.* Never make a negative assumption.

  - *No Echoes.* Rephrase the customers' responses; do not merely repeat them.

- Customers' responses are usually three-tiered: vague, clearer, and measurable. When it comes to selling compensated value, only the last one counts.

- The questioning process involves qualifying, clarifying, or verifying to transform customers' vague responses into measurable terms of time and money.

- Only verifying questions should seek yes-or-no answers.

Chapter Six

Leave the Brochures Behind

The time has come to take all the concepts, strategies, and tactics from the previous chapters, tie them together, and apply them to your sales calls. It is time to outvalue the competition and receive higher profits as your reward.

This chapter empowers you to evaluate every sales opportunity using cast-in-stone reference points to ensure that the efforts of you and your customers are worth the returns. It explains the following:

- How the framework of the MeasureMax ("Measure to Maximize") selling system works
- How you use its measuring tools to influence sales in progress
- How your sales orders become planned events, not random occurrences
- How you sell value in business environments that are constantly tempted by low prices
- How to conduct the first two selling phases—MP 1: Spark Interest and MP 2: Measure Potential—without mentioning specific products

How MeasureMax Works

The MeasureMax selling system is 90 percent planning and 10 percent doing. Therefore, it starts with your Product and Market Profile sheets. These sheets highlight which groups of customers share goals that connect to your unique strengths or strongest features. You then plan where you want to invest your selling efforts. The ability to sell value and to receive compensation for doing so depends on whom you contact.

MeasureMax is also about measurability. Like you, customers know they can only manage what they can measure. They eagerly wait for you to help them quantify their goals and filters. You motivate customers to rethink their purchasing decisions in terms of the quality and value of their goals, not just the quantity and price of products' features. It is difficult to dispute that it makes good business sense to measure twice, cut once, before you decide what to buy or sell. MeasureMax's format ensures that you are ready to evaluate sales opportunities as a marketing manager, competitor, sales manager, salesperson, and most important, customer.

Now, it is just a question of how you do it.

The four selling phases called Measurable Phases (MPs) (see pages 7 and 8 in the Introduction) are the how-to part. They break sales opportunities into four minisales in which customers give you a kind of "purchase order" to end each phase. These are not your typical purchase orders (except for the last one). Instead, they are measurable commitments, or Measurable Phase Changes (MPCs), you receive from customers that confirm it still makes sense to continue trying to achieve their goals. Each MPC brings you closer to receiving the fourth MPC (Agreement Confirmed), which is your typical purchase order. Receiving MPCs renders the purchase order as nothing more than the logical conclusion to a series of customer commitments.

You also use MPCs to gauge your progress. These sales milestones denote that you have completed one MP and are ready to start the next one. The faster you obtain MPCs in the right sequence, the faster you receive orders. Needing fewer in-person sales calls to get more orders is how you make productivity boom.

You will also see how the sequence of the MPCs affects your ability to sell value. If you receive MPC 1 to 4 in order you build value; if you go out of order, you diminish value. In addition, a failure to obtain an MPC means customers are not ready to go to the next MP. Chapter 8 explains how to handle these situations.

Note: Two case studies spanning this chapter and Chapters 7 and 8 demonstrate how MPs and MPCs work with new prospects.

Chapter 9 explains how to use them with existing customers. The first case study (which continues with Steven Smartsell) examines the steps conceptually in a business-to-business sale. At the end of these chapters, another case study takes a business-to-consumer sale from inception to conclusion. It details the steps and logistics of the four phases. (See Exhibit 6-1.)

Note: There are no submissive roles in this sales process. (Leave those for the needs-satisfaction type of salespeople). You and customers are equal partners who take turns leading in the four selling phases. In the first two, customers lead with their goals, filters, measurable benefits, and systems of evaluations (SOEs). In the last two, you lead with your unique strengths, features, and measurable benefits. In Chapter 7, you will see how the common measurable benefits connect goals to features.

Exhibit 6-1. The four selling steps.

THE FOUR SELLING STEPS

MPC 4: AGREEMENT CONFIRMED
MP 4: IMPLEMENT AGREEMENT

MPC 3: SOLUTION CONFIRMED
MP 3: CEMENT SOLUTION

MPC 2: POTENTIAL CONFIRMED
MP 2: MEASURE POTENTIAL

MPC 1: INTEREST CONFIRMED
MP 1: SPARK INTEREST

As you pick up speed, MPCs verify that you and customers are still in step with one another.

Let the Best Sales Method Win

Throughout these four selling phases, you follow strategies and steps in a prescribed order. This recommended sequence emerged after years of fine-tuning which order of steps achieved the best results. Yet, the strength of the selling system is that it is goal oriented, not task oriented. While it is important how you conduct the steps, it is more important that you achieve the objectives of each MP, which is obtaining an MPC. You can choose to follow these steps or modify them to better fit your style and personality.

Fortunately, you do not need to memorize logic-driven steps. You only need to remember to keep your focus on the customers' goals and filters. Applying the MeasureMax process and achieving success is all it takes to fine-tune the steps to the specifics of your selling situations.

If you choose to use a sales method with different steps or sequences, however, challenge their effectiveness. Also, make sure you know Chapter 8 inside out so you can handle the obstacles that arise from going out of sequence. MeasureMax's framework of MPs and MPCs allows you to measure the productivity of *any* sales method *on a per-sales-call basis.* You want to measure your progress by how many in-person sales calls it takes for you to obtain each MPC. Remember, sales calls are your limited resources that must provide an adequate return.

In addition, measure how long (days, weeks, months, or years) it takes you to achieve the MPCs. The measurable customer commitments of MPCs make it easy to know whether you obtained them or not. They leave no room for interpretation. Try using MeasureMax's steps and sequence on a few sales opportunities. Compare your current sales method's results to MeasureMax's, and let the best sales method win.

Note: Regardless of whether you sell one product or a hundred, a service rather than a product, or high-end to low-end on a quality scale, selling value that you receive higher profits for still depends on connecting features to the measurable benefits of the customer's goals via accurate and favorable SOEs. Following the order and steps of the Measurable Phases helps to make that happen.

MP 1: Spark Interest

Creating interest levels in existing customers, let alone new ones, is a formidable task. It is easy to understand why sales training programs start you off in front of customers. The tough part is how to get in front of the worthwhile ones. You need answers to the following three questions to know how to get in front of them:

1. How do you make customers feel your potential to provide value to them is worth a sales call?
2. How do you ensure that their potential to provide value to you warrants a sales call?
3. How do you accomplish this feat within the first thirty seconds of your initial phone contact without mentioning a *specific* product?

To make life easier, all three questions have the same answers. You plug information from the appropriate Market Profile sheet into the following MP 1: Spark Interest step. This helps you to qualify whether specific customers are bona fide members of your targeted market segments and share general goals that interest them. It is premature to try to make customers' goals measurable in this phase; you save that task for MP 2: Measure Potential. If your Market Profile sheets are accurate, your unique strengths or strongest features should connect to their goals. If they do, you are off to a good start.

Unless you do a lot of in-person cold calling, you usually conduct MP 1: Spark Interest over the telephone. Its purpose is to ensure customers and you that it is worthwhile for you to continue on to the second phase, MP 2: Measure Potential. If you and the customer decide it is worthwhile, you have reached MPC 1: Interest Confirmed. Another objective is to provide the basis to seek measurable specifics during MP 2: Measure Potential. You conduct MP 2 in person at the customer's place of business. (See Exhibit 6-2.)

Step One: Research and Membership

You want to demonstrate your understanding of your customer's business as quickly as possible. When you mention details of organizational characteristics—such as operating hours, number of employees, importance of downtime, code sensitivity, growth rates, and size—you build immediate credibility. After considering the characteristics of the organization and the customer's position, you suggest goals that should interest him or her. Customers know you did not randomly pick them out of a hat, off a mailing list, or

Exhibit 6-2. MP 1: Spark Interest.

MP 1: Spark Interest Steps

Step 1: Research and Membership

Confirms Organizational Characteristics and Position of Customer

Step 2: Take Your Pick

Customer Selects a Goal(s) from a Group the Salesperson Suggests as Key Issues in His Market Segment

Step 3: Track Record

Salesperson Provides Names from Same Market Segment Where She Achieved Similar Goals

MPC 1: Interest Confirmed

because they have a pulse. You eliminate the common tension that occurs when no clear understanding exists for why you made contact.

Note: A sure-fire way to demonstrate your knowledge of the customer's company or industry is to point out a goal that might make the customer more competitive against a specific competitor (just make sure it's one that you don't work with).

You confirm that the customer's company has the appropriate organizational characteristics to qualify it as being in your targeted market segment. You also confirm the customer's position and responsibilities. Make sure any suggested goals fall within his or her area of expertise and responsibility.

Note: Use the sources of information discussed in Chapter 3 under "Organizational Characteristics Affect Customers' Goals" to understand potential customers' goals.

However, no one should feel your research is invasive. You do not want anyone feeling that you violated his or her privacy. For instance, if you sell diet programs, you certainly would not start a sales call by saying, "Our records indicate that you are thirty pounds overweight. Is this correct?" Restrict your comments to ones that are indicative of hard work researching public knowledge.

Note: The more market details customers confirm as being accurate, the more likely that your suggested goals will be relevant to them.

Case Study

Steven Smartsell is a sales representative for FutureTech, which sells highly sophisticated products and services to personal computer manufacturers. Does this sound familiar? You reviewed his Product Profile sheet and Market Profile sheet in Chapter 2 and Chapter 3. Steven is about to contact Olivia Ontime, vice president of manufacturing for Positron, a personal computer manufacturer. The stage is set for the forces of positions, organizational characteristics, goals, measurable benefits, filters, systems of evaluations, and features to come together under Steve's guidance to create compensated value.

Using the Research and Membership step, Steven immediately mentions to Olivia why he contacted her. He stresses how FutureTech works exclusively with personal computer manufacturers. Specifically, companies that have more than five production facilities, sales of more than $1 billion, 20,000 employees, and operate around the clock (the organizational characteristics from his customer's Market Profile sheet). He just described Positron to Olivia. He then confirms with Olivia her position and that Positron shares these characteristics. Once confirmed, Steven continues to the second step.

Note: While Steven told Olivia the type of companies FutureTech works with, he did not mention specific products that would box him in prematurely. He does not want the initial contact to be product focused.

Note: This step combined with the next two, Take Your Pick and Track Record, creates your Spark Interest Statement. Use this scripted icebreaker for the first twenty seconds of contact with customers. You develop one Spark Interest Statement per market segment but get to use the same ones repeatedly. You do not have to reinvent the wheel; you benefit from the power of market segments sharing the same organizational characteristics and goals. With enough practice, you will not sound like you are reading it. Your Spark Interest Statement is the most important fifty words you will use with neutral and negative customers who do not know you or favor competitors. It also helps to decrease the time it takes to generate qualified interest with positive customers who do know you. Most of the information comes from the Market Profile sheets you developed in Chapter 2. See Exhibit 6-3, whose template can also be downloaded at www.measuremax.com.

Step Two: Take Your Pick

In this step, you mention two to four goals (or a compelling industry event) that should interest members of this market segment.

Exhibit 6-3. Spark interest statement template.

Spark Interest Statement		
Market Segment:		
Position:		
Key Organizational Characteristics:		
Last Three Successful Projects In Same Market Segment:		
Potential Customer Goals	**Past Benefits Achieved**	**Systems of Evaluation**
1.		
2.		
3.		
Notes:		
MP 1: SPARK INTEREST STATEMENT CHECKLIST		

☐ **Step 1: Research And Membership:** Immediately demonstrate and verify that research on targeted market segment applies to customer. Also, verify position of the contact.

☐ **Step 2: Take Your Pick:** Have customer select one or more potential goals you suggested. Suggest goals in the form of a question. Mention any new industry-specific systems of evaluation to spark interest.

☐ **Step 3: Track Record** Provide success stories in same market segment.

✓ *Spark Interest Statement* **(via telephone):**

You do not want to box customers in by only giving them one choice that requires a yes-or-no answer. If your Market Profile sheet is accurate, they should be interested in achieving at least one of your suggested goals. Ideally, these suggested goals or compelling events—such as changes in local, state, or federal regulations that would be costly to comply with, but which you can help them address—should connect to your unique strengths. If not, you gain a competitive advantage by demonstrating measurable value. In either case, you will be dealing from a position of strength if competitors arrive on the scene.

In this step, you also confidently state that if certain conditions exist, you could help the customer achieve goals that produce significant benefits. You highlight the general benefits you achieved with other customers in the same market segment. Be prepared to provide measurable and documented benefits when asked or if customers would consider your previous results as dramatic by market standards.

As both a seeker of long-term customers and an honest person, you shoot straight from the very beginning. You clearly inform customers (no small print allowed) that you are not guaranteeing the same outcomes, only their possibility. Let customers know up front that you cannot make broad-based claims without more facts.

You know you are not for everybody. Hey, that is why there are market segments. However, when customers' goals and your unique strengths match, no one can provide more value. In addition, determining whether these conditions exist provides the valid business reason to meet. It also provides the reasons for asking questions in MP 2: Measure Potential.

Case Study

Steven Smartsell mentions to Olivia Ontime that if *certain conditions* exist, FutureTech, with its wide range of manufacturing products and services, has had significant successes in preventing unscheduled production stoppages, reducing operating costs, increasing productivity, and eliminating the potential for code violations.

He then asks Olivia which one of these goals interests her. In addition, are there others she would like to pursue?

Note: If customers ask you what those "certain conditions" are—always tell them. Inform customers these conditions range from technical to operational to financial considerations. Again, you want to meet (if you get MPC 1: Interest Confirmed) to explore these considerations (filters, measurable benefits, and systems of evaluation) in detail with them.

Step Three: Track Record

Verify that customers have an interest in at least one of the goals. Whether they select a goal or not tells you whether your Market Profile sheet is on target or needs reassessing. It also indicates whether a cost-of-doing-nothing situation or create-and-wait situation exists. Once they select goal(s), you can reference documented successes in their market segment.

When you provide references from only their market segments, customers view you as a leader in their industry. For instance, do not use office buildings, schools, and hotels as references for hospitals. Review your reference lists and see if you segregated them by market segment.

Note: A word of caution: If you mention customers' competitors, make clear that each company is unique in its own way. Stress that your success with their competitors is due in part to your ability to keep trade secrets strictly confidential. Finally, point out that your expertise also lies in solving common industry problems.

Case Study

Olivia Ontime confirms that her interest lies in reducing downtime. Would you really expect any other goal from a vice president of manufacturing in a critical application where downtime has huge lost-dollar implications?

Steven Smartsell mentions how FutureTech helped vice presidents of manufacturing companies similar to Positron to achieve the same goal. He references companies such as Advanced Computer Co., Star Computers, and PC Power Ltd.

Measurable Phase Change 1: Interest Confirmed

You express and verify mutual interest to invest more time, effort, and resources in exploring the customer's stated goals. Your focus is on the customer's goals and benefits, not on your product's features and benefits. Do not mention specific products until MP 3: Cement Solution. You still need to perform a *test of reasonableness* on the customer's goals and filters before you know what the customer can achieve and what you can offer.

If customers ask about specific products or a price (a common customer question), tell them a few come to mind or give them a wide range. However, you really do not know which ones, if any, fit their circumstances until you understand them better. Do not box yourself in with a specific product—and without a specific product, you cannot provide a specific price. It is unfair to customers and to you to try to guess what, if any, products can help them before you know their measurable goals and filters.

You also risk coming across as presumptuous. After all, how can you, one or two minutes into a conversation, claim you can help them solve a problem or achieve a goal? Anything you do not say about specific products today, you can always say tomorrow. The reverse is not true. You cannot "unsay" something. If customers push you for detailed product information do the following two things:

1. Ask them specifically what they would like you to discuss—that is, operational, financial, or technical aspects of your products. Then, explain that without knowing the specifics of their goals, situation, and purchasing considerations (filters), you would not know which one to highlight yet.
2. Promise to bring a general product or company capabilities brochure to leave with him or her after you meet.

MP 1 ends with MPC 1: Interest Confirmed. Customers confirm there is an interest in achieving a goal and determining its potential. They agree to your call for action, which is a recommendation to the customer to implement a measurable and physical activity. Besides a purchase order, this could be a meeting, a survey, a review of past records, a job-site visit, a factory visit, or another sales call.

Note: Make sure you do not sound as if you are doing the customer a favor in pursuing this opportunity further. You just want to confirm that you are not the only one motivated to pursue their goals. Remember the pitfalls of being more motivated than customers (Chapter 1).

Case Study

Steven tells Olivia that he is willing to invest time in pursuing her goal of reducing downtime based on the potential benefits if she is willing to invest time also.

Steven schedules an appointment to meet in person with Olivia to conduct the second phase, MP 2: Measure Potential.

Using Voice Mail to Jump-Start MP 1

For salespeople, voice mail sounds more like voice jail. You find yourself locked into two less-than-ideal choices. Either you leave an awkward message that is not returned, or you leave customers with a lot of hang-up messages. Then, you keep calling back. You are now in a race. You hope you make contact with the person before he or she figures out that you are the one who keeps hanging up.

The key to leaving a voice mail that encourages customers to call you back is to have an abbreviated spark interest statement ready to go. Your objective now is to get the customer interested enough to return your call. If they call back, be ready to use their Spark Interest Statement (you might want to set up a Waiting for Returned Voice Message folder). If they don't, there is always speed dialing.

Example

Voice Mail: Hi, this is Olivia Ontime with Positron. I'm sorry that I missed your call. Please leave your name, number, time, and a brief message. I will get back to you as soon as I can. Beeeeeep.

Steven: Hello Olivia, I'm Steven Smartsell with FutureTech. We work exclusively with personal computer manufacturers that operate at least five production plants worldwide. Our global services and products have had one purpose for more than twenty-five years: We successfully help manufacturing managers of companies in highly competitive market places increase their productivity and profits without sacrificing quality and customer satisfaction.

I'm confident that when we speak, you'll know within five minutes whether we might be in a position to help you. At worst case, I'm sure our discussion will highlight key industry trends that could affect your operations. You can reach me at 888-999-7777. I look forward to our conversation. Thanks for your time and consideration. Have a great day!

In this example, Steven's forty-five-second voice message has all the qualities of a strong Spark Interest Statement. He shows evidence of research, lists some goals and general benefits, and indicates past successes. He also lets Olivia know that he possesses industry expertise (goals, system of evaluations, and the like)—and that her investment is only five minutes.

Using E-Mail to Jump-Start MP 2

After obtaining MPC 1: Interest Confirmed, let your contacts know that you would like to send them an e-mail or a fax. It will outline a tentative agenda of your in-person meeting. Let them know that the purpose of the e-mail is to give them the opportunity to make changes to the agenda. Stress how it will help to ensure that you fulfill their expectations of the meeting. Referencing the e-mail also serves as an excellent way to begin MP 2: Measure Potential.

The following e-mail example occurs after Marge Kane, a sales representative who sells financial services, completed MPC 1: Interest Confirmed. Her contact is Barbara Green. She is the chief financial officer for a high-tech start-up corporation called Advance Biotronics. (See Exhibit 6-4.)

Using an Assistant to Obtain MPC 1 and Set Up MP 2 Calls

Granted, not everyone has a sales or marketing assistant. However, if you do, and you use him to qualify and obtain MPC 1 and set up MP 2 sales calls, his productivity and yours soars. The following are some effective ways to do that:

- Set up MP 1 phone calls by market segment.
- Supply the appropriate Spark Interest Statements for those segments.
- Role-play on how to conduct MP 1.
- Communicate the blocks of time you have open to make sales calls (various software program with scheduling functions are available for this purpose).
- Have your assistant send a follow-up e-mail to the customer (make sure the assistant references your name and contact information). Your assistant then can e-mail the customer's reply to you. He or she should also be familiar with leaving voice messages.

MP 2: Measure Potential

MP 2: Measure Potential has four steps. You use these steps to help customers gather specifics about their goals and filters. You both

Exhibit 6-4. Sample e-mail agenda.

Dear Barbara:

   As we discussed, at CorpGrowth, we have one goal. We help growing biotech businesses have the financial power to move from one stage of their development to the next stage in a profitable manner. Therefore, to make the best use of our half-hour meeting, I would appreciate it you could review this tentative agenda. I welcome any additions, deletions, or modifications you might have. Just send them back to me and I'll make sure we address them.

   a) An overview of Advance Biotronics's asset situation today to determine your starting point.
   b) A review of your key asset management goals. In addition, how you will measure their achievement in order of importance to determine where you want to end up. You mentioned that "preservation of capital" is your top priority. For your consideration: some other typical financial goals for companies like yours that are shipping product and have positive cash flow are as follows:
       i.   High degree of liquidity
       ii.   Liquidity forecasting
       iii.   Competitive investment performance
   c) Review of industry trends in asset management to help you explore more options.

   I appreciate your time, efforts, and consideration. I look forward to meeting you on Tuesday at 10 A.M. I'm confident that it will be educational and productive for both of us.

Regards,

Marge Kane
Vice President, CorpGrowth
987-123-8833
(Fax) 987-123-8833
(E-mail) margek@corpgrowth.com

P.S.- Please feel free to visit our web site at www.corpgrowth.com to see what we have done for other companies in your industry.

   Note: Like any correspondence, make sure you do a spell check and read it aloud before sending it. Also, if you segment your Web site by market segments, insert the hyperlink to that section instead of to your home page.

---

perform a *test of reasonableness* to see if customers first, you second, can achieve their goals.

   If customers have multiple goals, rank them. Their goals are not equal in importance or value; the top one counts most. The secondary goals are typically luxury items rather than necessities. If customers have two or three number one goals, it is a sign that they have not yet assigned value to achieving them. When you make their goals measurable, they choose the one that produces the most value.

   Prioritizing their goals helps you to understand why they ranked them as they did. Often, numerous filters surface when you ask customers to explain why they chose a goal as the most important one to achieve. Use their top-ranked goal to uncover their filters. You will find that the influencers (goal motivation, current, situation, plans, alternatives, and past keys) will change, but the prerequisites (decision maker, dates, funding, and attainment measurement) will not. The attainment measurement of the top-ranked goal sets the purchasing requirements your products must meet.

You also have a tough choice to make if your products cannot achieve their primary goals. You can focus on their secondary ones if you think you can show them that they can produce as much or more value than their primary one. The difference between the measurable benefits of the primary and secondary goals will determine the outcome. The tough choice is whether this uphill battle is worth the effort.

Note: Customer etiquette dictates that you fulfill customers' expectations of a meeting—even if it means mentioning specific products in MP 1: Spark Interest and MP 2: Measure Potential. Therefore, make sure customers understand that the purpose of the meeting during MP 2: Measure Potential is to better understand what is involved in achieving their goals (measurable benefits, filters, and systems of evaluation). Be patient, customers expect product presentation at the first in-person sales calls. Keep reminding them and receiving agreement that it is their goals that will determine their product selections rather than the other way around.

Yet, one glaring exception exists when it might be necessary to describe specific products during MP 1: if it becomes the only way to spark interest. With technically advanced or unique products, customers might not have any reference points to relate to them. A description, sample, or demonstration might be the only way for them to realize that previously unattainable goals are achievable. However, make sure when you meet during MP 2 that you shift the focus from the product's features to the goals it can help the customer achieve. (See Exhibit 6-5.)

In addition, customers usually do not have all the details about goals, measurable benefits, filters, and SOEs at their fingertips. They need time to research information as do you. Typically, MP 2 takes at least two in-person sales calls to gather all the specifics and to find out any information you forgot to ask. However, this additional investment in the details shortens your sales cycle, not in-

Exhibit 6-5. MP 2: Measure Potential.

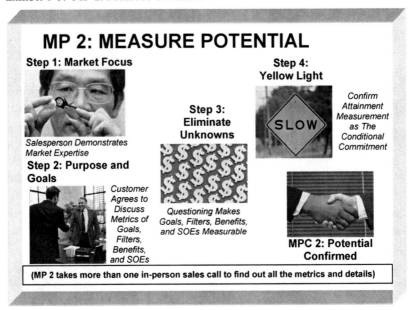

creases it. You and the customer only gather data that will decide if you can help them to achieve their goals. You then can make advance-or-abandon decisions sooner to prevent wasted efforts.

Step One: Market Focus

Display your knowledge of the customer's market segments by citing relevant facts. Technical statements about your features and benefits do not demonstrate expertise; your questions about their goals and filters do. Therefore, do not mention specific products during this phase either.

Note: Ask the customer if anyone else will be at your in-person meeting. If there are other people attending, ask for their titles and their fields of interest. Be prepared to discuss goals that are relevant to their positions and/or fields of interest.

Case Study

Steven Smartsell mentions how long FutureTech in general—and he, specifically—has worked with computer manufacturers like Positron.

He stresses how he is familiar with the issues that confront highly competitive industries like hers—such as fluctuating demand, high-dollar downtime for interrupted production, short product life, reliance on fewer suppliers, and constant manufacturing changes to accommodate new technological advances.

Step Two: Purpose and Goals

Start with dialogue questions to build rapport. Using customers' cues, be ready to shift into business gear. You achieve your first yes of the day when the customer agrees the meeting's purpose is to determine the potential of achieving her goals and your ability to help accomplish them. You then verify her stated goal(s). If you did not set a specific meeting purpose in MP 1: Spark Interest, ask customers, "What would you like to accomplish today that would make you feel that our time together was productive?" Once you acknowledge their purpose, then share with them what you would like to accomplish to make it productive. Remember, it's your business time also.

Case Study

Steven Smartsell confirms that the meeting's purpose is to get a better understanding of Olivia's stated goal of reducing downtime and whether FutureTech can help in this endeavor. He also verifies that Olivia has no other goals she wants to pursue at this time.

Olivia asks Steven to review with her some of his products and services that he thinks might be helpful to her operations. Steven tells her that while he has some general thoughts on what products might apply in her situation, he would not venture a guess until he understands her goals and purchasing considerations (filters) better. He will leave her some case studies of how FutureTech has helped other customers in her industry achieve goals such as reducing downtime or improving efficiency. He also offers to leave a general product and service catalog when their meeting concludes.

How to Handle the "Tell Me About Your Products" Request

As previously discussed, customers often want you to describe your products before you ask them any questions. Customers feel that you only ask questions to posture your products as the right solutions for them—regardless of whether you know their goals or not.

Therefore, they figure that they might as well ask you to become a "feature creature." When you finish your pitch, they will then let you know whether they are interested. Unfortunately, customer "interest" without defined goals can lead to unfulfilled expectations and disappointments for all involved.

The following is a more-detailed example (with strategies and tactics in italics) on how to handle a product pitch request at the start of either MP 1 or 2.

Example

Customer: Tell me about your products and services.

Salesperson: Nothing would make me happier than having the opportunity to talk to you about my products and services. However, I wouldn't know where to start without first understanding what you want to achieve.

I thought our objective today was to better understand your priorities and what it would take *you* to achieve them. Once I fully understood your parameters (*goals, measurable benefits, SOEs, and filters*), I'll take your information back to my team. Then, after careful analysis of the specifics of your situation, we'll see if we can custom-tailor a program (*Connecting Value sheet, Chapter 7*) that achieves your goals.

I promise that I'll send you a summary of our findings for your review (*see Scope of Work in Chapter 7*). How does this plan sound to you (*verifies agreement*)? Finally, I'm confident that you'll find out more about what we do by the questions I ask you about your company than any product presentation I could make (*positioning himself as a customer expert*).

Step Three: Eliminate Unknowns

Start making customers' goals measurable by making their benefits measurable. Build their safety zones as large as possible. The more measurable the goals, the larger are the safety zones. You then qualify, clarify, and verify each filter in terms of how it affects the customers' ability to achieve their goals.

When you connect customers' filters to their goals, and not to your products, they do not feel manipulated by the questions you ask. For instance, think of how you would feel if a computer sales-person, who did not know your goals, asked you, "How much money have you set aside to buy a new server?" Compare that question to this one from a computer salesperson who knows your measurable goal: "How much have you budgeted to reduce your system maintenance costs by $35,000 annually?" (See Exhibit 6-6.)

Customers appreciate how your questions help them to make better purchasing decisions. When you deal with measurable goals and the specifics of filters, the room for unmet expectations decreases dramatically. You also create an environment where it does not feel like you are grilling them with rapid-fire yes-or-no questions.

Reinforce to customers the concept that details of measurable benefits, filters, and systems of evaluation determine whether you can achieve their goals. They are offering you challenges that become more formidable as they disclose more filters. Readily accept these challenges. The requirements for achieving their goals become more difficult not only for you but also for competitors as well. Again, if you chose your market segment correctly, these requirements help you to provide more value than do competitors. You

Exhibit 6-6. Your questions should reference customers' goals.

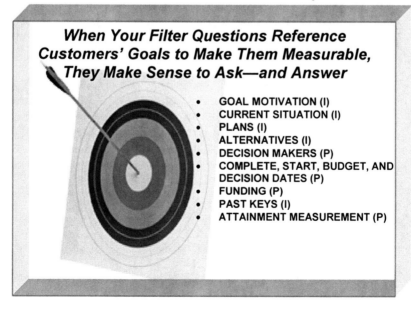

When Your Filter Questions Reference Customers' Goals to Make Them Measurable, They Make Sense to Ask—and Answer

- GOAL MOTIVATION (I)
- CURRENT SITUATION (I)
- PLANS (I)
- ALTERNATIVES (I)
- DECISION MAKERS (P)
- COMPLETE, START, BUDGET, AND DECISION DATES (P)
- FUNDING (P)
- PAST KEYS (I)
- ATTAINMENT MEASUREMENT (P)

are building your case to receive fair compensation for the unique or measurably better value your products provide.

Note: If you cannot achieve a customer's goal or satisfy the attainment measurement, the details enable you to explain why. You can tell the customer what goals you can achieve and why. You might need to forgo this sales opportunity but not the prospects for future business.

Although it is not the desired outcome, it beats wasting everyone's time, energy, and resources for one to three months. Typically, customers take this long to inform you that it does not make sense to do business with you. Ironically, positive customers who do not want to hurt your feelings might take longer, while negative customers usually require less time. They cannot wait to tell you why they are happy with their existing suppliers. Use the create-and-wait strategy in their case.

Case Study

In Step Three: Eliminate Unknowns, Steven uses his active listening and questioning skills to quantify and obtain details about Olivia's goal (reducing downtime) and her filters. Pay special attention to how Steven will link each of her responses to his next question concerning that filter or the next appropriate filter. Clarifying points and comments are in parentheses and italics. While her answers could probably take you to two or three different filters, the case study will follow them in the order prescribed in Exhibit 6-6.

Steven uses the vague-clearer-measurable questioning pattern to quantify Olivia's answers. His qualifying, clarifying, and verifying questions will be his tools to find out both Column 1 and Column 2 details. In real life, various filters can surface at the same time and one question often prompts the customer to provide measurable answers. For illustrative purposes, each filter will surface one at a time and require Steve to ask versions of the following three questions for most of the filters to get to measurable:

1. What does that involve?
2. How does that affect you?
3. How much does that cost? or What are those details?

Steven also receives *all* the details of the nine filters on this first call. Typically, salespeople need more than one meeting to find them out. They figure out which details they missed when they fill out their Quick-Entry Sales Management (Q) sheets. They then call to find them out or schedule another meeting to do so. Remember to make it a two-way street. If you want new information, you must give out new information.

In addition, when reading this section, ask yourself, "Where do you stop with your questions?" Do not stop until the answer to this question is when you receive measurable or detailed information. You and customers will reap the rewards as a result.

Continuing from Step 2: Purpose and Goals:

Steven: Olivia, what does reducing downtime mean to you? *(Steven seeks to quantify her vague goal.)*

Olivia: Our goal is to get our downtime reduced to no more than nine hours annually. *(Olivia provides a clearer answer.)*

Steven: What has prompted you to select that target figure at this time? *(He wants to understand the filter of goal motivation—and why nine hours.)*

Olivia: No matter what we do to address downtime, we still average about eighteen hours of production loss yearly. *(Olivia explains her negative motivation and provides an answer that still needs to be converted to dollars.)*

Steven: What does that end up costing you? *(He seeks to quantify the dollar amount of downtime.)*

Olivia: It costs us about $40,000 per hour of downtime. *(Olivia provides a measurable answer and her SOE—dollar per downtime.)*

Steven: So, you have been averaging about $360,000 of downtime annually? *(He turns an hourly figure into an annual dollar total.)*

Olivia: You got it. *(Steven uses his next question to link her measurable response to the filter of current situation.)*

Steven: What are you currently doing to reduce these costs?

Olivia: We have increased our monitoring of the equipment. *(Olivia provides a vague answer.)*

Steven: What does that involve?

Olivia: We dedicate two people per shift to constantly inspect the equipment for any warning signs. *(Olivia provides a clearer answer.)*

Steven: It sounds expensive. What do they cost?

Olivia: Each person costs about $40,000 annually; and with two shifts, that's a lot of money.

Steven: In other words, these four people add $160,000 to your production costs? *(Steven always wants to get to the total dollar amount.)*

Olivia: Hey, you seem pretty good with numbers. Yeah, $160,000 sounds about right. *(Olivia provides a measurable answer. Steven uses his next question to link her measurable response to the filter of plans.)*

Steven: So, what are you planning to do to get to those nine hours?

Olivia: We are looking at installing redundant equipment. *(Olivia provides a vague answer.)*

Steven: How many pieces of equipment will you need to buy?

Olivia: We are looking at purchasing three new pieces of production equipment. *(Olivia provides a clearer answer.)*

Steven: What will something like that cost?

Olivia: It could end up costing us almost $600,000. *(Olivia provides a measurable answer. Steven uses his next question to link her measurable response to the filter of alternatives, which might include other suppliers.)*

Steven: Besides purchasing new equipment, what other options are you looking at to reduce downtime?

Olivia: We might buy used equipment, which would cut our costs in half, although we might be risking reliability. Also, we have received presentations from PricePoint Services and FastShip Technology (Steven's competitors) about their predictive maintenance services and production equipment. For what it's worth, you are definitely making me think a lot more about my situation than they did.

Steven: Thanks. I hope you feel the information we are discussing will make it clearer what you want to accomplish and what it will take for a company to help you. *(Steven does not take the bait and go into a product pitch or fall for the "What do they do for you?" trap. He knows his competitors' strengths and weaknesses from his Competitor Product Profile sheets. Once he finds out Olivia's goals and filters, he will then know how to connect his products to them, and not have his solutions compared with his competitors' products. Let them compare their features to his features, and leave out Olivia's goals. In addition, he knows if he helps Olivia to define her purchasing requirements, she will view him more as an industry expert than his competitors.)*

Olivia: I will let you know when I don't think it's making things clearer.

(Steven uses his next question to link Olivia's previous measurable response [half the costs of new equipment or $300,000, and knowing his competitors' price ranges] to the filter of final decision maker [FDM].)

Steven: Fair enough. When you are evaluating these different options, who will be involved with approving these types of decisions?

Olivia: I'll make the initial recommendation to my boss, Ronald Reuters, the CEO of the company.

Steven: What will he do with your recommendation?

Olivia: I have final approval if it achieves our goals and stays within budget; otherwise, he needs to get corporate approval. *(Steven uses his next question to link Olivia's detailed response to the filter of dates [he could have also linked it to budgets].)*

Steven: Upon approval, when would you and Mr. Reuters want to start?

Olivia: When the new budget goes into effect on October 15.

Steven: With that budget date, when do you want to make your decision, and then begin and finish the project?

Olivia: Make our decision by August 1, begin the project no later than November 1, and complete by fourth quarter. *(Steven uses his next question to link Olivia's detailed response to the filter of funding.)*

Steven: In October, how would the project be funded to meet your deadlines?

Olivia: Out of our capital budget.

Steven: How much has been allocated for this project?

Olivia: We have set aside $1,080,000.

Steven: How did you establish that figure? *(He wants to see if she used a competitor's estimate to arrive at a dollar amount.)*

Olivia: Ron feels that we need at least a three-year payback to proceed. Being good with numbers, you have probably figured out that it's the potential $360,000 savings times three years. *(Steven will use his next question to link Olivia's measurable response to the filter of past keys.)*

Steven: What is the major reason why you approved or abandoned projects involving reducing downtime in the past?

Olivia: We stopped pursuing a project last year with one of your competitors because we didn't feel confident that their products would work in our situation.

Steven: What does it take for you to feel assured that a solution will work in your circumstances? *(Again, Steven does not want to get into a negative sale. Rather, he wants to find out what it will take to avoid his competitor's mistake and make sure that Olivia knows the reasons. If she doesn't, Steven will need to rethink and question what her role really is, and her importance in the decision-making process.)*

Olivia: We want to make sure they understand the nuances of our operations and demonstrate where their products work in similar situations. *(Olivia's answer, while clearer, still needs further clarification.)*

Steven: What would meet those requirements? *(This question requires Olivia to provide specific details.)*

Olivia: We would want a company to conduct an engineering survey of our equipment operations and provide documented results they achieved over a two-year period with one of our competitors. *(Steven will use his next question to link Olivia's measurable response to the most important filter, which is attainment measurement. With all the details discussed, Steven asks Olivia to review his summary on how she knows if she achieves her goal of reducing downtime. He wants to make sure nothing major is missing. Steven looks at his notes and begins.)*

Steven: Let me see if I understand what you said it will take to achieve your goal of minimizing downtime. You want to reduce your costs of $40,000 per downtime hour to no more than nine hours annually, save $360,000, begin in November and finish by December, not exceed $1,080,000 budget, get at least a three-year payback, and any solution must have proven performance. Is there anything that we missed? *(I'm glad that I took notes.)*

Olivia: If we can accomplish all that, there will be a lot of happy people here. Do you think you have any products that can do what we want to do?

Steven: Before I say a definite yes, I'd like to take everything we discussed today and run it past my engineering group to get their thoughts. Does that sound like a good plan to you? *(Steven is positive that he can help Olivia. However, he sticks to his MP 2 strategy. His objective is to gather details about goals and filters, review them with his sales and engineering team, and see if he needs* *more information. Furthermore, he wants to obtain MPC 2: Potential Confirmed via a conditional commitment, match features to measurable benefits in MP 3: Cement Solution, and only then make his presentation. Discipline will have its rewards.)*

Step Four: Yellow Light

Do a summary of the measurable benefits of the customer's goals to build momentum. Get her head nodding in approval. You are ready to have the *customer* separate the serious car buyers from the tire kickers.

Conditional Commitments

When you confirm a customer's attainment measurements, they become conditional commitments. Only customers who are serious about achieving their goals make these commitments. Conditional commitments are not trial closes used to flush out customers' receptiveness through specific product commitments. You know the product-focused approach of "If I can prove that I can do this, will you buy that?" You do not need trial closes when you have MPCs. The customers who acknowledge sales opportunities are moving forward when they proceed to the next MP. Conditional commitments ensure that there are no moving targets and that both you and customers can manage expectations.

Whether customers want to achieve their goals versus whether they want to buy your products are two separate and distinct issues. If you try to lump them together, you are a product advocate, not a customer advocate.

These commitments customers *make aloud to themselves.* They commit to achieving their goals, although a huge *if* exists: *If* they can achieve their goals within the constraints of their attainment measurements. These commitments are only valid if your yet-to-be determined products meet those requirements. Do not view these commitments as green lights, but rather as proceed-with-caution yellow lights.

Note: Often salespeople use a memorandum of understanding (MOU) to signify a customer's commitment level. A MOU outlines the investments (usually more time and labor than direct dollar costs) both organizations need to make to find out whether the customer's goals can be achieved within the conditional commitments. A signed time line outlining what steps need to be taken, by whom, and when goes a long way toward helping everyone manage expectations. If one date slips, everyone understands why subsequent dates might also slip.

Case Study

Steven uses the measurable specifics of Olivia's attainment measurement to create her conditional commitment. Making conditional commitments measurable requires calculations that competitors do not know how to do, but you do. Your sales approach just gave you another competitive advantage.

Continuing from Step Three: Eliminate Unknowns, Steven confirms Olivia's attainment measurement to turn it into the conditional commitment as follows:

Steven: In other words, if you could meet all those requirements, you would feel that you achieved your goal of reducing downtime?

Olivia: Yes. (*Note that Steven did not ask Olivia to commit to a specific product through trial closes, but rather commit to achieving her goals if the conditional commitment is met. As stated earlier, Steven would now take this information back to his sales team and use the full resources of his company to choose the right combination of products and services to meet Olivia's conditional commitment. The target of downtime is no longer a moving abstract concept but a static, well-defined one. Now, Steven needs to see if any products can hit it.*)

Measurable Phase Change 2: Potential Confirmed

MPC 2: Potential Confirmed ends this phase. Customers confirm that the potential for achieving their goals is qualified and warrants your call for action.

Case Study

Steven's next call for action is to conduct a paid survey of Positron's manufacturing facility. The cost of the survey reinforces Olivia's commitment, and addresses her concerns over the selected supplier's knowledge of their nuances. Steven will credit its cost to any subsequent work by FutureTech.

A survey benefits both parties because it eliminates unknowns. The fewer the unknowns, the fewer the risks, and the more accurately Steven can identify the project's costs.

Note: When you end MP 2 with trial closes and not conditional commitments, you are forced to start MP 3 with a product, not a goal focus.

Skipping the Order to Get the Order

Sometimes, it makes sense to skip or rush through one or more of the MPs. You might need to do so in any one of the following situations:

- *Costly sales expenses to conduct MP 2: Measure Potential in person.* Therefore, conduct MP 1: Spark Interest and as much of MP 2 as possible simultaneously via phone or e-mail to qualify long-distance prospects.
- *Customer emergency requires an immediate proposal; you go straight to MP 3: Cement Solution.* Again, try to establish customers' long-term goals, so short-term emergency solutions are consistent with them.
- *A strong MPC 3: Solution Confirmed leads you right into MP 4: Implement Agreement.* MP 4 becomes the logical conclusion to the previous MPC commitments. The stronger the measurable benefits, the greater the chances that MPC 3 and MPC 4 will occur at the same time.
- *With multiple decision makers, conduct MP 2 to MP 4 with gatekeepers.* Their MPC 4: Agreement Confirmed is their endorsement for you to meet with the advocates or final decision makers.

To Take Notes or Not to Take Notes, That Is the Question

What you record is what you build your sales strategies around. Therefore, a question that often comes up is whether to take notes in front of customers. The main reason customers react adversely to note taking is that they do not know what you are writing. They usually suspect the worst. Are you jotting down, "This person is a waste of time," or "Add $10,000 to price, sounds like he's in a jam."

The less paranoid may feel you cannot adequately keep the conversation flowing, pay attention, and take notes. That is probably true if you are trying to steer their conversation toward your products. In addition, most salespeople focus only on decision makers, deadlines, and budgets; there is not a lot to remember or jot down.

Given these considerations, do you or do you not take notes? If you plan on writing down specifics of customers' goals, filters, measurable benefits, and systems of evaluation you should take notes. Explain to customers why you need to accurately record their details. Most people will appreciate your keen interest in what they are saying. Offer to summarize your notes at the end of the call to verify that you did not "miss anything." This recap affords you the opportunity to build momentum by highlighting their conditional commitments right before you leave.

Use Quick-Entry Sales Management (Q) sheets specifically tailored for your use during MP 1 and MP 2. Think of them as loose-leaf paper with empty boxes on them that you fill out—if you can. You use them to measure, manage, and maximize your sales progress and results. You also use an updated sheet for MP 3: Cement Solution and MP 4: Implement Agreement.

You probably take notes on a loose-leaf pad now, so why not use a better note pad? With Qs, you quickly insert and retrieve information, complement your sales process, and evaluate each call using the same benchmarks. Additionally, show customers a Q sheet before you begin MP 2. Let them know how everything on the sheet helps them and you make well-thought-out decisions on how best to achieve their goals. There is nothing to hide when you work with measurable value. The case study at the end of this chapter illustrates how to use a Q sheet.

Note: Generate the appropriate Q sheets with the MP 1: Spark Interest section filled out before you make your MP 2: Measure Potential call on the customers—not afterward. Then complete the blank sections in MP 2 as soon as you can.

You Forgot Something

When you are back at your office trying to fill out your Q sheets, you sometimes find you missed a filter. When you notice a miss, make sure it is not attainment measurement. Find this out before you propose products to avoid any misses. Without the attainment measurements, it is difficult to make your customers' conditional commitments measurable—and difficult to figure out what it takes for them to say yes.

After reviewing your Q sheets, plan your follow-up questions (review Chapter 5) before you call the customer. The table in Exhibit 6-7 shows how Steven would plan his clarifying questions if he found out that his Q sheet had fluff in it (it doesn't) and he had to call Olivia back. It is divided into four columns as follows:

1. Q sheet remarks that lack details or measurable data (in dollars)
2. Clarifying questions you need to ask to make the data measurable
3. Reasons why you need to know this information
4. How you would handle the situation if the customer asked you to explain the reason for your question

Note: As a general rule of thumb, do not call customers unless you have new, relevant information for them. Give them new information before you try to obtain specifics from them. Make the exchange of information mutually beneficial. The customer should end the discussion by saying, "Interesting, I did not know that. Thanks." (A follow-up question planner can be found at www .measuremax.com.)

Exhibit 6-7. Call-back questions.

Q sheet boxes that lack details or measurable data (in dollars)	Call-back question to seek specifics	Reason for asking the question	Response to the customer asking, "What do you mean?"
Decision Makers: Olivia has final approval if it stays within her budget. Otherwise, she needs to get corporate approval.	What's involved with getting corporate approval?	Make sure Olivia knows what we need to do if we can achieve her goals, but we go over budget.	Let Olivia know that corporate approval procedures and timing might affect her ability (and yours) to meet her deadlines.

Handling Selling Situations with Multiple Decision Makers

You probably have sales opportunities in which you need to find out information from different decision makers. And some situations arise in which different salespeople are working on the same sales opportunities. Each salesperson is probably at a different stage in the process. It is important that you coordinate your efforts and follow one simple rule: Make sure the salesperson dealing with the lowest-level decision maker conducts MP 2: Measure Potential first. Then, you can always verify the requirements of that person's conditional commitments with the next-highest-level decision maker before conducting MP 2 with that person. For instance, salesperson number one verifies MP 2 information gathered from a gatekeeper with salesperson number two before she starts her MP 2 phase with the advocate.

You want to ensure that you proceed with accurate information. You build momentum by not having to return to a previously completed MP because of inaccurate or incomplete data. Make sure all conditional commitments are accurate. Verify all previously established goals or filters with your contact before starting the third phase of MP 3: Cement Solution.

Regardless of how many salespeople are involved, only one proceeds with product selections to MP 3 and MP 4 with the final decision maker. With gatekeepers and advocates, you still go through all four MPs with them until you reach MPC 4: Agreement Confirmed. Their commitments will not be purchase orders. More likely, they are recommendations, endorsements, and arranged meetings with the FDMs. These agreed-upon MPCs and calls for action by the gatekeepers and advocates signal their support for you to the FDM. Furthermore, you get to use their MPC commitments whether they participate in your meetings with the FDMs or not.

Note: Q sheets are especially valuable when there are various buying influences on the same sales opportunity. They record all the necessary information in one location. The more specific the information, the easier it is for you to determine a decision maker's authority and influence.

Case Study

To illustrate this point about different decision makers, Olivia, for this example only, is now the gatekeeper and advocate, not the final decision maker. Her role is to qualify suppliers' technical capabilities and then pass their proposals on to Ronald Reuters, the CEO.

Steven Smartsell completes MP 2: Measure Potential with Olivia Ontime. Steven's sales manager, Bobby Bigticket, is working with Ronald Reuters, the CEO of Positron, and the final decision maker. Steven makes sure his manager reviews a copy of his Q sheet with his MP 2: Measure Potential specifics and conditional commitment from Olivia before conducting MP 2 with the CEO to ensure consistency.

Bobby Bigticket will start his MP 2 meeting with the CEO by restating Olivia's conditional commitment he received from Steven to verify its accuracy.

Why Care If Customers Understand Their Purchasing Decisions?

You might be questioning the need to invest so much time and effort to ensure that customers understand their purchasing decisions. They are smart enough to know what they want on their own, right? It is easy to understand a mentality of "Who cares why customers make purchases as long as they buy from me." In both the short and long term, you care because sales are at stake.

You want your customers to buy for the right reasons. You do not want customers to feel their goals were not met. They should be able look back at any time and still be able to measure how your products met or exceeded their expectations. When customers can measure your achievements and their own, they act like long-term customers. Remember from the Introduction that the top-selling salespeople are the ones who have the most long-term customers. Additional sales become easy to obtain from long-term customers when you are in the relationship selling mode. In addition, documented and measurable successes become competitor-proof references to help you earn and win your next sale.

The following page shows how Steven fills out the front page of his Q sheet after completing MP 1 and MP 2 with Olivia. (See Exhibit 6-8.)

Note: In this example, Olivia is the gatekeeper, advocate, and final decision maker. She is also the technical, operational, and financial person. If Steven met with her boss, Ronald Reuters, he would verify the data on a copy of this Q sheet to confirm the accuracy of Olivia's information. He would seek clarification on any differences, note them on Ronald's Q sheet, and then discuss them with Olivia.

Exhibit 6-8. Quick-entry sales management sheet.

Quick-Entry Sales Management Sheet

□ Won	□ Lost	☑ In-Progress	□ Positive	☑ Neutral	□ Negative
Organization Name: Positron			**Contact Name/Phone #:** Olivia Ontime, 456-908-3456		**Position:** VP of manufacturing
Confirmed Goals:			**Measurable or Perceived Benefits with Dollar Values:**		**Systems of Evaluation:**
1. Reduce downtime			Prevent 9 hours of downtime and save $360,000		Dollar per downtime ($40,000 per hour)

MEASURABLE or SPECIFIC FILTERS

Goal Motivation:
Positive:

Negative: Lost 18 hours and $720,000 of production output to downtime last year

☑ **Current Situation:** Use two people for two shifts to monitor equipment at $40,000 per person. Costs them $160,000 a year

☑ **Future Plans:** Install redundant equipment that will cost $600,000

☑ **Alternatives:** Buy used equipment for $300,000. Solicit competitive presentations from Fastship Technology and PricePoint Services

(continues)

Exhibit 6-8. (Continued.)

☑ Decision Makers:	☑ Name and Position	☑ Sway (1-3):
Gatekeeper: Technical, Operational, or Financial	Direct Supervisor: Ronald Reuters, CEO	2
Advocate: Technical, Operational, or Financial	Direct Report: Don't know	?
FDM: Technical, Operational, or Financial	Staff Report: "Corporate," don't know	?

☑ Complete Date: Finish by 4th quarter	☑ Decision Date: August 1st	☑ Budget Date: October 15th	☑ Start Date: November 1st or sooner

☑ **Funding:**
Operating Budget ($): Will be funded out of capital investments

Capital Investment ($): $1,080,000

☑ **Past Keys:**
Successes: Engineering study of operations and documented successes with companies in their industry

Failures: Didn't feel products and services would work in *their* situation

☑ **Attainment Measurement:** reduce costs of $40,000 per downtime hour to no more than nine hours annually, save $360,000, begin in November and finish by December, not exceed $1,080,000 budget, get at least a three-year payback, and any solution must have "proven" performance

☑ **YES, customer confirmed the attainment measurement as his or her conditional commitment**
☐ **NO (why not?):**

Notes: I still need to find out what "proven performance" means, who at corporate would get involved, and what would make them approve this project. I also want to find out whom Olivia's direct report is and the role he or she will play.

Case Study: MP 1 and MP 2 Business-to-Consumer Transactions

John Peters is a salesperson for Water Heaters Inc. He sells high-efficiency water heaters. Brian Walters is a homeowner who might need a water heater. John Peters will illustrate how to apply the steps of MP 1 and MP 2 in business-to-consumer transactions in which the salesperson must take the lead in suggesting the goals and SOEs. Most consumers are not as technically oriented as businesspeople. After all, their position as homeowner is not a technical one. So, salespeople must also use everyday terms. In addition, commercials and advertisements condition consumers to think in terms of perceived value, emotions, or low price, not measurable value and objective decision making. What a great opportunity for value-driven salespeople!

As you review John's Market Profile sheet in Exhibit 6-9 on page 182, you can see that John's product, the XLX 9000, has no unique strengths. Yet, John knows that his strongest features, sold collectively, can produce more value than those of competitors—if he can make them measurable. He also knows that in the replacement market he must use a SOE that can offset the costs of doing nothing (replacing an old water heater that still works for a so-called new and better one). His challenge is to find market segments whose goals can be achieved by those features.

John identified Water Heater Replacement Opportunities as a market segment. He developed a modified-for-consumers Market Profile sheet for it by defining its organizational characteristics (in italics). His marketing logic for defining this market segment is as follows:

- *Homeowners.* Renters are not interested in making investments in assets they do not own.

- *2,200-Square-Foot or Larger Houses.* Larger homes usually house larger families. In addition, larger homes require larger water heaters and have higher utility costs to justify a reasonable payback (if necessary).

- *Built Before 1971.* Oil embargoes were not in vogue yet, and therefore energy efficiency was not a major concern for American homeowners.

- *Families with Five or More Members.* They require lots of hot water. (See Exhibit 6-9.)

As you review his Market Profile sheet, notice how the four organizational characteristics produce goals that match his features.

How far you need to segment markets depends on the point at which you can link your strongest feature or unique strength. Sometimes, you need to consider your unique strengths at the company level not, just at the product level.

Thinking in terms of organizational characteristics, John also knows there are other reasons why people might increase their water-heating requirements. For instance, when people purchase Jacuzzis, they often increase their hot water requirements. Therefore, John would create a market segment for Jacuzzi owners. He might even want to offer Jacuzzi companies a commission on every sale that results from a lead they give him.

Note: To simplify the case study, there is only one decision maker and only one of John's products, the XLX 9000, can satisfy Brian Walters's goals. In your selling situations, numerous products might help customers achieve their goals. The only requirement is that their features connect to the stated goals. In addition, all the benefits are internal because consumers do not have customers.

MP 1: Spark Interest

The following steps make up MP 1: Spark Interest.

Step One: Research and Membership

John: Good evening, Mr. Walters. This is John Peters with Water Heaters Inc. I'm calling you because of our successes in helping your neighbors with their water-heating requirements. We achieve our best results in 2,200-square-foot or larger homes built before 1971 that still use their original water heaters. Real estate records indicate your home falls into those categories; is that correct? (*The only yes-or-no question John asks. He needs to verify that Mr. Walters shares these organizational characteristics. If Mr. Walters does, he gets to start with a positive customer response, a yes. Don't worry; he has used up only twenty seconds.*)

Brian: Yeah, That's right. But, my water heater still works just fine. (*He confirms that it is the original one.*)

Step Two: Take Your Pick

John: Well, Mr. Walters, regardless of how well your water heater works, if it's still the original one, we might be able to help

Exhibit 6-9. Market profile sheet.

Market Segment: Replacement opportunities					
Market Segment Location: Homes on Elm, Oak, and Pine Streets					
Position: Owner, not renter					
Organizational Characteristics: Homeowners, houses built before 1971, greater than 2,200 square feet, family of five people or more a higher priority					
Previous Success Stories: More than 25 houses on these streets					
Homeowner's Goals	Homeowner's Benefits	Systems of Evaluation	XLX 9000 Features/Benefits	Unique Strengths	
Reduce energy usage	Saves money	Kilowatts or therms (gas) used per BTU	High efficiency rating (lowers electrical or gas consumption)	No (MV)	
Improve efficiency	Reduces reheat time	Minutes per reheat	Fast heat transfer (decreases downtime between showers)	No (MV)	
	Increases supply of hot water	Gallons of available hot water	Large water tank (stores more hot water than standard tanks)	No (MV)	
Improve reliability	Minimizes inconvenience of no hot water	Number of moving parts	Solid-state design (reduces number of moving parts)	No (PV)	
Reduce maintenance	Lowers repairs and maintenance costs	Unscheduled repair costs	5-year parts and labor warranty	No (PV)	

you reduce your electrical or gas bill costs significantly while greatly increasing your hot water capacity. Are these goals that you'd like to pursue, or are there other ones that might be more important to you? *(John suggests two broad goals that reflect Mr. Walters's organizational characteristics and potentially connect to John's XLX 9000 features. John also asks a clarifying question.)*

Step Three: Track Record

Brian: Well I actually haven't given my water heater a lot of thought other than when it doesn't work, I get it fixed. However, you got my interest, so keep going. *(John receives his first customer confirmation and some indication that Mr. Walters has had problems with his water heater in the past. He will explore that issue in MP 2: Measure Potential.)*

John: Mr. Walters, judging by our results in the Justinville area, we might be able to achieve the same results with your home. Their homes are similar in size and age as yours. In more than twenty-five Justinville homes that still had the original water heaters we averaged 38 percent energy savings while increasing capacity by an average of 40 percent during the last year. *(John validates his proven performance in the same market segment.)*

MPC 1: Interest Confirmed

John: However, Mr. Walters, do you feel it's worth pursuing these opportunities to lower your utility costs and increase capacity? I would welcome the opportunity to see whether you can achieve the same improvements at your home that others achieved in similar situations. *(John indicates that he and Mr. Walters will need to make an investment of time. He uses a yes-or-no question to verify that there is customer agreement.)*

Brian: I'm willing to find out. *(John receives a confirmed customer's agreement.)*

John: Well, thanks for your time. Can we meet next Thursday if that's convenient for you? It will take about a half hour. *(John's call for action is a meeting to conduct MP 2. In addition, because this is a telephone call, he lets Mr. Walters know how long a meeting would take. He makes sure he schedules the meeting before concluding the call.)*

Brian: Thursday is good; see you then. *(John receives MPC 1: Interest Confirmed to end MP 1.)*

Note: Of course, sometimes sales calls do not go as planned (Chapter 8 examines this topic in detail). However, like everything else in the MeasureMax selling system, if you can find your way back to the customers' goals, you can get back on track. Suppose our Mr. Walters cut John short and said, "What are you selling, John?" All John would have to say is the truth. His reply would resemble this goal statement: "Hopefully, cost-justified reliability, improved efficiency, increased capacity, and utility savings in the form of a water heater. I will need to get more information, though, to determine if we can achieve the same success with you that we have had with similar customers."

Again, the reason to meet is to see what the unique circumstances of Mr. Walters' filters are and the measurable benefits these goals can produce. John can proceed to the second phase after obtaining MPC 1: Interest Confirmed.

MP 2: Measure Potential

The case study continues with the second phase of MP 2: Measure Potential. It begins with John meeting Mr. Walters for the first time at his house. The italics in parentheses will reference the active listening and questioning skills discussed in Chapter 5. Please note how John uses Mr. Walters's responses to acknowledge that he understands his comments. Active listening also gives John time to formulate his follow-up comments and questions. He uses these to reinforce the goals and gather the specifics of the measurable benefits, filters, and systems of evaluations.

Step One: Market Focus

John: Hi, Mr. Walters, John Peters with Water Heaters Inc. Thanks for taking the time to meet with me. As promised, I'll only be about thirty minutes. *(John builds an initial trust level by committing to honor his telephone promise about the length of the meeting.)*

Brian: Please, John. Call me Brian.

John: OK, Brian. Thanks. I'd like to point out before we start that Water Heaters Inc. has been serving single-family homes' water-heating requirements for over fifty years. Our special emphasis is on homes built before 1971. I'm in my tenth year with the company and have worked successfully with over eight hundred homeowners. *(John establishes his and his company's credibility.)*

Brian: That's a lot of homes!

John: And a lot of good references. *(John acknowledges Brian's comments.)*

Step Two: Purpose and Goals

Brian: Well, John. How do you think you can help us? *(Brian is ready to discuss business.)*

John: Well, Brian, as we discussed on the phone, the reason for our meeting tonight is to first understand your water-heating requirements (goals) and the specifics of your situation. We can then determine what opportunities might exist. In order to gather the details, I'll need to ask you a few questions. How does this approach sound to you? *(John verifies the purpose of meeting and seeks his first agreement.)*

Brian: Sounds like a good place to start. *(customer's agreement)*

John: Then, let's get to it. You expressed an interest in reducing your utility bill (goal) as it relates to heating your water. Is that right, and are there any other hot-water issues you have an interest in? *(John verifies goal and sees if any others exist before moving on to the filters.)*

Brian: Yes, cutting our electric bill wouldn't hurt, but we never seem to have enough hot water in the morning. *(Brian explains his goal motivation of avoiding a past negative result; the first influencer filter surfaces.)*

John: No one likes a cold shower! How do these two issues rate in importance to you so that we know which one to focus our efforts on first? *(John acknowledges his reply by summing up the ramifications of small capacity and why ranking the goals is necessary. This ranking also determines which goal John will use as his safety zone [see Chapter 5]. If necessary, John will reference his questions to Brian's goal to understand how he thinks a filter affects his ability to achieve that goal.)*

Brian: I'd rather be warm than save a few bucks. *(Capacity is the safety zone goal around which John will reference his filter questions.)*

John: Well, let's see if we can't do both. First, we'll need to find out what your specific situation is, OK? *(John knows the priority of the goals and reconfirms the need to gather more information.)*

Brian: Okay, but I don't have all night. (Customer's verification and a not-too-subtle verbal clue to pick up the pace.)

Step Three: Eliminate Unknowns

Note how John's questions move Brian's response from vague to clearer to measurable. As a reminder, filters are either *influencers (I)* or *prerequisites (P)*. *(Note how John links Brian's measurable answers to the next filter still lacking measurable details.)*

John: You're right. I only have twenty minutes left so I'll make each one count. How does your family make do with not enough hot water? *(John acknowledges previous response and is seeking current situation [I].)*

Brian: Currently, between the five of us, we have to wait between showers. So, we take turns who goes first. It sometimes makes one of us late for work.

John: Typically, how long is your wait? *(Clarifying question to get specifics.)*

Brian: Oh, about forty-five minutes. It's definitely an inconvenience.

John: Yeah, no one likes waiting—especially if on a tight schedule. How were you planning to shorten your wait time? *(John verifies with rephrasing that focuses on the ramifications of the current situation. John then seeks the details of the plans [I].)*

Brian: We were looking at adding another water heater for the Jacuzzi we were going to put in, but it didn't make sense to do it at the time.

John: Oh, why's that? *(John follows the customer's lead by using a clarifying question to find out specifics concerning plans and alternatives [I].)*

Brian: The space limitations wouldn't allow it, and Heating Vessels' single unit wasn't large enough. *(John finds out about key to previous failure filter and alternatives, too [I].)*

John: If you were able to meet all your requirements, when would you want to do it? *(John knows it is still too early to start selling large capacity. He needs to continue qualifying to find out the next filters of budget, decision, start, and complete dates [P]. John knows his goal is to build an inventory of opportunities and then capitalize on them when his strategy dictates. This opportunity occurs when he knows the specifics of the attainment measurement [P].)*

Brian: I would do it next week if it could fit our budget. *(John is starting to build Brian's attainment measurement [P] and provides start date [P].)*

John: What budget have you set for yourself? *(John found out two of the dates [P] and took lead from customer to obtain funding [P].)*

Brian: I really haven't. I know I don't want to spend more than $600. What does your product cost? *(The attainment measurement continues to develop [P]. John has his work cut out for him because XLX 9000 costs around $750.)*

John: Yeah, no one wants to spend money without being able to justify it in his mind. Depending on what specific product makes sense for your application, it can cost around $750. However, will that cost difference be an issue if you felt it was worth the money? *(John rephrased, verified, and used a clarifying question to seek attainment measurement [P] to determine what Column 2 measurable benefits Brian needs to go ahead with achieving his goals. He also addresses the $600 budget in terms of return on investment.)*

Brian: What do you mean?

John: Well, most homeowners think it makes sense to invest in a new water heater if they can recoup their money in less than three years. What are your feelings? *(John, as a customer expert, had the SOE of payback ready to discuss with Brian. He did miss an opportunity to find out why Brian has a $600 budget figure. Is it from the previous year's proposal, or just some number he threw out? He can always ask about the figure before he makes his proposal in MP 3: Cement Solution if he or his manager deems it important to know in light of all his other goals and filters.)*

Brian: How would I recoup my money in three years?

John: Well, besides energy savings, you won't have any parts or labor repair costs for five years because every new unit has a full parts-and-labor warranty. Before we make any proposal, we will conduct a savings analysis to see exactly what your water heater has been costing you to determine your potential savings and to see if a new one makes financial sense for you. Does this approach work for you? *(John shows Brian that he has experience in determining which SOEs might justify a new water heater—and that he does not throw out numbers without researching Brian's situation.)*

Brian: Yeah, it does, and a three-year payback seems reasonable. But, not so fast, I still want to be positive that at least three people can take a shower during a one-hour period. *(Customer uses systems of evaluation of three-year payback and showers per hour to calculate measurable benefits.)*

John: What would make you feel reassured? *(John wants to know what will give Brian the reassurances he needs.)*

Brian: I'd like to talk to some of your customers who used your products for at least three years. By the way, what product do you have in mind for my situation?

John: I'll send you a list tomorrow of ten people who meet those requirements. I will let them know you'll be calling them. In addition, I can also include their annual savings. As for what specific product to offer, I'd like to see the findings of our survey first. In the interim, I can leave you a brochure that will give you a general overview of our product lines. Also, once we select the best product for your application, I can send you more specific brochures, or even have you visit our showroom to see an actual unit at work. As for the list, will that give you the reassurances about our ability to deliver on our commitments? *(John wants Brian to start focusing on dollar savings besides documented performance to help offset his $750 price. He also does not want to get prematurely drawn into a detailed product selection on a yet-to-be determined solution.)*

Brian: That'll work.

Step Four: Yellow Light

John: Brian, we went over a lot of details tonight, and I just want to make sure before I leave that I have my facts straight. It seems that if you could get enough hot water for three people in an hour, have a three-year payback savings of $200 annually, and meet your budget of $600—or, if slightly higher, still provide a three-year payback—you would consider that you achieved your goals of reducing electrical costs and increasing capacity. Did I get it right? *(John summarizes the attainment measurement, quantifies measurable benefits, and verifies them as Brian's conditional commitment. He does not tie Brian's conditional commitment to any of his specific products. John also recognizes that he will need to address the issue of the $600 budget. He chooses to wait for Brian to talk to his references, and to see if he can beat a three-year payback after conducting his survey. He feels confident Brian will increase his budget to $750 if he can show him a three-year payback or offer a financing program to spread the price over two years.)*

Brian: I would definitely go ahead with any water heater that could meet those requirements. *(He confirms the requirements of his conditional commitment.)*

MPC 2: Potential Confirmed

John: Brian, I would like to suggest that I survey your existing water heater to determine its size, efficiency, and perform the savings analysis. I'll then pursue some possible solutions with my engineering and applications group. This will help me determine what product will work best in your situation. We can then plan to meet next week to review our findings. How does that sound? Is Thursday at the same time good for you? *(John verifies the call for action [survey] to work up a yet-to-be-determined product. John does not want to start mentioning products yet. He needs to review all his data with his sales and engineering groups before he commits to a particular product. Furthermore, it sets the purpose for the next meeting—to review his findings. John would also give Brian the opportunity to add, subtract, or modify any goals, filters, systems of evaluations, or measurable benefits.)*

Brian: Let's look at my water heater, and then I'll see you next Thursday.

John: Thanks for all your time. I look forward to our meeting. *(John got his information; now it's time to go. Anything else said would detract from his efforts. Keep in mind that selling is the ability to gather customer information beneficial to you at a greater rate than you give out product information detrimental to you.)*

John Peters has the ability to evaluate his progress by the use of the following modified Q sheet. He generated the appropriate MP 1: Spark Interest before he made his MP 2: Measure Potential in-person sales call to Brian—not afterward. John completes the blank sections in his Q sheet as soon as his in-person sales call ends to evaluate the *details* he gathered.

You also could use these sheets to measure, manage, and maximize your selling efforts. This recording of essential information takes into account another adage: Sales geniuses know in detail why they are successful so they can repeat their triumphs and avoid failures. (See Exhibits 6-10 and 6-11.)

SUMMARY

- MeasureMax has four Measurable Phases (MPs) that break sales opportunities into four minisales. A kind of purchase order ends each phase.
- Measurable Phase Changes (MPCs) are the four so-called purchase orders.

(Text continues on page 194)

Exhibit 6-10. Front page of Q sheet.

Quick-Entry Sales Management Sheet (front page)

☐ Won	☐ Lost	☑ In-Progress	☐ Positive	☑ Neutral	☐ Negative
Market Segment: Replacement opportunities		**Organization Name:** House built before 1971, average 2,200 or more square feet, family of five people or more a plus			
Contact Name: Brian Walters		**Address:** 11 Elm Street, Carleton, IA			
Phone #: 446-9807		**E-Mail:** zzwalters@aol.com		**References:** Elm and Oak houses	

Confirmed Goals:	Measurable Benefits:	Systems of Evaluation:
1. Increase shower capability	Three people can take a shower within one hour, no more waiting	Tank size, speed of reheating, and cost of waiting (late for work?)
2. Reduce electrical costs	Reduce water heater electrical consumption by ? (Need results of survey and savings analysis)	Difference between kilowatt per BTU of existing water heater compared to new one
3. Achieve 3-year or better payback	Use electrical and repair savings to pay for new water heater in less than three years	Difference between repair, maintenance, and electrical costs of old and new units

(continues)

Exhibit 6-10. (Continued.)

☐ **Goal Motivation**			
☑ **Negative:** Brian and two other people need to wait forty-five minutes between showers			
☑ **Current Situation:** They take turns on who goes first; pay for repairs as needed			
☑ **Plans:** Put in a Jacuzzi			
☑ **Alternatives:** Heating Vessel's proposal, unit couldn't handle capacity, space limitations			
☑ **Decision Makers:** Find out if he's married or has a girlfriend; what role does partner play?			
☑ Complete: **Takes 2 days**	☑ Start: **ASAP**	☑ Budget Date: **N/A**	☑ Decision: **ASAP**
☑ **Funding:** $600			
☑ **Past Keys:** Couldn't get necessary capacity (failure), needs references of at least 3 years			
☑ **Attainment Measurement:** Three people take a shower in an hour without waiting, 3 year or less payback, and not exceed $600, budget			
☑ **Conditional Commitment:** Confirmed attainment measurement			

Exhibit 6-11. Back page of Q sheet.

Sales Efforts By Measurable Phases (back page)

MP 1: Spark Interest

MP 1: Dates:	MP 1: Notes:
4/18	Called, satisfied with his existing water heater, but still would like to meet. Find out if they have a lot of guests who stay over to determine any unusual requirements

☑ MPC 1: Interest Confirmed	Date: 4/18	Total MP 1 Sales Calls: 0 (phone calls do not count; only in-person sales calls)

☑ Call For Action: Meet next week to conduct MP 1. Bring general capabilities brochure

MP 2: Measure Potential

MP 2: Dates:	MP 2 Notes:
4/25	Make sure of reheat capacity and energy use of existing water heater to compare against our efficiency. Might need to look at spreading costs over 2 years if the $600 budget is a cast-in-stone figure (it didn't seem like it)
5/12	Met again to nail down budget and dates

☑ MPC 2: Potential Confirmed	Date: 5/23	Total MP 2 Sales Calls: 2

☑ Call for Action: Survey equipment, do savings analysis, and provide list of 3-year references. Meet next week to review findings and make a recommendation; the XLX 9000 looks like it fits

(continues)

Exhibit 6-11. (Continued.)

MP 3: Cement Solution

MP 3: Dates:	MP 3 Notes:		
☐ MPC 3: Solution Confirmed	Date:	Total MP 3 Sales Calls:	
☐ Call for Action:			

MP 4: Implement Agreement

MP 4: Dates:	MP 4 Notes:		
☐ MPC 4: Agreement Confirmed	Date:	Total MP 4 Sales Calls:	
☐ Call for Action:			

Quote Date:	Quote #:
Close Date:	Purchase Order #:
Winning Supplier:	Dollar Amount: $

- The sequence in which you conduct the MPs affects your ability to build value. Moving out of sequence diminishes value.

- The first two MPs are MP 1: Spark Interest and MP 2: Measure Potential.

- You do not mention specific products during the first two phases.

- You plug information from your Product Profile sheets and Market Profile sheets into the MP 1: Spark Interest steps.

- MP 1: Spark Interest consists of the following three steps:

  1. *Research and Membership.* Confirm organizational characteristics and position.

  2. *Take Your Pick.* Customers choose goals.

  3. *Track Record.* Provide references from market segment.

- These first two steps form your Spark Interest Statement, which you use for specific market segments.

- MP 1: Spark Interest ends with MPC 1: Interest Confirmed.

- MP 2: Measure Potential consists of the following four steps:

  1. *Market Focus.* Display expertise in customers' market segment.

  2. *Purpose and Goals.* Confirm purpose of meeting to understand requirements of goals.

  3. *Eliminate Unknowns.* Make goals, filters, and conditional commitments measurable.

  4. *Yellow Light.* Customers make conditional commitments.

- This second phase ends with MPC 2: Potential Confirmed. Customers confirm they want to achieve their goals.

- In sales with various decision makers, conduct MP 2: Measure Potential with the lowest-level decision maker before conducting it with the next highest-level decision maker. You always begin the next sales call with a different advocate or the FDM by verifying the conditional commitments from the previous contact. Make sure you have valid and accurate information.

- Customers make conditional commitments to themselves. They commit to achieve their goals. A huge *if* exists—*If* they can achieve their goals within the constraints of their attainment measurements. Conditional commitments are not trial closes. They are not committing to a specific product, but rather attaining a specific goal.

- After MP 2: Measure Potential, any time you contact customers to gather missed information, provide them with new and relevant information first.

- Ask customers with multiple goals to rank them, and use their top one to flush out their filters.
- If you plan on writing down specifics of customers' goals and filters, you should take notes.
- Use Quick-Entry Sales Management (Q) sheets to measure and manage your selling efforts objectively against the same benchmarks.

Chapter Seven

Every Reason to Say Yes

It will feel a little backward, but powerful. Thinking like a customer, not a salesperson, to present your products will feel awkward the first few times. When you begin presentations with the goals and measurable benefits of the conditional commitments, and not features and benefits, it runs contrary to your training and selling habits. When it becomes apparent that old habits get in the way of selling value, you will find it easy to get rid of them.

This chapter provides customers with every reason to say yes to your product selections by explaining:

- How you turn products into *solutions* that achieve customers' goals
- How to conduct MP 3: Cement Solution and MP 4: Implement Agreement so purchase orders become foregone conclusions
- How to make powerful technical presentations to nontechnical buyers
- How to make sure your proposals (formal offers to customers) are pulled through by customers and not pushed through by you

MP 3: Cement Solution

The third Measurable Phase (MP) consists of six steps. The first three occur before you meet with customers; the next three take place during your meetings with them. Again, memorizing the steps is not important. Just remember what you are trying to accomplish. When you present products that meet their conditional commitments, you value-earn purchase orders and long-term customers. (See Exhibit 7-1.)

Exhibit 7-1. MP 3: Cement Solution (before presentation).

MPC 3: Cement Solution (before presentation)

Step 1: No Blanks

Step 2: Benchmarks
Match Features of Selected Solutions to Measurable Benefits of Customers' Goals

Determine What Filters are Missing Measurable Details, and How They Affect Your Selection of Products and/or Services

Step 3: Oops!
Be Prepared to Explain How Any Unmatched Benefits Are Not Show-Stoppers

Note: You will continue to follow the two case studies from the previous chapter for these last two Measurable Phases. Steven Smartsell and Olivia Ontime highlight the business-to-business concepts while John Peters and Brian Walters focus on the business-to-consumer ones.

Before Meeting with Customer MP 3 Steps

Preparation is a key to success. The following three steps ensure that you highlight how you built the selected solutions from the customer's goals down, not your product's features up.

Step One: No Blanks

Review your Quick-Entry Sales Management (Q) sheet to determine what else you need to find out. Its format makes it easy to see what measurable details you know or do not know. Your knowledge of sales opportunities will be apparent. If you use loose-leaf notes (and can find all of them), how you piece your information together will probably differ for every sale. Yet, sales success comes from consistently repeating the same steps that achieve the same outcomes. Loose-leaf notes make that a difficult task. Q sheets do not.

Either way, be on the lookout for either sketchy (that is, immeasurable) or missing information. An unknown or vague goal, filter, or conditional commitment can doom a sale to failure. With unknowns, you gamble that any filter or goal you do not know will not affect the outcome of the sale. Again, you can call customers to get missing details. Be sure to provide them with new, relevant information when you do.

Step Two: Benchmarks

With your product selections, you seek to accomplish two objectives. First, you connect the features of your products that produce the measurable benefits of customers' goals. While you should strive to achieve all their goals, achieving the top-ranked one included in the conditional commitment is mandatory. Include as many unique strengths as you can. Do not forget how packaging or corporate-level features help you in this endeavor. Avoid any *diluting features* that do not connect to a measurable benefit.

Second, if you are not the existing supplier, make sure the measurable benefits in Column 2 can offset the assigned dollar value of price, delivery, supplier relationship, and cost of changing suppliers or products in Column 1. If you are the existing supplier, make sure Column 2 value can overcome the costs of doing nothing.

Note: If your product selection contains no unique strengths, question the validity of your Market Profile sheet. Without any unique strengths, you often end up doing battle with me-too competitors that offer low prices. However, you can still earn sales even without any unique strengths. Just show how the features of your products produce more measurable benefits than those of competitors.

Steven Smartsell starts with Olivia's only stated goal of reducing downtime. He fills in the details from the MP 2: Measure Potential section of his Q sheet (another strong argument for taking notes) into his Connecting Value sheet. He matches only the appropriate product features to her goals, measurable benefits, and conditional commitment. For illustrative purposes, Olivia has only one goal while your customers might have two or three goals (as in the water heater case study). A Connecting Value sheet becomes invaluable in matching features when you have more than one product that can achieve customers' goals. (See Exhibit 7-2.)

Step Three: Oops!

Be ready to explain any misses. These occur when your products do not fulfill all the requirements of the conditional commitments. Misses also occur when goals with measurable benefits have no features connected to them. You offset any misses with additional benefits customers did not consider. Steven Smartsell has no misses, but Chapter 8 provides several examples of the skills and strategies used to compensate for misses.

Are Your Proposed Solutions Pushed or Pulled Through?

Do not be more motivated than your customers are to achieve their goals. Therefore, before you continue with the second half of MP 3, conduct one last reality check. Verify that your proposals are *pulled through* by the customers and not *pushed through* by you. If you obtained the first two MPCs (Interest Confirmed and Potential Confirmed), they should feel pulled through.

However, sometimes in your zealousness to help customers, it is difficult to identify the category in which your proposals fall. Make that determination by taking the following "Does Your Proposal Pass the Pulled-Through Test?" in Exhibit 7-3. No boxes should be marked off in the left pushed-through column, while all the boxes should be checked in the right pulled-through column.

Classify your proposal's status before you present it. If it is pushed through, revisit MP 1 and MP 2 as the checklist indicates. If pulled through, continue on to the rest of MP 3 and MP 4. This checklist helps you to avoid the disappointment of working up proposals doomed to "maybe next year" or lost for unclear or unstated

Exhibit 7-2. Connecting value sheet.

CONNECTING VALUE SHEET

Customer Goals	Benefits of Achieving Goals (Time or Money)	Systems of Evaluation	Products	Specifics of Features and Benefits (features are in italics)	Value Type and Focus (Internal, External, or Both)	Unique Strength/ Feature Value Rating
					Perceived value. Both; it ensures uninterrupted shipments to their customers (E) and saves them money from lost production (I).	Yes/ 5
Reduce downtime	Prevent production stoppages from 18 hours annually to 9, which generate savings of $360,000 annually	Hours of downtime	Predicto Services	*Variance Alerts* prevent unscheduled breakdowns		
				Tolerance Checks prevents unscheduled breakdowns	Same as above	Yes/ 5

Conditional Commitment: Reduce the costs of $40,000 per downtime hour (SOE) to no more than nine hours annually (goal), save $360,000 (measurable benefit), begin in November and finish by December (start and completion dates), not exceed $1,080,000 budget (funding), get at least a three-year payback (SOE).

Exhibit 7-3. Pushed-through vs. pulled-through test.

DOES YOUR PROPOSAL PASS THE PULLED-THROUGH TEST?	
"Pushed-Through" (Salesperson-Generated)	"Pulled-Through" (Customers-Generated/MeasureMax)
☐ Goals, systems of evaluations, and filters are not measurable or specific	☒ Goals, systems of evaluations, and filters are measurable or specific
☐ No verifications of MPCs	☒ Verifications of Measurable Phase Changes
☐ No conditional commitment or attainment measurement exists	☒ Conditional commitment or attainment measurements exists
☐ Uncertainty over what prompted the proposal	☒ Proposal generated at customers' request using well-defined goals
☐ Proposal contains limited customer input	☒ Proposal uses customer's input to fill out Q sheet
☐ MPs not conducted in proper sequence	☒ MPs conducted in proper sequence
☐ Salesperson avoids or supplies own numbers for cost justification	☒ Customer supplies the means for direct or indirect cost justification
☐ Proposal considered as a means to flush out concerns or undisclosed goals and filters	☒ Proposal used to formalize agreed-upon MPCs
☐ Clarification calls to customers before making presentations are nonexistent	☒ Numerous clarification calls, and customers understand the reasons for them.
☐ Unclear time frame for starting	☒ Well-defined time frame for starting
☐ Uncertainty over chances of success	☒ Proposal status is well known
☐ Proposal focuses on numerous product features without connecting to specific customers' goals and measurable benefits	☒ Proposal focuses on customers' agreed-upon goals and measurable benefits, and demonstrates connections between them and products' features

reasons. Another sure-fire way exists to determine the status of your proposals. See how much of a Q sheet you filled out.

Note: If you are dealing with a customer that you have not done business with before, the larger the dollar amount of the proposal, the more risk the customer feels he or she is taking. Measurable goals, performance guarantees, and documented success will help the customer to feel less at risk. However, sometimes it's better to eat an elephant one chunk at a time. If need be, divide your proposal into smaller scopes of project and dollar amounts. Make sure the customer understands the projects are cascaded with no significant redundant costs (such as administrative, labor, and set-up charges).

Sign a memorandum of understanding with a time line on

when each smaller project will be completed. This fragment strategy also works when there are budgetary constraints. The customer can spread out costs to encompass more than one fiscal year. Caution: Do not use a fragment strategy if your unbreakable package as a whole provides you with unique strengths to sell compensated value and create competitive barriers.

Note: Boilerplate proposals often use a product-oriented format that leaves it up to customers to determine which features apply—and their value. They are always risky. Only highlight features that connect to measurable goals and create maximum value. The customers know they are only paying for what they need to achieve their stated goals.

At the Meeting MP 3 Steps

The big moment is here. You are ready to decommoditize your selected solutions by showing how, feature by feature, they achieve the measurable benefits of the customer's goals. (See Exhibit 7-4.) The final three MP 3 steps are as follows.

Exhibit 7-4. MP 3: Cement Solution (at presentation).

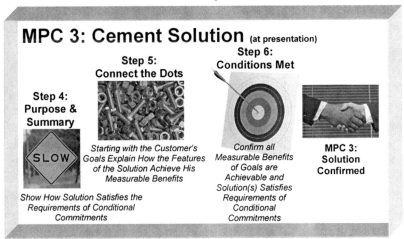

Step Four: Purpose and Summary

You are in front of the customers again—and eager to make great product presentations. You are sitting on *G* waiting for *O*, just rearing to GO! Leading with open-ended dialogue questions, you are ready to shift to business mode when customers indicate it is time. You still do not ask about the sailboat pictures on the wall. The customers let you know they are eager to see what you came up with. Go (slowly)!

Confirm the purpose of your meeting. Let customers know you are going to explain how the products you selected achieve their goals within their purchasing requirements. Do a summary of their goals, measurable benefits, and conditional commitments.

Wait for them to confirm your details as accurate. Before you proceed, make sure you built your proposals on valid information. If any goal, measurable benefit, filter, or system of evaluation has changed, qualify your proposal against these new requirements before beginning the next step. If you find any *new* misses, understand whether they prevent either you or customers from achieving their goals before you proceed.

Note: Do not mention any products by trade name. You want to focus on the customers' goals. Trade names surface during the next step, Connect the Dots.

Step Five: Connect the Dots

This step makes or breaks the sales. Either you explain how the features of your products achieve customers' measurable benefits and conditional commitments—or you do not. When you are explaining highly technical features, verify that customers agree it produces benefits by asking, "Have I explained that so it makes sense?" Take responsibility for customers' comprehension.

Explaining is one of those sales skills you usually take for granted. Most salespeople consider explaining a reflection of their technical expertise and product knowledge. They also like the fact that it is more of a monologue than a dialogue. Customers find it hard to interrupt them as salespeople tick off their features and benefits. Sometimes, product monologues tick off customers who think they are on the receiving end of a technical feature dump.

Yet, explaining is about thinking like customers. Your explanations will be well received if customers accept that at the feature level, your products fulfill their conditional commitments.

How You Connect the Dots

Features of your products and the goals of customers both have benefits. Knowing this tidbit makes connecting them easier to understand and accomplish. Otherwise, you end up pointing out product benefits in the mistaken belief that you are highlighting the benefits of customer goals. It becomes especially difficult to connect features to benefits with perceived value because they can mean anything. Your products create the most value when you can connect their features and benefits to the measurable benefits of a customer's goals. Look to make sure the benefit has a "by" in it, followed by the dollar amount, to ensure that it is measurable. *By* equals "buy," which means compensated value.

Example

Rich Darling sells protective enclosures for electronic components. Jane Austin runs the assembly plant that inserts electronic parts into different types of enclosures for various manufacturers such as computers, telephones, or stereo equipment. Jane's goal is to reduce the number of products damaged in transit by $50,000.

In his MP 3 presentation, Rich does what most product-focused salespeople do: He talks about the benefits of his enclosures thinking he is talking about the benefits of Jane's goals. For instance, he explains how one of the features of his enclosures is shatter-resistant plastic that protects the electronic parts better (benefit of feature). Sounds like a good feature and benefit. However, there is one slight problem.

He does not relate this benefit directly to Jane's goal. Granted, it must surely provide value to Jane, but he is leaving it up to her to decide exactly how. Therefore, Rich should directly connect the benefits of shatter-resistant plastic to reducing returns by $50,000. For instance, he could find out how many of Jane's shipments were damaged by incidents that his shatter-resistant plastic could have prevented.

When customers provide measurable dollar benefits, ask them why they chose that amount. In the previous example, Rich should have asked Jane why $50,000 and not $25,000, or $75,000. Knowing those reasons will help you to determine how customers calculate value—and to make sure those dollar amounts are not just out-of-the-blue figures. Measurable dollar benefits will also determine how you can cost-justify your product selections.

Note: In cases where you cannot define measurable value, perceived value must suffice, such as the example in Exhibit 7-5.

Exhibit 7-5. Connecting goals, benefits, features.

Case Study: Olivia's goal is to reduce downtime by nine hours annually (the benefit becomes measurable once you know what an hour of downtime costs). Steven's *variance alerts* feature prevents unscheduled breakdowns. They connect as follows:		
Customer's Goals	**Common Benefits**	**Product's Features**
Reduce downtime	Cut production stoppages by nine hours annually (benefit of goal) by preventing unscheduled breakdowns (benefit of feature)	*Variance Alerts*

The Verbal Structure of Explaining

The structure of explaining highlights the difference between the benefits of goals and the benefits of features. Start your explanations with customers' goals and they will value them more as they listen to how you connect features to them. Avoid leading with the features of products and making customers wait as you work your way back to their goals. It takes a little practice becoming comfortable starting explanations with customers' goals—not product's features. It is like visiting a country where they drive on the wrong side of the road (at least, according to Americans). The steering wheel is where the passenger sits from our perspective. Although it feels a little awkward jumping into the passenger seat, it is still the fastest way to get where you want to go.

In addition, you connect all the features and benefits of one goal before you proceed to the next one. These connections require concentration (fortunately driven by logic) when customers might have two or more goals, one goal might have two or more benefits, and one benefit might have two or more features that can connect to it. Again, the case studies give you plenty of examples of the explaining process.

Explaining consists of the following four-step process:

1. Start with the customer's first goal (top ranked) and that goal's first measurable benefit.
2. Highlight and explain which feature(s) of which product(s) achieve that first benefit.
3. If there is a second benefit of the first goal, again highlight and explain which features of which product(s) achieve that benefit.
4. Exhaust the benefits and features that achieve the first goal before proceeding to the second goal by following this same pattern.

Another sure-fire way to determine if customers accept your explanations is to let customers know that you accept responsibility for their understanding of what you said. A helpful question is: "Does that make sense the way I explained it?"

Note: The following examples make this concept easier to understand; otherwise explaining them is like trying to give someone a haircut over the telephone. You can either chart out the relationships among goals, measurable benefits, and features on your connecting value sheet or create one for your customers. Use modified versions of these sheets in your formal proposals and presentation packages tailored to your audiences' areas of expertise. Customers find them easy to read and understand.

The Tactics Behind Crystal-Clear Explanations

In the course of explaining, use the fewest words possible to connect the features of your products to the benefits of the customers' goals. Your explanations take into account the following six guidelines:

1. *Simple.* Use your customer's terms and jargon to explain technical features and benefits. Remember, your goal is to make customers feel smart about their business decisions, not dumb about technical details that might not have any impact on their decisions. Limit your technical knowledge to the features that produce measurable benefits, nothing else.

Example

Explaining the waterproof feature of a watch as being a "hermetically sealed chamber resistant to external pressures of seven atmospheres before liquid infiltration occurs" is technobabble. Explaining how it only leaks at 250 feet or deeper is plain English.

2. *Vivid.* Use descriptions that create powerful images.

Example

Saying that the face cover of a watch is scratch resistant is boring. Explaining how the watch can land facedown after falling from a three-story building and still look brand-new is exciting. It may not work any longer, but it will look brand-new.

3. *No Return.* Stay focused on one measurable benefit and its features, exhaust them, and then go to the next. To keep momentum building and to keep customer comprehension high, do not go back and speak about a benefit you have already covered.

Example

Explain all the features (construction, material, and warranty) of the watch that improve quality as a group. Mixing them with features that increase functions (stopwatch, countdown timer, and alarm) could confuse customers.

4. *Analogies.* As illustrated in Chapter 2, provide everyday parallels that the customer can relate to. Typically, choose a unique strength to build your analogy around.

Example

Explain the watch's wireless connection to your e-mail as an electronic post office box on your wrist. You receive your mail anywhere.

Note: Competitors' use of analogies tells you about how they try to sell value. An abundance of them indicates they are customer oriented (keep things simple)—a lack of them suggests a product orientation that rely on technically astute customers

5. *Power Words.* Use terms that express confidence such as *confident, convinced,* or *know* and avoid using weak words such as *think, feel, maybe,* or *might.*

Example

Do not say, "I think you will be pleased with the watch's performance." Your display of enthusiasm will underwhelm customers and probably cast doubt on their purchasing decisions. Instead, boldly proclaim, "I know the watch will exceed your expectations." When you know measurable benefits of goals and conditional commitments, you know how much value your products provide. While the meek may inherit the earth, they do not get the sale.

6. *Do Not Use "Never" or "Always."* You do not want to put yourself in an awkward position if exceptions exist—and exceptions always, oops, often, seem to surface.

Example

Do not say the watch never needs an adjustment. Rather, say that it should not. However, if it ever does, there is no charge for the service.

Explaining Technical Products to Nontechnical Buyers

When selling technical products, take the responsibility to ensure that customers understand your features. Let customers know up front that if they do not understand something, it is because you did not explain it properly. You win when customers feel smart.

Two issues affect how smart you need to make customers feel.

The first issue involves how easy it is for customers to accept that a feature produces the benefit the way you described it. For instance, it is difficult to accept on face value that 800 MHz computers process information 50 percent quicker than 600 MHz computers. After all, their 200 MHz difference suggests they would be 33 percent, not 50 percent faster. Yet, it is easy to understand how a computer with 128 MB of RAM has twice as much RAM as one with 64 MB.

The second issue is the technical expertise of the customers. The greater the gap between your technical expertise and that of you customers, the more you should explain concepts in their jargon. Conversely, if your customer has a strong technical background, you do not need to elaborate as much.

How Technical Should You Get

"Less is more" is a good rule to follow on how technical you should get. Use your technical knowledge to support your points, not to make them. Let the technical depth of customers' questions about your products provide the platform to display your expertise. If a customer asks you about the amperage draw and power factor of a piece of electrical equipment, answer him or her by using technical terms. In addition, use the customers' systems of evaluations as indicators of their expertise.

Example

Arlene Hartman wants to purchase a laptop that can handle numerous peripheral pieces of equipment (printers, modem, and DVD burner) at fast speeds. Mike Boone, the salesperson, asks Arlene what she is looking for in a laptop. He can suggest goals and terms that range from the elementary (fast speed and huge memory) to the high-tech (bandwidth connections and cache size).

She points out that the *number of USB ports* (SOE) will play a major role in her decision. When she asks Mike about data transmission speeds, he knows that if his explanations are technical in nature he will be speaking Arlene's language.

Note: Buzzwords or acronyms are mostly position related. Be careful whom you use them with. For instance, a hotel manager probably does not know the technical terms used by the director of engineering.

Note: PowerPoint presentations have become commonplace. Exhibit 7-6 shows some sample slides on how you can incorporate the MeasureMax approach.

Step Six: Conditions Met

All the measurable benefits of the customer's confirmed goals have product features that help to achieve them. Verify that customers agree that the features of your product selections are on target. You now recap how your proposals satisfy their conditional commitments.

Exhibit 7-6. PowerPoint presentation.

1. Cover slide: Use customer's logo and yours with stated goal(s)	2. Conditional commitment slide: List (and reconfirm) the customers' measurable expectations
POSITRON *The Technology Behind Information* **and** **FutureTech** *Tomorrow's Technology Today* **Working together to prevent costly production stoppages**	**Making Your Expectations Measurable** ☐ **Cut downtime from 18 to 9 hours annually** ☐ **Save $360,000 ($40,000/hr)** ☐ **Start November and finish by December** ☐ **Don't exceed $1,080,000 budget** ☐ **Payback of less than three years**
Variance Alerts • **Warns operators of impending failures**  **Prevents Unscheduled Breakdowns (downtime)**	**Achieving Measurable Expectations** ☑ **Cut downtime from 18 to 9 hours annually** ☑ **Save $360,000 ($40,000/hr)** ☑ **Start November and finish by December** ☑ **Don't exceed $1,080,000 budget** ☑ **Payback of less than three years**
3. Goal banner slide: No feature gets presented unless it achieves a goal. Use a goal banner at the bottom to remind the audience and yourself of goal that is achieved by feature.	4. Goal achievement summary slide: Show how each requirement of the conditional commitment has been achieved.

Measurable Phase Change 3: Solution Confirmed

Once they agree with your summations, customers turn your products into solutions (products that customers confirm achieve their goals and satisfy their conditional commitments). Your products now *solved* the question of how to achieve customers' goals. You are almost ready to ask for orders. Some steps remain to make orders foregone conclusions rooted in logic and known facts—not leaps of faith revolving around emotions and unknowns. Patience and discipline will pay off. Upon receipt of this third MPC, immediately proceed to the final selling phase, which is MP 4: Implement Agreement.

Scopes of Work

Send the highest-level decision maker you contacted a Scope of Work sheet to review before generating your proposal. Send it via fax, postal mail, or e-mail (do not invest an in-person sales call on a Scope of Work that a customer has not had time to review yet). This informal proposal is an outline that lists the details of customers' goals, measurable benefits, and conditional commitments, and explains how features of your products connect to them.

Encourage customers to review the connections and edit anything that does not meet their requirements. If any discrepancies surface, correct them before making your formal proposals. Scopes of work allow customers to perform one last check before you make your final presentations and proposals. As always, the final decision makers' comments count most. If sales opportunities involve advocates or gatekeepers, the FDM will contact them if he or she thinks their review is necessary.

Although scopes of work *do not* include pricing, you let customers know they satisfy their conditional commitments. You highlight that fact in the budget section. A scope of work combines the Q sheet from Chapter 6 with the Connecting Value sheet in this chapter. You explain that you will firm up pricing once they confirm that the current product(s) and feature selection(s) achieve their goals. Without firm prices to squabble over, you avoid the "one from column A, two from column B" quagmire that wastes everyone's time and effort. If pressed for cost details, verbal pricing works. A sample of a scope of work cover letter and a scope of work checklist follow in Exhibits 7-7, below and 7-8 (page 214), respectively.

Note: All the templates shown in this chapter can be downloaded from www.measuremax.com.

Although Steven still has questions that need answers and issues that need resolving, at least he and Olivia are working together to

Exhibit 7-7. Scope of work cover letter.

FutureTech

Tomorrow's Technology Today

8/5/2001

The Positron Corporation
Ms. Olivia Ontime
Vice President of Manufacturing
124 Centre Place
Randolph, MI 89768

Dear Olivia,

Our evaluation of the survey of your operations is complete. I appreciate your offer to review the following Positron scope of work based on our findings. It will help ensure that any solution we offer achieves your goals within your purchasing requirements.

The scope of work recaps the details you shared with me as I understood them. Its checklist format allows you to make any additions, deletions, or modifications you deem necessary. It also provides a space for you to record your notes.

When you complete it, please fax me a copy at 678-908-9878 or e-mail me at smartsell@futuretech.com. After I review it, we can discuss any changes you would like to see and answer any questions you might have. Once we address all issues to your satisfaction, I will work up a formal proposal to present to you. I also will send a brochure on the *Predicto Services* with the appropriate features highlighted for your review.

Thank you in advance for your investment of time, effort, and consideration. It will be well worth the return.

Regards,
Steven Smartsell
Steven Smartsell

Cc: FutureTech Engineering Group

Note: Steven would send the Scope of Work checklist to Olivia with her column blank.

---

solve them. (See Exhibit 7-8.) In addition, note that you need only one or two features to achieve the measurable benefits of a customer's goal.

Case Study

Continuing the case study from Step Four: Purpose and Summary, and after resolving all the issues from the scope of work, Steven reconfirms that Olivia's goal is to reduce downtime from eighteen hours to nine hours a year. He also verifies that her conditional commitment requires a three-year payback and a price not to exceed $1,080,000. He also confirms that a lost hour of production costs $40,000. His explanation begins with her goal of reducing downtime. Watch for the goal-benefit-feature-explaining pattern.

> **Steven:** Olivia, you want to reduce downtime *(goal)* by nine hours annually to save $360,000 in lost production time *(measurable benefit)*. Our Predicto Services use variance alert monitors *(feature)*. They warn of impending failures if the equipment is working outside its normal operating range to prevent breakdowns *(benefit)*.
>
> Furthermore, variance alert monitors (feature) could have prevented four failure instances last year for a savings total of three hours, which represents production savings of $120,000 *(measurable benefit)*. Olivia, have I explained it where you can see how it does that? *(Steven verifies that Olivia understands how feature connects to measurable benefits—and lets Olivia know that he takes responsibility for making sure she understood his explanation.)*
>
> **Olivia:** It makes sense.
>
> **Steven:** *(Steven then connects the second feature that achieves this goal.)* In addition, our service includes tolerance checks *(feature)*. They analyze critical components on a weekly basis for wear and tear *(benefit)*. There were two cases last year where this service could have prevented production stoppages totaling five hours, or $200,000, in lost production *(measurable benefit)*.

Steven then would proceed to a second goal, if there was one, or to another benefit or feature of the first goal.

Exhibit 7-8. Scope of work checklist.

Scope of Work Checklist

Positron Requirements	FutureTech Comments	Positron Comments
Primary goal: Prevent production stoppages from 18 hours to 9 hours annually	☑ Can do it with it with *Predicto Services*	☐ What can we do to reduce downtime to six hours?
Downtime costs: $40,000 per hour	☑ Confirmed costs using your past records	☐ Let's review your calculations again
Projected savings: 9 hours decrease save $360,000	☑ Confirmed savings using your past records	☐ Let's shoot for six hours
Start date: November	☑ No problem if order released by September 15th	☐ No problem
Finish date: December	☑ No problem if project begins by November 15th	☐ What happens if we run into the holidays?
Budget date: Not to exceed $1,080,000	☑ Current selection of products fit within this budget figure	☐ What will the actual price be?
Payback: Three years or less	☑ Current selection of products fit within this payback figure	☐ Did the survey indicate that there might be a way to lower our payback to two years?
General notes: Very similar situation that we have encountered on four other projects.	**General notes:** Survey really documents some significant opportunities to decrease downtime.	**General notes:** Still want to see some sort of guarantee on the savings.

(continues)

Exhibit 7-8. (Continued.)

Solution Selection and Review

Measurable Benefits	Product or Service	Feature and How It Works	Benefits of Features	FutureTech Comments	Positron Comments
Prevent production stoppages from 18 hours annually to 9		*Variance Alerts* prevents unscheduled breakdowns by warning operators of impending failure	It ensures uninterrupted shipments to your customers and saves money from lost production.	Only company in industry that provides this type of service	How come no one else offers it?
	Predicto Services	*Tolerance Checks* prevents unscheduled breakdowns by electronically analyzing critical components for wear and tear on a weekly basis	Same as above	By increasing tolerance checks to a daily basis, your records indicate that you can reduce downtime to six hours	What will that do to both cost and payback?
General Product Selection Notes for FutureTech: Suggest you visit a working installation.			**General Product Selection Notes for Positron:** Great idea. Which one will best resemble our operations?		

The Steps of MP 4: Implement Agreement

You are now ready to conduct MP 4: Implement Agreement. (See Exhibit 7-9.) Its purpose is to set up the contractual relationships necessary to start the sale. It has two steps.

Step One: Deal

Verify customers are ready to implement your proposals. Use the momentum that has been building as a direct result of the three Measurable Phase Changes previously obtained. Confidently and directly, ask customers to use your solutions to achieve their goals. You do not need trial and assumptive closes after showing how your features achieve the measurable benefits and requirements of their conditional commitments.

Step Two: Logistics

Reassure customers that their purchasing decisions are well thought out and will achieve their goals. Then, explain what you need to start. Have the necessary paperwork ready to sign. It demonstrates

Exhibit 7-9. MP 4: Implement Agreement.

MP 4: IMPLEMENT AGREEMENT

Step 2: Logistics

Step 1: Deal

MPC 4:
Agreement
Confirmed

*Direct Request for Earned Order;
Logical Conclusion to a Series of
Previous Commitments (MPCs)*

*Documents and Schedule
Required to Meet Conditional
Commitment. Plan Follow-up Visit
to Confirm Achievement of
Measurable Benefits*

your confidence that you and the customers already had a tacit agreement on what was required to conduct business. After receiving MPC 2: Potential Confirmed, but before your presentation, provide customers with a blank contract so that they can review terms and conditions. Do not let paperwork become an issue during MPC 4, especially if company lawyers need to review documents. Furthermore, you never know what will happen when support people review contracts with big numbers on them that they feel do not directly benefit them.

Measurable Phase Change 4: Agreement Confirmed

This last phase ends with the final Measurable Phase Change— MPC 4: Agreement Confirmed. Customers confirm they will proceed with your proposals and issue formal commitments.

Steven now completes his sale and receives the order. While it would make a great sequel, there are no cliffhangers today with the audience wondering whether Steven Smartsell received the order. What would your commission be on a $1,080,000, high-profit, value-driven sale? You find out when you make value measurable.

Case Study

Steven confidently asks Olivia if she is ready to start this program to reduce her downtime by 50 percent. Once she confirms that she is, Steven reinforces how her decision pays for itself many times over. He then discusses the logistics and deadlines. He also gets the necessary documents signed or purchase orders issued.

Note: Steven would then schedule a follow-up visit to confirm that his solution satisfied Olivia's conditional commitment. He focuses on the systems of evaluation Olivia used to calculate the measurable benefits of her goals. Documented successes make the best references—and ensure that if Olivia leaves, her replacement knows the measurable value Steven has provided Positron.

Just the Logical Conclusion

Selling value that you receive compensation for requires sweating the details. However, when you continuously verify that you and customers are at the same step in the same Measurable Phase, you eliminate wasted efforts and guesswork. The order becomes the logical conclusion to a series of engineered commitments (MPCs).

Case Study: Business-to-Consumer Transaction

John Peters is now ready to move to the next measurable phase in this case study of a business-to-consumer transaction.

MP 3: Cement Solution

John Peters illustrates how to apply the steps and strategies of this chapter in detail as he concludes the last two phases with Brian Walters.

Before Meeting the Customer MP 3 Steps

The three steps that occur before John Peters meets again with the customer in person are as follows.

Step One: No Blanks

John Peters fills out his Connecting Value sheet before making his presentation. He uses the specifics gathered during MP 2: Measure Potential to select the features. Although his product has no unique strengths, his confidence is building because of all the features he connects to the measurable benefits of Brian's goals. (Note that he omits the Focus column. Brian is not a business, so the benefits can only be internal. Also, because none of the features are unique strengths that column is omitted also. See Exhibit 7-10.)

Note: The key point: Even if your products don't have any unique strengths, how you make value measurable becomes your unique strength.

Note: The key points and commentary are in italics and parentheses for easy reference.

Step Two: Benchmarks

John Peters connects the features to the measurable benefits as defined in Exhibit 7-10.

Step Three: Oops!

All of Brian Walters's measurable benefits have a feature connected to them. There are no misses (until Chapter 8).

Exhibit 7-10. Connecting value sheet.

CONNECTING VALUE SHEET

Customer Goals	Benefits of Achieving Goals (time or money)	Systems of Evaluation	Products	Specifics of Features and Benefits (features are in italics)	Value Type and Focus (all focus is internal with consumer sales)	Unique Strength/ Feature Value Rating
	Reduces wait between showers by 67%	Time between showers	XLX 9000	*90-gallon tank*	Measurable	No (1)
Increase shower water capacity	50% more capacity than existing heater to accommodate three showers in one hour		XLX 9000	*60% more heating coils*	Measurable	No (1)
		Size of water tank	XLX 9000	*90-gallon tank*	Measurable	No (1)
Improve energy efficiency	Reduces utility costs by $18 a month; $648 over three-years	Energy required to heat water	XLX 9000	*Most efficient heat transfer surface*	Measurable	No (1)
Receive 3-year payback	Saves $180 on warranty costs	Costs of typical or past repairs	XLX 9000	*Five-year parts warranty*	Measurable	No (1)

Conditional Commitment: Three people can take a shower during a one-hour period, the new hot water heater will provide a three-year payback, stay within a $600 budget, and be installed by the end of next week.

At Meeting MPC 3 Steps

John Peters is now prepared to let Brian Walters know that he understands Brian's goals—and can help him to achieve them.

Step Four: Purpose and Summary

Brian: Good to see you again, John. I look forward to seeing what you came up with. (*Brian indicates he is ready to discuss business.*)

John: Brian, good to see you, too. Thanks for taking the time to meet with me again. I'd like to explain over the next ten minutes how you can have enough hot water for three people in an hour, justify a $750 price, and achieve a three-year payback by reducing utility costs. I almost forgot, and have it installed by the end of next week—if these requirements are met. Is there anything else you'd like to cover? (*John puts Brian at ease by telling him how much time he needs. Brian does not have to wonder how long the presentation will take. John does not mention any products by name yet; he instead focuses on Brian's goals. He makes the "agreement" subject to meeting all of Brian's stated requirements. Finally, John verifies there is nothing else to address.*)

Brian: No, John. If you can satisfy all those issues, I'm ready to go. (*John receives his confirmed conditional commitment to ensure he has accurate details.*)

Step Five: Connect the Dots

John takes out a cutaway, 3-D model of the XLX 9000 to show Brian as he explains how its features achieve his goals.

John: Brian, I'm confident that our high-efficiency water heater (*at this point in the sales process, he gives the product a "name" to encompass the features and benefits*), the XLX 9000, can meet all your requirements. Let's start with increasing your capacity (*first goal*) to provide enough hot water for three people to take a shower in one hour (*first measurable benefit of goal*). The XLX 9000 has the largest tank size available at 90 gallons (*first feature*). It's 50 percent larger than your current 60-gallon capacity (*first benefit of this feature*). Additionally, with 60 percent more coils and heat transfer surface than your current unit (*second feature*), the XLX 9000 requires just one third the reheat time (*second benefit of the second feature*). Instead of needing sixty minutes to reheat fully, you only need twenty minutes (*second measurable benefit of goal*). You'll have plenty of hot water whenever your family needs it. No more taking turns on who goes first.

A second priority of yours is to improve energy efficiency and reduce utility costs *(second goal and vague benefit)*. The XLX 9000, with its increased heat transfer surface *(third feature)*, has the highest energy efficiency *(first benefit of third feature)* on the market today. It will cost $18 a month less than your current system *(first measurable benefit of second goal)* while providing 50 percent more hot water *(second benefit of third feature)*. You could almost think of the XLX 9000 as a new savings account. *(Analogy)*.

In addition, with a price of $750, you achieve a three-year payback *(third goal)* and justify its price. You can save $648 on your utility bill over the next three years *(first measurable benefit of third goal)*. In addition, due to the XLX 9000's five-year parts-and-labor warranty *(fourth feature)*, another $60 a year can be saved on your existing warranty contract *(first benefit of fourth feature)*. This increases your three-year savings to over $820 *(second benefit of fourth feature)*. *(Note how John connected all the appropriate benefits and features to each goal before proceeding to the next one. The explanations were simple and vivid, one had an analogy, and John was brimming with confidence.)*

Step Six: Conditions Met

John: Brian, can you see how the XLX 9000 can meet all your hot-water requirements of capacity and efficiency and save you over $800 over the next three years and exceed your payback schedule based on its price of $750? This price also includes a five-year full warranty. *(John satisfies conditional commitment ands keep the focus on the Column 2 benefits, not the features. He also makes Column 1 price what it is, just another function of the requirements of the conditional commitment, not a stand-alone issue)*

MPC 3: Solution Confirmed

Brian: Yes I can. You did a very good job of explaining how the XLX 9000 could benefit us.

MP 4: Implement Agreement

John is now ready to implement the agreement.

Step One: Deal

John: Brian, are you ready to go ahead with the purchase of the XLX 9000? *(John feels confident enough to make a well-earned direct request.)*

Brian: You bet. We have ourselves a deal. *(John receives final verification.)*

Step Two: Logistics

John: Great, you made a good decision and will be happy with the results. All we need to do to start is for you to sign this standard contract you reviewed previously and a $200 deposit. I can then order the materials and schedule the installation for next Tuesday. *(John provides good positive reinforcement. In addition, he explains the need to get the "paperwork" out of the way so they can finish by next week.)*

MPC 4: Agreement Confirmed

Brian: Here's my John Hancock and a check for $200. *(Nothing is more professionally satisfying than customer-oriented solutions that result in well-thought-out and well-earned orders.)*

Note: John would schedule a follow-up visit in six months to confirm the XLX 9000 is fulfilling Brian's conditional commitment. John wants to add Brian to his list of documented and measurable successes and references.

SUMMARY

For a chart depicting the MeasureMax phases, see Exhibit 7-11.

- MP 3: Cement Solution consists of (prior to meeting with the customer):
  - *Step One: No Blanks.* Make sure you can fill out a Quick-Entry Sales Management sheet completely.
  - *Step Two: Benchmarks.* Connect features to measurable benefits and verify that they satisfy conditional commitment using a connecting value sheet.
  - *Step Three: Oops!* Be ready to offset any missed measurable benefits of goals or requirements of conditional commitments.
- Use the *Does Your Proposal Pass the Pulled-Through Test?* to determine if you are ready to continue to MP 3 or must return to MP 1 or MP 2.
- At the meeting:
  - *Step Four: Purpose and Summary.* Confirm that the meeting is to explain how your proposal achieves their goals and satisfies conditional commitment.

Exhibit 7-11. The four phases of the MeasureMax selling system.

MP 1: Spark Interest
Step One. Research and Membership
Step Two. Take Your Pick
Step Three. Track Record
MPC 1: Interest Confirmed

MP 2: Measure Potential
Step One.   Market Focus
Step Two.   Purpose And Goals
Step Three. Eliminate Unknowns
Step Four.   Yellow Light
MPC 2: Potential Confirmed

MP 3: Cement Solution
Before Meeting:
Step One.   No Blanks
Step Two.   Benchmarks
Step Three. Oops!
At Meeting:
Step Four.   Purpose & Summary
Step Five.   Connect the Dots
Step Six.   Conditions Met
MPC 3: Solution Confirmed

MP 4: Implement Agreement
Step One.   Deal
Step Two.   Logistics
MPC 4: Agreement Confirmed

- *Step Five: Connect the Dots.* Start with goals and measurable benefits and explain how your products achieve them. Do not start with your products' features first.
- *Step Six: Conditions Met.* Recap how the proposal satisfies the conditional commitment.
- *MPC 3: Solution Confirmed.* Customers agree your products achieve their goals, but it is still too early to ask for an order.
- Explaining is illustrating how your features connect to their measurable benefits.
- A good explanation uses simple, vivid, analogies, no return, power words, and avoids using the words *never* or *always.*
- Speak in your customers' terms.
- Use your technical knowledge to support points, not to make them.
- Start at the same technical level as the customers' attainment measurements.
- The verbal structure of explaining always starts with the customers' goals, then the benefits of the goals, and finally your product's features and benefits.
- Customers might have two or more goals, one goal might have two or more benefits, and one benefit might connect with two or more of your product's features.
- MP 4: Implement Agreement consists of:
  - *Step One: Deal.* Verify customer is ready to start.
  - *Step Two: Logistics.* Explain what customers need to do to start.
  - *MPC 4: Agreement Confirmed.* Customers confirm they will proceed with your solutions.
- A scope of work provides different decision makers with the opportunity to review a preliminary proposal and make one last check before you make your final presentation.

Chapter Eight

When the World Isn't Perfect

The famous Scottish poet Robert Burns is credited with the old adage: "The best laid plans of mice and men often go astray." While it is hard to vouch for the mice, this passage definitely applies to salespeople. Often, customers' less-than-ideal comments or actions derail your plans and wreck sales opportunities.

Traditional selling methods refer to these potential sale wreckers as *obstacles* or *objections.* Yet, these terms create a negative perception for something that can be a positive event. Therefore, a more appropriate term is *hinges.* The outcome of a sales opportunity *hinges* on how you resolve obstacles.

This chapter provides you with the strategies and tactics to turn these so-called negative situations into orders by explaining:

- How hinges form
- How to handle hinges

Nip Them in the Bud

Hinges prevent your sales plans from moving forward. Your sales plan is simple: Obtain the four Measurable Phase Changes (MPCs) in the proper order to earn high-value orders. Proof that MPCs have occurred comes when customers confirm Interest (MPC 1), Potential (MPC 2), Solution (MPC 3), and Agreement (MPC 4). They agree to your calls for actions (meetings, surveys, presentations, or purchase orders) that move you to the next Measurable Phase (MP). Therefore, to wreak havoc on your sales plans, hinges must prevent you from:

- Conducting the four MPs and MPCs in sequence
- Obtaining the MPCs and their respective calls for action

If either one of the above happens, it stops the forward motion of the sale. Your ability to sell value is in jeopardy. As you will see, when it comes to hinges, an ounce of prevention is worth a pound of cure. Good salespeople know how to handle hinges to stay on plan; great ones know how to prevent them from occurring.

The Three General Categories of Hinges

If you know the MP in which the hinges occur, you will know what strategies and tactics to use to remedy them. The three general categories of hinges tell you where they occur and how they form. They are *natural, leveraged,* or *hidden* hinges.

Natural Hinges

If you must contend with hinges, natural hinges are the most desirable. They arise in MP 2: Measure Potential. Although they might have an adverse effect on your selling efforts, customers are unaware of any potential problems. They do not view these hinges as problems because they surface during the natural flow of MP 2. They occur before you attempt to obtain MPC 2: Potential Confirmed—and *before you mention specific products.* Customers consider them to be nothing more than details about their goals, measurable benefits, filters, and systems of evaluation. While you might deem these details to be potential problems, customers do not because they are without any specific products to reference them to.

You weigh the effects of natural hinges and determine how they affect customers or you from achieving their goals. You think about how to handle them on a proactive and strategic basis at your office, rather than on a reactive and tactical one in front of customers. While not a problem *yet* to customers, any potential inability to achieve their goals that surfaces can jeopardize your ability to provide value if ignored or mishandled.

Example

One of Olivia Ontime's other goals is to increase productivity by 15 percent. She tells Steven Smartsell during MP 2: Measure Potential that any purchase must not exceed her $50,000 budget (*funding filter*). Steven knows his products typically cost $75,000. At this time, Olivia does not consider the budget constraint an issue because Steven has not yet mentioned any specific products that exceed her $50,000 limit. However, Steven knows that he must solve the potential problem that Olivia's budget figure is less than his products' price range to earn a sale.

Steven also knows better than to address Olivia's budget issue without first reviewing the specifics of his Quick-Entry Sales Management (Q) sheet. Therefore, he returns to his office to review his Q sheet. Either by himself or by using the resources of his sales team, the details from the Q sheet will help him plan how he will handle a hinge that has arisen during MP 2.

Leveraged Hinge

When customers use details of your products to *leverage* their concerns, you have a *leveraged* hinge. Therefore, a leveraged hinge occurs when you mention specific products and services as solutions in MP 1 and MP 2 before you know the details of goals, measurable benefits, filters, and SOEs. Customers block your attempts to obtain MPCs and do not agree to your calls for action. Sales opportunities start to regress into the brinkmanship selling mode. You must defend your product selections while discussions about undesirable features, prices, delivery dates, and budgets dominate the sales calls.

Example

In sharp contrast to the previous example, Steven now pursues the first product-positioning opportunity that surfaces when Olivia mentions her 15 percent productivity goal. He tells her that one of his specific services, ProdoGain, deals with increasing productivity. He mentions this service before he quantifies her productivity increase in dollar terms or knows the details of her filters. Buyers and sellers beware.

After Steven explains its features, Olivia asks Steven what the service costs. He states about $75,000. Olivia tells him that she cannot spend more than $50,000. Olivia now leverages her budget hinge against the price of his service. Now Steven must defend his price—without knowing any measurable benefits. The focus shifts from productivity goals to price. Olivia probably views any additional information Steven requests as an attempt to justify his budget-busting price. Steven cannot obtain MPC 2: Potential Confirmed.

Note: As the "Handling Hinges" section illustrates, the most effective way to deal with hinges is to make Column 2 benefits measurable to offset concerns that arise in Column 1 over price, delivery, relationships, and costs of changing suppliers.

The good news is that salespeople create leveraged hinges, not customers. The better news is that more often than not, you can prevent them from occurring. You can make them surface as the more innocuous natural hinges, if you conduct MP 1: Spark Interest and MP 2: Measure Potential more thoroughly—and avoid mentioning specific products. For instance, in the previous example, all Steven had to do in MP 2 to make the budget hinge natural instead of leveraged would have been either of the following two things:

1. *Not* mention specific products or services.
2. Keep asking questions that gathered details about Olivia's goals, measurable benefits, filters, and SOEs. (If you review the MP 2 dialogue between Steven and Olivia in Chapter 6, you will see how many times Steven needed patience and discipline not to interject product discussions.)

In MP 1 and MP 2, if you encourage more measurable customer input and less product output, you can avoid most leveraged hinges.

Hidden Hinge

Hidden hinges are either leveraged or natural hinges that customers do not want to disclose. They believe that disclosure creates negative impressions of them or their company, or your products or company. Hidden hinges are typically caused by customers' reluctance to admit the following for this sales opportunity:

- They cannot make the purchasing decision.
- They cannot get the funding.
- They have already committed to one of your competitors.
- They do not feel your products are justifiable or beneficial.

Typically, neutral or negative customers bring up hidden hinges faster than positive customers do. They usually like to reaffirm and challenge you on why they do not conduct business with your company. They feel you justify their decisions when you cannot change their minds in ten seconds. Here is where it is essential to have a Spark Interest statement or references with documented and measurable savings at one's fingertips.

Positive customers are usually more reluctant to discuss negative issues with you. They feel it might jeopardize your friendship. Instead, they use *smokescreens* to conceal their hidden hinges.

Smokescreens

Smokescreens are business issues that customers claim are beyond their control that prevent sales from occurring. It is ironic (and unfortunate) how sometimes your personal relationships work against you. The customers make unilateral decisions to spare your personal feelings. They do not disclose the professional reasons why they do not want to conduct business (which is another reason why you want professional bonds to be as strong as personal ones).

Note: Qualifying customers first on their ability to achieve their goals, not buy your products, encourages them to share information. The more information customers share, the less reason they have to create smokescreens. Constantly reinforce to customers that you seek disclosure about their ability and authority to achieve their goals, regardless of the outcome on you.

You usually sense a hidden hinge when customers:

- React adversely to a clarifying question that seeks a better understanding of their smokescreens
- Dismiss without consideration your handling of the smokescreen
- Keep bringing up one smokescreen after another, regardless of how they are handled (like a hurdle race that never ends; as you clear one hurdle, another pops up)
- Will not make goals, benefits, or filters measurable or discuss SOEs

Example

Steven asks Olivia if she can increase her budget. She says no. She does not want to admit to Steven that any project over $50,000 needs corporate approval. Olivia feels embarrassed that she will no longer be the final decision maker.

Again, the "Handling Hinges" section explains how to address hidden hinges. Hint: Using yes-or-no questions does not work very well.

The Four Types of Hinges

Whether they are leveraged, natural, or hidden, hinges fall into one of four types. This additional classification makes them easier to handle. Each hinge has its own nuances, which you handle somewhat differently. Their number designation signifies in which MP the hinge occurs. For example: Type I, occurs in MP 1: Spark Interest, Type II, in MP 2: Measure Potential, and so forth. (Use the hinge charts and examples on Exhibits 8-7, 8-9, 8-11, and 8-13 to look up the details of each hinge and the strategies and tactics to remedy them.)

Type I: Pulse Check

Customers show no interest in your suggested goals and potential benefits—you wonder if they are even alive. This hinge occurs in MP 1: Spark Interest. It is the most difficult one to handle because it occurs so early in the sales call. Not a lot of information exists to help determine your next step.

Type II: Iceberg Ahead

Look out; this hinge could spell disaster for your "Titanic" sales opportunities. It occurs when filters impede your or your customers' ability to achieve their goals. It also arises when customers view your products as commodities. When customers cannot distinguish between products, the filters of funding (price) or dates (delivery) become their goals. The bid system (described in Chapter 1) is a key catalyst in these two filters becoming goals. This hinge can surface either in MP 2: Measure Potential or MP 3: Cement Solution. If you conduct MP 2 thoroughly, the hinge surfaces as the preferred natural type. Otherwise, it becomes a leveraged one in MP 3 after you disclose your product selections.

Type III: Gutter Ball

Your products do not completely fulfill the requirements of the conditional commitments. Instead of rolling a strike, you let loose a gutter ball. It is leveraged and occurs during the disclosure of your product selections in MP 3: Cement Solution. Avoid this hinge at all costs. It can end up with the sale, like the bowling pins, waiting to be knocked down by customers and competitors.

Type IV: Rip-Off

Its name says it all: Customers perceive the price of your products as being excessive. They feel you are counting on this one sale to send your kids through college. It occurs during MP 4: Implement Agreement and is leveraged against product or service selections. Three factors influence what customers expect of price: (1) Perceived manufacturing costs multiplied by a reasonable markup, (2) the value of perceived and measurable benefits, and (3) pricing of similar products (measurable benefits make them different).

Handling Hinges

The Safety Zone and How's Zat? questioning strategies from Chapter 5 form the foundation for handling hinges. They help you and customers understand how and why they assign a negative perception to a goal or filter, or how they connect a filter to a goal. You take customers' responses and reference them to "how does that" affect:

- Their ability to achieve their goals or conditional commitments
- Your product selections or calls for action
- Your decision to invest more time and efforts in the sales opportunities

Any time you respond to a hinge with a statement and not a question, you are trying to explain away something you cannot fully understand. Make "How's Zat?" the first two words to start a question concerning a hinge and you are well on your way to handling it. Use these two words to clarify how customers view the *measurable* effects of their hinges. More than likely, they have not considered their measurable ramifications, only perceived ones. Use these two words to quantify their perceptions.

How's Zat? Prevents Responses on Automatic Pilot

Do not try to explain away a hinge before you understand the measurable (and motivating) reasons behind it. While it is good to think about how you might handle hinges that arise before you go on sales calls, this preparation can work against you too.

Planning your replies assumes you know the reasons why customers bring up the hinges. Therefore, when customers bring up hinges, it is natural for you to go on automatic pilot with your well-thought-out responses. However, you might bring up concerns that did not exist until you brought them up. Knowing *your* reasons for why there is a hinge is not the same as knowing *their* reasons. Contain your urge to blurt out canned responses by remembering the following two sayings:

1. "Seek to understand before you seek to be understood."
2. "What part of 'no' didn't you understand?" Treat the word *no* as a knee-jerk reaction to your comments, not as a steadfast position. Customers usually mean no in the following context:
   - "No, I need more time to think through my goal, measurable benefits, filters, SOEs, and your product selections."

- "No, I need more information about your products or my goals."
- "No, I didn't understand how you help me achieve my goals."

Your handling of hinges involves clarifying what part of no you must address: time, information, or comprehension.

How's Zat Tactics

While How's Zat? is the overall strategy for handling hinges, the following are its ministrategies and tactics. They make the Safety Zone and How's Zat? strategies work better.

The *Silence Is Golden* Tactic

This tactic helps you handle a hinge initially by doing nothing, nada, zilch . . . silence! Use the fact that most people in a conversation dread the sound of silence. Four to five seconds of quiet seems like an eternity.

The following benefits result from this time-out:

- It allows you to collect your thoughts and ask yourself, "Wow, I wonder how I am going to handle this one?"
- It prevents an automatic response that otherwise sounds canned or defensive.
- It gives you the opportunity to remind yourself that customers are not attacking you personally. They are just reacting to MPCs or calls for action they feel are unwarranted or unjustifiable. Take hinges personally and you become subjective, rather than objective, in handling them.
- You can use the pause to let customers know you are giving their comments proper consideration.
- You can give customers the opportunity to clarify or even answer their own hinges. They might skip over this one to bring up hinges that are more important.

The *Pat from Saturday Night Live* Tactic

This tactic treats hinges like the androgynous character Pat from the television show *Saturday Night Live* whom no one could identify as either man or woman. With hinges, you often face situations where you cannot tell what you have. Is it a hinge or a request for more information, a better explanation, or more documentation?

Therefore, when clarifying and verifying customers' responses, do not assume they are hinges until you gather more information. In addition, do not sound like you agree it is a hinge by validating their comments.

Example

Olivia: Your service costs $25,000 more than we budgeted!

Steven: (on automatic pilot): I assumed your $50,000 budget was just an estimate, not a firm number.
A better way to respond is with the following tactic:

Steven: How will that affect your purchasing decision? (If she says it does not, leave it alone. If she states that it does, handle it by using the next tactic.)

The *Lose the Battle, Win the War* Tactic

Use this tactic to build credibility by acknowledging that customers' hinges, if accurate, have merit. However, demonstrate that in the grand scheme of things, the hinge—even with merit—is not a deterrent to continuing the sale. You can resolve a hinge with merit. Just transform hinges into benefits.

Customers appreciate it when you tackle their valid concerns head on and turn them into benefits. Heck, you usually impress yourself when you do it. You convert a liability into an asset by showing customers how their hinges help them to achieve their goals.

Example

Olivia: Your ProdoGain service costs $25,000 more than we budgeted. I will not be able to get more money without getting corporate involved.

Steven: It does. Yet, the $25,000 is for the *single operator control* feature (see Steven's Market Profile Sheet in Chapter 3) that only FutureTech provides, which lowers your payback from two years to one. We can also extend payment terms so you pay the additional $25,000 in your next fiscal year. It will not affect this year's budget. Can you see where the $25,000 pays for itself within a year—and won't require corporate approval?

The *You Can't Do Both* Tactic

Sometimes your products achieve customers' goals, but not all their prerequisites. This hinge usually involves difficulty meeting funding requirements or delivery dates. Unless you arbitrarily lower your price or miraculously speed up deliveries, use this tactic. Explain that your products cannot do both. Let customers choose which one is more important, the prerequisite or the goal. If the value of their goals is measurable, chances are high that the customer will choose the goal.

Example

Olivia: We can only go with your proposal if you meet your competitor's bid price, which is $18,000 less.

Steven (on automatic pilot): There's no way I can meet that price! *(Unless, Steven arbitrarily lowers his price and watches the bidding wars begin! Steven might also say, "OK, let me talk to my sales manager. I'll see if I can get her to lower the price." Both responses hurt his ability to sell value and protect profit levels.)*
A better reply would be to use the following tactic:

Steven: I understand the need to cost-justify any difference in price. Using your figures, *you* justified our price. I would like to work with you; however, the only way to lower my price by $18,000 is to change our product selections. If we do that, we cannot help you achieve your goals. Olivia, do you understand why I cannot just lower my price and still achieve your goal of improving productivity by 15 percent or $240,000 *(converting percentages to dollars make them powerful allies)*?

The Basic Steps in Handling Hinges

You know the hinge categories, types, strategies, and tactics. The following four steps in Exhibit 8-1 show how to combine them so that you can effectively handle hinges. The case studies at the end of this section also highlight the logistics and strategies of each step. The steps are as follows:

Step 1. Damage Report

In the damage report step, the salesperson evaluates the impact of the hinge.

- Pause and implement *Silence Is Golden*. If you say to yourself, "Uh-oh, I wonder how I am going to get out of this one?" you waited the recommended five seconds.
- Use the Safety Zone strategy and the *Pat from Saturday Night Live* tactic and evaluate the impact or potential damage of the hinge. Ask yourself, "Do I understand how the hinge impacts their goals, my sales strategy, product, or call for action? Is it just a request for more

Exhibit 8-1. Basic steps for handling hinges.

information?" Formulate your clarifying question on what you need to know to answer these questions.

Example

Olivia: I *really* do not want to exceed our $50,000 budget.

Steven asks himself: *What is determining the $50,000 budget limit; how will that affect their goals or product selections; what does "really" mean?*
Those answers hold the key to understanding and handling the hinge.

Step 2. How's Zat?

This step clarifies the impact of the hinge.

- Ask a clarifying question concerning the hinge's impact without confirming a negative. This sometimes requires two or three open-ended questions before you can verify that you have a measurable reply.

Example

Steven: Why is that? *(Clarifying question)*
Olivia: Exceeding the $50,000 figure means getting corporate approval, which could delay the project a year.

Step 3. Target Confirmed

In this step, the salesperson verifies the impact of the hinge.

- Verify your understanding of how they feel the hinge affects their goals or your product selections without agreeing with them.
- Verifying requires yes-or-no questions. If necessary, phrase your clarifying question so that it relates to their goals (*safety zone*).
- The customers' responses should be a challenge that states, "Here's my concern. If you make it go away, we can move forward."

238 The Science of Sales Success

Example

Steven: So, your concern is that you might have to wait a year if you need to get corporate approval and delay receiving the projected cost savings.

Olivia: Exactly, I do not want to wait a year to get the savings. *(She verifies hinge and issues her challenge.)*

Step 4. Downplay

In this step, the salesperson minimizes the impact of the hinge.

- Use the following three tactics to apply for the now-defined hinge by:

1. *Explaining.* Provide additional information or clarification to "explain away" a customer's misconception or misinterpretation. Use this tactic during any of the four MPs.

Example

Olivia: Exactly, I do not want to wait a year to get the savings.

Steven explains: We can use progressive billing to spread the price over a two-year budget period. You wouldn't exceed the $50,000 level in a single year and you wouldn't require corporate approval.

2. *Outweighing.* You remedy an actual liability by showing how the overall benefits in achieving their goals "outweigh" their concerns. Depending on whether you mentioned specific products, you use this tactic during MP 2: Cement Solution or MP 3: Implement Agreement phases. This strategy requires measurable benefits. Outweighing is like an accounting ledger with credits and debits—with the total sum carrying the most weight.

Example

Olivia: Exactly, I do not want to wait a year to get the savings.

Steven outweighs: The project exceeds your $50,000 budget. *(It is a fact, and he hits it head on).* However, if I can help you demonstrate to corporate how waiting a year delays saving $180,000 *(lost opportunity costs or the costs of doing nothing)* in operating expenses, will that bring about an approval this year?

3. *Revising.* You offer a new call for action in MP 3: Cement Solution because the filters in MP 2: Measure Potential were not fully qualified. Your original proposed solution does not address all the customers' goals and filters. Use this tactic as a means of last resort. First, return to MP 2 and try to establish new goals or new *attainment measurement* filters before changing product selections.

Example

Olivia: Exactly, I do not want to wait a year to realize the savings.

Steven revises: I suggest breaking this one major project into smaller projects implemented over a multiyear period.

- Ask a yes/no question to verify that customers agree that you have remedied the hinge to their satisfaction. Once you verified that you removed the hinge, reenter the Measurable Phases at the immediate step beyond which the hinge stopped you.

Example

Verifying to customer: Do you think corporate would approve a project that saves $180,000 this budget year although it exceeds the $50,000 budget limit?

Customer: Yes, I do. (Reenter sale at MP 4: Implement Agreement.)

Let the Customer Go First

Handling hinges comes down to understanding how they affect the ability of customers or your products or services to achieve their goals. Discipline yourself to keep from automatically trying to explain away the hinge as your first response. Instead, save that step until after you ask the customer to explain its details away with some version of Safety Zone and How's Zat? The impact of these powerful tools is immediate and significant.

Overview of the General Steps for Handling Hinges

An overview of the four steps for handling hinges is show in Exhibit 8-2.

Case Study

John Peters's sales call with Brian Walters now encounters unexpected twists and hinges. These examples demonstrate how to apply the strategies and tactics for handling hinges inside the Measurable Phases.

Review the following steps for active questioning to see how they are applied in the case study.

1. *Follow the Customers' Lead.* Relate all clarifying questions to customers' last responses on how their hinges affect their goals and filters.
2. *Ask Specific but Open-Ended Questions.* Do not use yes-or-no questions unless you need to verify a point.
3. *No Loose Ends.* Verify that a goal or filter is measurable before pursuing another.
4. *Don't Shoot Yourself.* Never confirm a negative statement.
5. *Think Positively.* Never make a negative assumption.
6. *No Echoes.* Rephrase the customers' responses; do not repeat them verbatim.

Type I: Pulse Check—No Interest in Any Goals in MP 1 (Leveraged)

John: Mr. Walters, we have helped some homeowners to reduce utility costs, sometimes by as much as one third, and other homeowners to increase hot water capacity by 50 percent. Are either of these areas of interest to you or are there any other ones more pertinent? *(Uses spark interest statement to generate and verify interest.)*

Exhibit 8-2. Overview of the four steps.

DAMAGE REPORT
1. Pause and implement *Silence Is Golden.*
2. Implement *Pat from Saturday Night Live* and evaluate the impact of the hinge. Ask yourself, "Do I understand how the hinge impacts their goals, my MP sequence, product selections, or call for actions (MPC)? Is it just a request for more information?"
3. Formulate your clarifying How's Zat? question to take the narrow focus of the hinge to encompass the above.

HOW'S ZAT?
1. Ask clarifying questions concerning the hinge's impact (How's Zat?) without confirming a negative. Sometimes, you require two or three open-ended questions before you can verify customers' responses.

TARGET CONFIRMED
1. Verify you understand (without agreeing) how the customer thinks the hinge affects his or her goals or product selections.
2. Phrase clarifying question so it relates to the customer's goals (*Safety Zone*).

DOWNPLAY
1. Handle the hinge by:
(a) Explaining away the hinge. Provide additional information that might cause the customer to remove his or her own hinge.
(b) Neutralizing the hinge by outweighing its apparent liability and converting it into new benefits.
(c) Revise a new call for action or product selections.
2. Verify that customers agree you have remedied the hinge to their satisfaction.

Brian: I am not interested at this time. *(Disregards spark interest statement.)*

(See Exhibit 8-3.)

Type II: Iceberg Ahead—Unfavorable Filter Surfaces in MP 2 (Natural)

Brian: I don't want to exceed my budget. *(A vague response that needs clarifying.)*

Exhibit 8-3. Pulse check scenario.

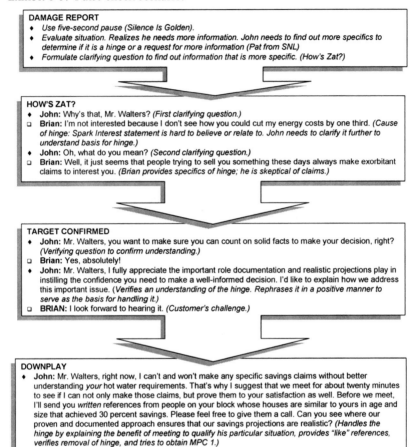

DAMAGE REPORT
- Use five-second pause (Silence Is Golden).
- Evaluate situation. Realizes he needs more information. John needs to find out more specifics to determine if it is a hinge or a request for more information (Pat from SNL)
- Formulate clarifying question to find out information that is more specific. (How's Zat?)

HOW'S ZAT?
- **John:** Why's that, Mr. Walters? (First clarifying question.)
- **Brian:** I'm not interested because I don't see how you could cut my energy costs by one third. (Cause of hinge: Spark Interest statement is hard to believe or relate to. John needs to clarify it further to understand basis for hinge.)
- **John:** Oh, what do you mean? (Second clarifying question.)
- **Brian:** Well, it just seems that people trying to sell you something these days always make exorbitant claims to interest you. (Brian provides specifics of hinge; he is skeptical of claims.)

TARGET CONFIRMED
- **John:** Mr. Walters, you want to make sure you can count on solid facts to make your decision, right? (Verifying question to confirm understanding.)
- **Brian:** Yes, absolutely!
- **John:** Mr. Walters, I fully appreciate the important role documentation and realistic projections play in instilling the confidence you need to make a well-informed decision. I'd like to explain how we address this important issue. (Verifies an understanding of the hinge. Rephrases it in a positive manner to serve as the basis for handling it.)
- **BRIAN:** I look forward to hearing it. (Customer's challenge.)

DOWNPLAY
- **John:** Mr. Walters, right now, I can't and won't make any specific savings claims without better understanding *your* hot water requirements. That's why I suggest that we meet for about twenty minutes to see if I can not only make those claims, but prove them to your satisfaction as well. Before we meet, I'll send you *written* references from people on your block whose houses are similar to yours in age and size that achieved 30 percent savings. Please feel free to give them a call. Can you see where our proven and documented approach ensures that our savings projections are realistic? (Handles the hinge by explaining the benefit of meeting to qualify his particular situation, provides "like" references, verifies removal of hinge, and tries to obtain MPC 1.)
- **Brian:** Yes, I can. Let's get together on Tuesday to look at my specifics. (Bingo.)

John: Mr. Walters, what price range have you set? (*Clarifying question.*)

Brian: I really don't want to exceed $500. (*An unfavorable filter—product lines start at $750.*)

(See Exhibit 8-4.)

Type III: Gutter Ball—Unfulfilled Commitment in MP 3 (Leveraged)

John: Brian, can you see how the XLX 9000 meets all your hot-water requirements of capacity and efficiency? In addition, it saves

Exhibit 8-4. Iceberg ahead scenario.

DAMAGE REPORT
- *Use five-second pause (Silence Is Golden).*
- *Evaluates comment and realizes he needs more information to determine how flexible the $500 figure is. Where does the figure come from, and is it a hinge? (Pat from SNL)*
- *Formulate clarifying question to find out information that is more specific. (How's Zat?)*

HOW's ZAT?
- **John:** Mr. Walters, why did you choose a $500 figure? *(Clarifying question to get specifics.)*
- **Brian:** Well, it just seems that whenever you discuss a budget number, the final price always seems to come out higher. I figure it's better to start out lower. Besides, my friends told me I should be able to get a something good for less than $500. *(Actually, not bad logic unless Brian is dealing with a professional, like John, who helps customers establish conditional commitments to measure the value of purchases.)*
- **John:** You're right; justifying a price on whether it meets a budget does everyone a disservice because it ignores the real issue. Regardless of what you spend, whether it's $100 or $500 like your friends suggested, or even a $1,000, it must meet the conditions you set. What conditions have you or your friends set to justify your investment? *(Acknowledges and verifies customers' comment. Also, uses second clarifying question to find out attainment measurement.)*
- **Brian:** Make sure that whatever I purchase pays for itself in at least three years--and I can tell you right now, there's no way I'll spend more than $900. *(The hinge involves getting specifics about, attainment measurement. The term "make sure" still needs clarification.)*

TARGET CONFIRMED
- **John:** Mr. Walters if we could guarantee your savings would you feel confident enough to go ahead with it? *(Uses a verifying statement to confirm an understanding of the hinge. Rephrases it in a positive manner to handle it better; Safety Zone strategy.)*
- **Brian:** Yeah, I would.

DOWNPLAY
- **John:** OK. Once we finish our survey and know the savings of a solution pays for itself in three years, we'll guarantee them. Does that meet your requirements? *(Handles the hinge by explaining the benefits of "no guarantees without the facts survey." Verifies removal of hinge and tries to obtain MPC 2.)*
- **Brian:** Absolutely. When can we arrange a survey? *(Bingo.)*

you more than \$800 over the next three years and exceeds your payback schedule with its \$750 price. It also includes a five-year warranty.

Brian: John, I don't see how the XLX 9000 meets all my requirements. *(Unfulfilled conditional commitment.)*

(See Exhibit 8-5.)

Type IV: Rip-Off—Views Price as Excessive in MP 4 (Leveraged)

John: So, Brian, can you see how the XLX 9000 meets all your hot-water requirements of capacity and efficiency? In addition, it

Exhibit 8-5. Gutter ball scenario.

DAMAGE REPORT
- *Use five-second pause (Silence Is Golden.)*
- *Evaluates situation and realizes he needs more information. John needs to find out more specifics to determine if it is a hinge or a request for more information. (Pat from SNL)*
- *Formulate clarifying question to find out information that is more specific. (How's Zat?)*

HOW'S ZAT?
- John: Brian, what do you mean? *(First clarifying question.)*
- Brian: Well, I don't see how you can reheat my water faster and still use less power. *(Cause of hinge: the technical explanation is not easy to comprehend. It did not explain how the features produce the benefits of the goals in a manner Brian accepts.)*

TARGET CONFIRMED
- John: Brian, I understand how those two benefits seem mutually exclusive. Let me provide a clearer explanation of how the technological advantages of the XLX 9000 achieve them. OK? *(Uses a verifying statement to confirm an understanding of the hinge. Rephrases it in a positive manner to serve as the basis for handling it by taking responsibility for the need for a better explanation.)*
- Brian: OK, fire away. *(Customer's challenge.)*

DOWNPLAY
- John: The key issue in how fast and inexpensively you heat the water depends on how much of the water goes through the coils. The heat either transfers to the water or gets wasted. The more contact, the faster the heat transfer--and the less wasted energy. Have I explained it clearly so far where it make sense? *(Simplifies the explanation by breaking it down into smaller components. Verifying understanding of each one before going to the next concept. John also takes responsibility for the explanation.)*
- Brian: Yeah, so far so good.
- John: Well, the XLX 9000 has 60 percent more coil surface than your existing water heater, so it heats 60 percent more water. In addition, because the XLX 9000 coils are a better conductor of heat than your current water heater, 25 percent more heat actually goes into the water. Otherwise, this heat ends up wasted as exhaust heat. So, Brian, can you see where the XLX 9000 provides you with both faster and less-costly heating? *(Simplified explanation and a verifying question to obtain MPC 3.)*
- Brian: Yes, that makes a lot more sense. *(Bingo.)*

saves you more than $800 over the next three years and exceeds your payback schedule based on its price of $750. It also includes a five-year full warranty. *(Rephrases to focus on the benefits, not the features. John also makes price what it should be—just another function of the requirements of the conditional commitment and not a stand-alone issue.)*

Brian: Yes, I can see where it can benefit my situation, but the price is a lot higher than I thought it should be. *(Perceives price as excessive.)*

(See Exhibit 8-6.)

How to Handle Type I: Pulse Check

Exhibit 8-7 and Exhibit 8-8 demonstrate how to handle the pulse check hinge.

How to Handle Type II: Iceberg Ahead

Exhibit 8-9 and Exhibit 8-10 demonstrate how to handle the iceberg ahead hinge.

How to Handle Type III: Gutter Ball

Exhibit 8-11 and Exhibit 8-12 demonstrate how to handle the gutter ball hinge.

How to Handle Type IV: Rip-Off

Exhibit 8-13 and Exhibit 8-14 demonstrate how to handle the rip-off hinge.

(Text continues on page 255)

Exhibit 8-6. Rip-off scenario.

DAMAGE REPORT

♦ *Use five-second pause (Silence Is Golden.)*
♦ *Evaluates situation and realizes he needs more information. John needs to find out more specifics to determine if it is a hinge or a request for more information (Pat from SNL)*
♦ *Formulate clarifying question to find out specific information (How's Zat?)*

HOW'S ZAT?

♦ **John:** Why's that, Mr. Walters? *(First clarifying question using How's Zat?)*
❑ **Brian:** The previous water heater proposal I received from your competitor was only $600, 20 percent less than yours. *(Cause of hinge is comparison to a competitor's price. Brian provides specifics about the hinge. John needs no further clarification.)*

TARGET CONFIRMED

♦ **John:** Mr. Walters, it's often difficult to understand price differences between what appear to be similar products. I understand the importance of explaining how the unique benefits and savings achieved by the XLX 9000 more than offset the $150 price difference. I'll point them out now, OK? *(Uses verifying statement to confirm an understanding of the hinge. Rephrases it in a positive manner to serve as the basis for handling it.)*
❑ **Brian:** I'm all ears. *(Customer's challenge.)*

DOWNPLAY

♦ **John:** First, the XLX 9000 costs more to make. It uses a better conductor for its coils and has 60 percent more of them than any other product on the market. These two features enable you to cut your reheat time in half, and your energy costs by a third giving you a three-year payback. Additionally, the tank costs more because it is 50 percent larger than a standard tank. Again, with this feature you meet your requirement of three people being able to take showers within one hour. Can you now see why there is a price difference because of the superior construction qualities and technical capabilities of the XLX 9000? In addition, how you can easily cost-justify them in your situation? *(Handles the hinge by explaining how the cost differences are a result of the features that achieves his goals. Also, he cost-justifies them using measurable value to gain a competitive advantage.)*
❑ **Brian:** Yes, I can. Here's my check. *(The price difference did not water down the value of anything, other than the competitor's proposal.)*

Exhibit 8-7. Type I: Pulse check.

Type I: Pulse Check	
Synopsis: This hinge occurs when customers show no interest in the broad array of goals, benefits, or potential rewards you described in *MP 1: Spark Interest*. It is the most difficult hinge to handle because it occurs so early. You do not have a lot of information to clarify to determine your next step.	
Category of Hinge: Leveraged	
Surfaces: *MP 1: Spark Interest* **Re-enter Sale At:** *MP 1: Spark Interest*	
Result: You cannot obtain *MPC 1: Interest Confirmed.*	

Causes:	Remedies:
• Customers show no interest or cannot identify with the goals you suggested.	• Suggest more goals from your Market Profile sheet. • Review accuracy of organizational characteristics and positions and how they should affect potential goals; adjust accordingly. • Review similar market segment customers you do business with. See if your selected goals fit them. If not, replace the ones you selected with their goals. • Offer to end call, try again later, and start with references. • Provide a specific product description, send a sample, or make a demonstration.
• Customers do not feel the expected benefits are worth the effort or are not aware your suggested goals are achievable.	• Share references and success stories. If possible, point out higher returns, consequences, or costs of doing nothing in their current situation.
• Customers are not a member of your targeted market segment or you contacted wrong position.	• Create a new Market Profile sheet to accurately reflect this type of customer. Review your existing Market Profile sheet to see if other customers should be in this new segment.
• A potential benefit statement is hard to relate to or believe.	• Check the Spark Interest steps against its rules to follow from Chapter 6. Also, review rules of a good explanation from Chapter 7. • Reconfirm validity of evidence of research or references. • Provide a specific product description, send a sample, or make a demonstration.
• Unknown filters prevent interest at this time.	• Follow up later date to see if an interest exists at that time.
• Wrong contact level.	• Go one position higher with broader goals.

Exhibit 8-8. How to handle the pulse check hinge.

DAMAGE REPORT

- Relax and pause.
- Evaluate why customers show limited interest and what you need to find out.
- Formulate your clarifying question.

HOW'S ZAT?

- Clarify why there is not an interest or where there might be a stronger one.

TARGET CONFIRMED

- Verify that you understand how it influences their goals without validating the hinge. If necessary, phrase clarifying question so it relates to their goals (Safety Zone).

DOWNPLAY

- Suggest more objectives and benefits.
- Explain the costs or consequences of not achieving these goals or doing nothing.
- Reclassify their market segment and suggest goals that are more relevant.
- Provide better validation of claims or references that are more similar.
- Try to determine if an unfavorable filter exists and suggest alternatives or revisit at a later date.
- Verify removal of any detrimental impact and obtain MPC 1 before proceeding to MP 2.

Reenter at MP1

MP 1: Spark Interest

MP 2: Measure Potential

MP 3: Cement Solution

MP 4: Implement Agreement

Exhibit 8-9. Type II: Iceberg ahead.

Type II: Iceberg Ahead

Synopsis: This hinge occurs when customers disclose goals, filters, or conditional commitments that impede their or your ability to achieve or satisfy them. In addition, this hinge occurs when price or delivery become customers' goals.

Category of Hinge: Natural or Leveraged

Surfaces: Usually occurs in *MP 2: Measure Potential* as a natural hinge. It also arises in *MP 3: Cement Solution* as a leveraged hinge. Anytime a hinge is leveraged, it is much more difficult to handle.

Reenter Sale at: *MP 2: Measure Potential* or *MP 3: Cement Solution*

Result: Salesperson cannot obtain *MPC 2: Potential Confirmed*

Causes:	Remedies:
• You did not ask about or obtain the specifics of all the filters during *MP 2: Measure Potential.*	• Review and practice the use of effective qualifying, clarifying, and verifying questioning skills (Chapter 5).
• You did not have a strong enough customer goal commitment from *MP 1: Spark Interest* against which to reference questions.	• Better verification of stated goal during beginning of *MP 2: Measure Potential.* See *Safety Zone* strategy from Chapter 5.
• You did not obtain a measurable *MPC 2: Potential Confirmed.*	• Make sure *MPC 2: Potential Confirmed* is not vague or too general. It needs to be specific enough to define value.
• Customer did not feel comfortable enough to disclose specific filters.	• Review principles of active questioning in Chapter 5. You need to reaffirm customer's interest in achieving their goals or suggest stronger ones.
• Customer did not know specifics of filters.	• Confirm customer is the final decision maker by validating his or her ability to release funds and establish or approve the attainment measurements. • Ask customer how best to obtain unknown specifics.
• Filters of *funding* or *start or complete date* (i.e., price or delivery) become the stated goals.	• Provide a system of evaluation favorable to measuring goals that connect to your unique strengths. • Determine if your unique strengths match up to these two filters; if not, continue to the next remedy. • Ask customer how these two filters impact any of the other goal(s) from *MP 1: Spark Interest*, and which one is more important; then try to define and create value other than these two filters.

Exhibit 8-10. How to handle the iceberg ahead hinge.

DAMAGE REPORT
- Relax and pause.
- Evaluate how the filters affect customers' goals, your sales strategy (natural), or any proposed products (leveraged).
- Formulate your clarifying question.

HOW'S ZAT?
- Clarify how customer feels filters affect goals or your products.

TARGET CONFIRMED
- Verify you understand how customer thinks he or she influences goals or your products. If necessary, phrase clarifying question so it relates to their goals *(Safety Zone)*.

DOWNPLAY

Natural (MP 2):
- If necessary, ask or suggest how to change filters or SOEs to achieve goals and introduce new benefits.
- Ask or suggest if customer can alter goals to accommodate hinge and introduce new benefits.
- Ask or suggest to customer the best way to get missing goals and filters.
- Verify final decision maker again.
- Verify removal of any detrimental impact and obtain *MPC 2* before proceeding to *MP 3.*

Leveraged (MP 3):
- Try to handle same as above first.
- Determine if you can change product selections to accommodate filters and introduce new benefits.
- Verify removal of any detrimental impact and obtain *MPC 3* before proceeding to *MP 4.*

Reenter at either MP 2 or MP 3

MP 1: Spark Interest

MP 2: Measure Potential

MP 3: Cement Solution

MP 4: Implement Agreement

Exhibit 8-11. Type III: Gutter ball.

Type III: Gutter Ball	
Synopsis: This hinge occurs when customers perceive your products as not fulfilling their goals, measurable benefits, or conditional commitments.	
Category of Hinge: Leveraged	
Surfaces: *MP 3: Cement Solution* **Reenter Sale at:** *MP 3: Cement Solution*	
Result: You cannot obtain *MPC 3: Solution Confirmed.*	
Causes:	**Remedies:**
• Your explanation does not adequately describe how the features of the solution achieve the benefits of the customer's goals.	• Review the concept of explaining in Chapter 7 with special emphasis on simplifying technical solutions.
• The customer has doubts about whether your products achieve his or her goals.	• Have references from similar market segments available. • Be prepared to offer forms of assurance or guarantees. • Be prepared to explain in detail direct or indirect cost-justification numbers. • Redefine value with a different SOE.
• Previously verified filters change unexpectedly and adversely affect your products' ability to achieve customer's goals.	• Reassess with customer whether goals are still realistic in light of these new filters. If they still are achievable, determine: ▪ If you can offer any new product selections to achieve goals. ▪ If you can modify the system of evaluation to produce additional value from goals. ▪ If it is time to walk away because the new filters restrict your ability to help the customer achieve goals, a create-and-wait strategy might be appropriate.

Exhibit 8-12. How to handle the gutter ball hinge.

DAMAGE REPORT

- Relax and pause.
- Evaluate what you need to know to understand why the customer feels your products do not fulfill expectations.
- Formulate your clarifying question.

HOW'S ZAT?

- Clarify why customer feels you did not satisfy his or her conditional commitment.

TARGET CONFIRMED

- Verify you understand how customer feels it affects goals or your products. If necessary, phrase clarifying question so it relates to goals (*Safety Zone*).

DOWNPLAY

- Provide a less technical, simplified explanation. Focus solely on satisfying the conditional commitment.
- Offer additional references, assurances, calculations, guarantees, or documentation.
- Ask or suggest if you can modify the conditional commitment or SOE to accommodate your products and introduce new benefits.
- Ask or suggest how you can change your product selections if necessary to satisfy customer's conditional commitment. Introduce new benefits.
- Verify removal of any detrimental impact and obtain *MPC 3* before proceeding to *MP 4*.

Reenter at Measurable Phase

MP 1: Spark Interest

MP 2: Measure Potential

MP 3: Cement Solution

MP 4: Implement Agreement

Exhibit 8-13. Type IV: Rip-off.

Type IV: Rip-Off	
Synopsis: This hinge occurs when you disclose the price of your products. Customers consider your price excessive although it meets their conditional commitments. Three factors influence what customers expect the price level to be: (1) What they guess it costs to manufacture the product or provide the service multiplied by a reasonable mark-up. (2) The total value of the perceived and measurable benefits. (3) The price levels of what customers consider similar products.	
Category of Hinge: Leveraged	
Surfaces: *MP 4: Implement Agreement* **Reenter Sale at:** *MP 3: Cement Solution* or *MP 4: Implement Agreement.*	
Result: Salesperson cannot obtain *MPC 4: Agreement Confirmed*	
Causes:	**Remedies:**
• The price of the proposed solution seems excessive compared with their guesstimates of costs.	• Be ready to explain costs customers do not associate with the products. These are items such as special manufacturing processes, extensive testing procedures, strict tolerances, expensive materials, included warranties, and the likes.
• The price of the products seems excessive compared to fair market value.	• Be ready to explain significant quality differences between your products and other "similar, but definitely not the same" competitors' products. Acknowledge that your unique strengths do add costs to your products in order to achieve the customer's measurable goals and benefits.
• The price of the proposed products is marked up beyond a reasonable expectation even when accounting for all your investments.	• Best of luck, our sincerest wishes, and let us know how it worked out for you.

Exhibit 8-14. How to handle the rip-off hinge.

DAMAGE REPORT

- Relax and pause.
- Evaluate what you need to know to understand why the customer feels there is something objectionable about your pricing.
- Formulate your clarifying question.

HOW'S ZAT?

- Clarify why the customer thinks the price is too high.

TARGET CONFIRMED

- Verify that you understand how the customer feels the pricing affects your proposed solution. If necessary, phrase clarifying question so it relates to goals *(Safety Zone)*.

DOWNPLAY

- Explain hidden costs they can easily accept.
- Explain the significant quality and feature differences between your product and those of competitors. Relate them back to the customer's goals and benefits.
- Suggest scaled-down products similar in quality and price to a competitor's. Try to cost-justify the quality and feature differences.
- Verify removal of any detrimental impact and try to obtain *MPC 4* again.

Reenter at MP 4

MP 1: Spark Interest

MP 2: Measure Potential

MP 3: Cement Solution

MP 4: Implement Agreement

SUMMARY

- Hinges prevent you from conducting the Measurable Phases in their proper order or create an inability to obtain a Measurable Phase Change and its respective calls for action.
- Hinges fall into the categories of natural, leveraged, or hidden.
- Natural hinges occur during MP 2: Measure Potential. Customers do not view them as negatives because they are a response to your questions, not your actions or comments. They occur before you mention specific products.
- Leveraged hinges are adverse reactions from customers to your comments or calls for action. Customers leverage them against specific products.
- Hidden hinges are concerns customers are reluctant to disclose; they might have negative implications for the customer or for your company because:
  - The contact cannot make or is not involved with the decision.
  - The contact cannot obtain the funding for the project.
  - The contact committed to a solution from another company.
  - The contact does not feel your product selections are justifiable or beneficial.
- Customers use smokescreens to protect hidden hinges from disclosure.
- You encourage customers to disclose information, regardless of its impact on your business potential, by referencing your questions to their goals. There are four types of hinges:

  Type I: Pulse check (Natural—MP 1: Spark Interest)

  Type II: Iceberg Ahead (Leveraged or Natural—MP 2: Measure Potential or MP 3: Cement Solution)

  Type III: Gutter Ball (Leveraged—MP 3: Cement Solution)

  Type IV: Rip-off (Leveraged—MP 4: Implement Agreement)
- Use the How's Zat? to make measurable the effects of hinges. Start your initial responses to every hinge with some version of How's Zat?
- How's Zat? tactics are:
  - *Silence Is Golden.* Gives you time to collect your thoughts.
  - *Pat from SNL.* Are they hinges or requests for more information?
  - *Lose the Battle, Win the War.* Acknowledge legitimacy and outweigh.

- *You Can't Do Both.* Customers choose between filters or goals.
- The four basic steps in handling hinges:
  1. Damage report
  2. How's Zat?
  3. Target confirmed
  4. Downplay
- Strategies for removing hinges:
  - *Explaining.* Provide additional information or clarification to "explain away" customers' misconceptions.
  - *Outweighing.* Show how the overall benefits of achieving their goals still more than offsets existing liabilities they mentioned.
  - *Revising.* Means of last resort; change your product selections.

Chapter Nine

Using MeasureMax Your Way

It is time to make your investment in MeasureMax pay off. It is time to benefit from building a sales foundation where you make sales successes direct results of your planning. In this chapter, you unleash the power of measurability to your products, customers, and sales opportunities on an everyday basis by understanding:

- How to get out of the numbers game
- How to use the five steps to set MeasureMax in motion
- How to set measurable sales goals to gauge your potential and progress
- How to use personal benchmarks to enhance performance—not judge it
- How to make your output from using sales tools greater than your input

Get Out of the Numbers Game

Traditional selling methods teach you that sales is a numbers game. Take its 80/20 rule that proclaims 80 percent of your sales come from just 20 percent of your customers. In other words, 80 percent of your customers give you *only* 20 percent of your business. Figuring out which customers fall into the 20 percent category can waste a lot of time.

Customers have their 80/20 rule, too. Only one out of every five salespeople who contact them has something of interest. Now you know why when you call they might seem skeptical or reluctant to meet. The numbers are against you. Therefore, you overcompensate by making more sales calls.

Yet, when you increase the quantity of your sales calls, often the quality suffers. You become less choosy about whom you contact. You figure that with enough sales calls, you are bound to stumble upon opportunities. It becomes easy to take paths of least resistance and pursue sales opportunities that show minimal interest.

Granted, even with 80 percent of customers being nonproductive, more sales calls mean more orders. "Make more sales calls" becomes your (or your sales manager's) battle cry. Let the call reports fly. A sales manager once captured the essence of this sales strategy when he said, "Even a blind squirrel gathers some nuts." Twenty years later, no one is sure if he was commending tenacity, criticizing inefficiency, or just making an astute observation.

Although 80/20 makes sense from a volume standpoint, it does not from a productivity standpoint. Making hit-or-miss sales calls does not place a premium on efficiency. You want to lower the number of sales calls it takes to get an order, not raise it. Therefore, the key is to increase the quality of your sales calls, as well as the quantity.

However, two fundamental questions loom:

1. How do you apply MeasureMax to positive customers who are comfortable with your existing sales approach?
2. How do you apply MeasureMax to neutral or negative prospects who are accustomed to product pitches on the first sales call? The answers lie in how much selling effort you invest in account management and market development.

Account Management

In account management, you protect and grow your base of positive customers (see Chapter 4). You count on their untapped opportunities to grow your sales production at a faster rate than their market segments (or, at least, your sales quotas) grow. You concentrate on ensuring that their goals, filters, and systems of evaluations still favor your company.

You want to be at the joint planning level (where you progress from vendor to supplier to partner) and help customers set and achieve their long-term goals. Your sphere of influence should be at the *C* and *D* levels. Jim Bujold, of Johnson Controls, succinctly described account management as helping customers forget how to achieve their goals without you.

Positive customers become comfortable doing business with you a certain way. A way that might not have anything to do with making goals, benefits, filters, and systems of evaluation measurable. For example, a customer is accustomed to your responding to their requests for making product presentations or proposals. The customer might find it unusual that after all these years you now seek to find out their goals. Yet, the pitfalls of not making your professional bonds with organizations as strong as your personal bonds with contacts are well documented. So, how do you change established precedents for conducting business to benefit both you and your customers?

First, ensure that you honor the most important rule of customer etiquette: Fulfill customers' *expectations* of the purpose of the sales call before trying to fulfill yours. If customers *expect* to discuss specific products and prices, etiquette requires you to comply. Unfortunately, this compliance might diminish your ability to sell value. Therefore, change their expectations. Make the purpose of the meeting relate to the Measurable Phases (MPs). For instance, before you start MP 2: Measure Potential, customers should agree the purpose of a meeting is to gather specifics of their goals and filters.

Introduce positive customers to MeasureMax concepts by encouraging them to think about their goals chronologically. This thought process is a natural and comfortable way for customers to discuss their goals, the first step in MP 1: Spark Interest. Your questions take them from their past goals to current ones to future ones. In other words, you begin with the known goals of yesterday and today, and then work your way to their speculative goals of tomorrow. Let their thought process evolve logically. Build on their and your accomplishments. Ask them how you can continue to help them in their endeavors as you uncover the specifics of their goals or the filters affecting them during MP 2: Measure Potential.

Example

Steven: Olivia, how do you feel your goals changed from a year ago to now?

Olivia: Steven, reliability was our major concern, but now it is to reduce operating costs.

Steven: Why is that?

Olivia: A corporate edict states that we have to cut expenses by 8 percent.

Steven continues by focusing on how Olivia thinks his company can help her cut operating costs by 8 percent. In addition, he seeks answers to making her goals measurable. (What do operating costs entail? How much does 8 percent equal?) He gathers specifics by referencing the filters to her goals. Her answers determine his next questions per Chapter 5 strategies and tactics.

Making positive customers' goals and filters measurable builds stronger professional and personal relationships—and price and delivery-resistant barriers to competition. Customers can look back on any sale they completed with you and measure how your solutions met or exceeded their goals. Your last sale is a reference for the next one, even if your contacts or sponsors change. You always can point to your documented performance. Remember, you want to be a business partner who helps customers to achieve long-terms goals, not a product vendor who satisfies random short-term needs.

Market Development

In market development, your sales responsibility is to turn neutral or negative customers into positive ones. If you are a new sales hire, you also inherit existing customers from senior salespeople who find them nonproductive (meaning *dead ends*). *Inherit* is probably the correct word because you seek to receive benefits from someone considered "dead" by others.

You apply the goals, measurable benefits, and systems of evaluations from your past successes in their market segments to them. Market development is ideal for MeasureMax because you:

- *Start with a blank slate.* Unlike account development, no established method of conducting business exists (or very limited ones with your inherited customers) that might interfere with using MeasureMax.
- *Help customers make value measurable.* You focus on goals, not products, to set you apart from competitors.
- *Use Spark Interest Statements, which highlight customers' goals in specific market segments, as excellent icebreakers.* They eliminate the usual randomness of initial contacts and the risks of pulse check hinges. You generate interest on the first call as a customer advocate, not a product one.
- *Sell top down.* Again, unlike account development, you have no established pecking order. You can start higher with decision makers more receptive to change.
- *Avoid the constant and sometimes irresistible urge of the negative sell in which you start explaining why your products are better than those of competitors.* Do not force customers to defend their existing suppliers and decisions to use them. Eliminate these sales traps by keeping a positive emphasis on the customers' goals and how you help achieve them.

The following sales tools set MeasureMax into motion so that the quality and productivity of your selling efforts and the results in both account management and market development soar.

Note: To spare you the effort of looking up the various sales tools in their respective chapters, a sample is provided for each one.

Create Product Profile Sheets

Create one Product Profile sheet for each of your products or services as instructed in Chapter 2. To simplify matters if you have numerous ones, just do your top five with their top three features (or, at least, all their unique strengths). Then, do one for your key competitors, but list only their unique strengths. Make a separate profile for your company strengths. Treat them as universal features that might fit on every sales opportunity.

Use a pay-as-you-go strategy; create a new profile when the customers' goals and filters from MP 2: Measure Potential dictate. (Go to the www.measuremax.com Web site to download the Microsoft Word templates for these tools.) Samples of Product Profile sheets are shown in Exhibit 9-1 and Exhibit 9-2 on the following pages.

Develop Your Market Profile Sheets

Create one Market Profile sheet for each of your individual market segments as instructed in Chapter 3. If you have numerous segments, just do your top five. Use a pay-as-you-go strategy with these profiles as well. Create them as you need them and before you do MP 1: Spark Interest.

This sheet builds on the Product Profile sheets, so only the first four rows have new information. A sample of a Market Profile sheet is shown in Exhibit 9-3.

Use Quick-Entry Sales Management Sheets

No one likes to do paperwork—unless it is worth the return. You are motivated to fill out tax forms if you are getting a refund. Quick-Entry Sales Management (Q) sheets work the same way. Again, if you think of selling methods as diet plans, Qs are the scales you get on to see how they are working. With Qs, you know you are using the same scale every time to see how well you are doing.

Use them to measure, manage, and maximize your sales efforts in black and white, no gray areas allowed. Either you know the specifics of customers' goals, filters, benefits, systems of evaluations, conditional commitments—and how your solutions match up to them—or you do not.

Use the two-page Qs for the first two phases—MP 1: Spark Interest and MP 2: Measure Potential. Think of them as loose-leaf paper with columns and rows you fill in. (A Microsoft Word template for this tool is also found on the www.measuremax.com Web site so you can fine-tune them to your selling situations.)

A Q sheet takes about ten minutes to complete before you use it, and about ten minutes to fill out after you leave your meeting with the customer. This twenty-minute investment changes the 80/20 rule to the 80/80 law. With measurable information, you can make 80 percent of filled-out Qs generate proposals that produce 80 percent of your sales. It is not 100/100 because 20 percent of your sales still come from commodity-driven customers who equate low price with high-value regardless of your efforts.

Use Qs to record and coordinate your sales activities by market segments, goals, projects, and by contact levels (one Q sheet per decision maker on the same sale).

Step by Step

Qs also guide you through MP 1 and MP 2 by reminding you to get the necessary specifics and their Measurable Phase Changes. Fill in all the information you know before the initial Spark Interest phone call. Leave blank what you need to find out for MP 2: Measure Potential. Once you complete MP 1 and MP 2, you enter in the missing information. You then review your sheets to reflect what you need to achieve during MP 3: Cement Solution and MP 4: Implement Agreement.

Typically, you see patterns emerge when you use Qs as self-management tools. You usually are consistent in what information you make measurable and what you do not. Review whether you are asking the right questions to find them out. If you are asking the right questions, but still are not getting specifics, review your wording and reread Chapter 5. In addition, consider reviewing your Qs at your sales meeting to solicit group input and help. These reviews will help everyone improve his or her command of the process.

On joint sales calls, tell your manager and/or fellow salesperson what you want him to observe that you think you do well on a sales call (i.e., link customers' measurable answers to the next filter that needs details). Also ask him to observe a specific sales skill (i.e., suggesting SOEs if the customer doesn't know any to measure the value of achieving his goals) that you think you can do better. When you prompt someone on what to observe on a sales call beforehand, everyone's sales increase. Like customers, salespeople also win when you manage their expectations.

Finally, Qs also capture the reasons (goals, benefits, filters, SOEs, and conditional commitments) why you won or lost the sale. Use this historical information to concentrate on customers' goals and keep yourself razor sharp. Granted, you must fill in the data, but the more you do, the more valuable the information becomes for you. Keep thinking loose-leaf pad with rows and columns versus scattered notes.

(Text continues on page 272)

Exhibit 9-1. Product profile sheet.

Product Profile

Product: Predicto Services

Features (Adjective/Noun, Specific Characteristic, 2 to 3 Words)	Benefits (Verb/Noun, Time or Money; 3 to 5 Words)	Value (MV or (PV)	Focus (Internal; External; Both)	Unique Strengths (Y Or N)	Value Rating (1 or 5)
Variance alerts (on-site monitors)	Prevents unscheduled breakdowns	Measurable value (calculate the costs of downtime)	Both. It ensures uninterrupted shipments to their customers (E) and saves money from lost production (I).	Yes	5

Analogy for *Variance Alerts*: It is like the low-fuel warning in your car. You look for a gas station before your tank hits empty.

Exhibit 9-2. Competitor's product profile sheet.

Competitor Product Profile

Our Product: Predicto Services

Competitor Name: PricePoint Services | **List Price $:** (if known)

Product Name: Early Alarm Network | **Gross Margins %:** (if known)

Features (Specific Characteristic; Adjective/Noun)	Benefits (Time or Money; Verb/Noun)	Value (MV or PV)	Focus (Internal; External; Both)	Unique Strengths Only	Value Rating Of 5
Trends Tracker (remote monitoring)	Prevents unscheduled breakdowns	Measurable value (calculate the costs of downtime)	Both. It ensures uninterrupted shipments to their customers (E) and saves money from lost production (I).	Yes	5

Exhibit 9-3. Market profile sheet.

Market Profile		
Customer Name: Positron		**Profit Levels:** 30%
Market Segment: Global computer manufacturers	**Economic Sensitivity:** Cyclical	**Annual Sales $:** 3 Billion
Organizational Characteristics: 7/24 operations, high-dollar downtime, critical manufacturing tolerances, on-time deliveries and inventory levels critical, sensitive to competitors, receptive to state-of-the-art technologies, revenues of $3 billion, 20,000 employees		**# Of Employees:** 20,000
		Annual Growth Rate: 28%
Position: VP of Operations **Contact Name:** Olivia Ontime		**Current Use of Similar Products or Services in $:** 2 million
Previous Success Stories: Advanced Computer Co., Star Computers, PC Power Ltd., and Computer Giant Inc		**Potential Use of Similar Products or Services In $:** 3 million

(continues)

Exhibit 9-3. (Continued.)

General Goal Category (broad groupings)	Typical Goals (more specific by position)	Benefits of Achieving Goals (in time or money terms; insert an "I" for internal benefits, an "E" for external ones, and a "B" for both)	Systems of Evaluation (calculations used to determine if goal is achieved)	Products	Feature Rating and Their Benefits (insert a value rating of 1 for regular feature or 5 for unique strength)
Operations	Reduce downtime	Prevent production stoppages (B) and lost revenues (I)	Hours of downtime	Predicto Services	Variance Alerts prevents unscheduled breakdowns (5)

Top Two Competitors	Competitor Product	Competitive Unique Strengths
1. PricePoint Services	Early Warning Network	Trends Tracker's remote monitoring

Exhibit 9-4. Front page of Q sheet.

Quick-Entry Sales Management Sheet

☐ Won	☐ Lost	☑ In-Progress	☐ Positive	☑ Neutral	☐ Negative

Organization Name: Positron

Contact Name/Phone #: Olivia Ontime, 456-908-3456

Position: VP of manufacturing

Confirmed Goals:	Measurable or Perceived Benefits with Dollar Values:	Systems of Evaluation:
1. Reduce downtime	Prevent 9 hours of downtime and save $360,000	Dollar per downtime ($40,000 per hour)

MEASURABLE or SPECIFIC FILTERS

☑ **Goal Motivation:**
Positive:
Negative: Lost 18 hours and $720,000 of production output to downtime last year

☑ **Current Situation:** Use two people for two shifts to monitor equipment at $40,000 per person. Costs them $160,00 a year

☑ **Future Plans:** Install redundant equipment that will cost $600,000

☑ **Alternatives:** Buy used equipment for $300,000. Solicit competitive presentations from Fastship Technology and PricePoint Services

(continues)

Exhibit 9-4. (Continued.)

☑ Decision-Makers:	☑ Name and Position	☑ Sway (1-3):
Gatekeeper: Technical, Operational, or Financial	Direct Supervisor: Ronald Reuters, CEO	2
Advocate: Technical, Operational, or Financial	Direct Report: Don't know	?
FDM: Technical, Operational, or Financial	Staff Report: "Corporate," don't know	?

☑ Budget Date:	☑ Decision Date:	☑ Start Date:	☑ Complete Date:
October 15	August 1	November 1 or sooner	Finish by 4th quarter

☑ **Funding:**
Operating Budget ($): Will be funded out of capital investments

Capital Investment ($): $1,080,000

☑ **Past Keys:**

Successes: Engineering study of operations and documented successes with companies in their industry

Failures: Didn't feel products and services would work in *their* situation

☑ **Attainment Measurement:** reduce costs of $40,000 per downtime hour to no more than nine hours annually, save $360,000, begin in November and finish by December, not exceed $1,080,000 budget, get at least a three-year payback, and any solution must have proven performance

☑ YES, customer confirmed the attainment measurement as his or her conditional commitment
☐ NO (why not?):

Notes: I still need to find out what *proven performance* means, who at corporate would get involved, and what would make them approve this project. I also want to find out who Olivia's direct report is and the role he or she will play.

Exhibit 9-5. Back page of Q sheet.

Sales Efforts by Measurable Phases

MP 1: Spark Interest

MP 1: Dates:	MP 1: Notes:	
2/20	Spoke briefly about experience in computer industry	
2/26	Expressed interest in reducing downtime, meet next Tuesday, focus on similar companies	
☑ MPC 1: Interest Confirmed	Date: 2/26	Total MP 1 Sales Calls: 0 (phone calls do not count; only in-person sales calls
☑ Call for Action: Meet next Tuesday to discuss what "reduce down time" means		

MP 2: Measure Potential

MP 2: Dates:	MP 2 Notes:	
3/5	Great meeting, need to guarantee results	
3/12	Met again to nail down budget and dates	
☑ MPC 2: Potential Confirmed	Date: 3/23	Total MP 2 Sales Calls: 2
☑ Call for Action: Customer demonstration at similar company		

(continues)

Exhibit 9-5. (Continued.)

MP 3: Cement Solution

MP 3: Dates:	MP 3 Notes:	
3/19	Reviewing Q sheet with sales team and marketing to pick highest-value solutions; e-mailed scope of work to Olivia	
☐ MPC 3: Solution Confirmed	Date:	Total MP 3 Sales Calls:
☐ Call for Action:		

MP 4: Implement Agreement

MP 4: Dates:	MP 4 Notes:	
☐ MPC 4: Agreement Confirmed	Date:	Total MP 4 Sales Calls:
☐ Call for Action:		

Quote Date:	Quote #:
Close Date:	Purchase Order #:
Winning Supplier:	Dollar Amount: $

Team Effort

Qs help coordinate your team-selling effort. Few things are worse in a joint sales effort than two or more salespeople working at different contact levels and not sharing a common language or system for evaluating their progress. You use Qs to eliminate this concern. The Qs display information by salesperson and contact levels. Everyone in a team sell is aware of which MP each salesperson is in. Everyone views the most current information of the different salespeople working on the same sales opportunity. You can make strategic decisions on how each salesperson should conduct the next MP.

In addition, Qs help you to track the different contacts when you are working with multiple decision makers on a sales opportunity. You view the goals and filters columns for each contact level in a sales opportunity. Compare the information from gatekeepers, advocates, and final-decision makers for consistency (or lack thereof). Use any discrepancies to guide the different contacts involved on what goals and filters need clarification.

For the front page of the Steven Smartsell sample Q sheet, see Exhibit 9-4 on a preceding spread.

For the back page of the Steven Smartsell sample Q sheet, see Exhibit 9-5 on a preceding spread.

Connect the Value Sheet

You use this sales tool during MP 3: Cement Solution. You take the information you gathered on your Q sheets to build the customers' solutions from their goals down, not from your products' features up. You follow the MP 3 steps as instructed in Chapter 7. The downloadable, electronic template for this sheet is found on www .measuremax.com. (See Exhibit 9-6.)

Take the Pulled-Through Test

This sales tool allows you perform a simple test on whether customers are pulling your proposals through the sales process or whether you are pushing them through. As discussed in Chapter 1, you want customers to be at least as motivated as you are about achieving their goals. Otherwise, value and productivity suffer. Like the other sales tools, the Microsoft Word template can be found on the www .measuremax.com Web site. (See Exhibit 9-7.)

Exhibit 9-6. Connecting value sheet.

Connecting Value Sheet

Customer: Positron

Contact: Olivia Ontime

Specific Goals	Measurable Benefits	Systems of Evaluation	Solutions	Features	Value & Focus (Internal, External, or Both)	U.S. & Value Rating
Reduce downtime	Prevent production stoppages from 18 hours annually to 9, which generate savings of $360,000 annually	Hours of downtime	Predicto Services	Variance Alerts prevent unscheduled breakdowns	Perceived Value. Both. Ensures uninterrupted shipments to their customers (E) and saves them money from lost production (I).	Yes/5
			Predicto Services	Tolerance Checks prevent unscheduled breakdowns	Same as above	Yes/5
Improve capacity	Increase production by 15%	Units per hour	ProdoGain	200-nit capacity	Measurable value and internal	No/1

Conditional Commitment: Reduce the costs of $40,000 per downtime hour (SOE) to no more than nine hours annually (goal), save $360,000 (measurable benefit), begin in November and finish by December (start and completion dates), not exceed $1,080,000 budget (funding), get at least a three-year payback (SOE).

Do Proposed Solutions Satisfy It?

☑ Yes

☐ No. Why Not?

Exhibit 9-7. Passing the pulled-through test.

Does Your Proposal Pass the Pulled-Through Test?	
Sales Opportunity Name: Central Plant Upgrade	
Contact Name: Olivia Ontime	
Position: VP of manufacturing	
Date Customer Received Proposal: 4/10	
Date of Last Customer Contact: 4/17	
☑ **MPC 1: Interest Confirmed obtained**	☑ **MPC 2: Potential Confirmed obtained**
"Pushed-Through" (Salesperson-Generated)	**"Pulled-Through"** (Customers-Generated/Measuremax)
☐ Goals and filters are not measurable or specific	☑ Goals and filters are measurable or specific
☐ No verifications of Measurable Phase Changes	☑ Verifications of Measurable Phase Changes
☐ No conditional commitment or attainment measurement exists	☑ Conditional commitment or attainment measurements exists
☐ Uncertainty over what prompted the proposal	☑ Proposal generated at customers' request using well-defined goals
☐ Proposal contains limited customer's input	☑ Proposal uses customer's input to fill out Q sheet
☐ MPs not conducted in proper sequence	☑ MPs conducted in proper sequence
☐ Salesperson avoids or supplies own numbers for cost justifications	☑ Customer supplies the means for direct or indirect cost justification
☐ Proposal considered as a means to flush out concerns or undisclosed goals and filters	☑ Proposal used to formalize agreed upon MPCs
☐ Clarification calls to customers before making presentations are nonexistent	☑ Numerous clarification calls and the customers understand the reasons for them.
☐ Unclear time frame for starting	☑ Well-defined time frame for starting
☐ Uncertainty over chances of success	☑ Proposal status is well known
☐ Proposal focuses on numerous product features without connecting to specific customers' goals and measurable benefits	☑ Proposal focuses on customers' agreed-upon goals and measurable benefits, and demonstrates connections between them and products' features
Total Check Marks: 0	**Total Check Marks: 13**
☐ Pushed-Through	☑ Pulled-Through

Sales Consistency and Time Management

The amount of time (in-person sales calls) you spend in each Measurable Phase (MP) has a big impact on your sales consistency. In-person sales calls are your currency. You only have so many you can invest, and each one must provide a return to warrant further ones with the same customers. Making in-person sales calls is also like farming. You have three stages, and you want to strike the right balance between them to ensure a strong harvest. They are as follows:

1. *Planting Seeds.* This stage consists of MP 1: Spark Interest and MP 2: Measure Potential. You try to generate new sales opportunities and determine what it will take for them to grow (be worthwhile to plant).
2. *Watering Crops.* This stage consists of MP 3: Cement Solution. You demonstrate how your watering (solutions) makes their yield (measurable benefits) bountiful.
3. *Harvesting Crops.* This stage consists of MP 4: Implement Agreement. You are ready to bring the crop to market (purchase orders).

The right balance ensures that your sales performance does not encounter droughts. For instance, assume that you bat 50 percent. Half of your MP 1 telephone sales calls make it to MP 2 in-person sales calls, and half of those make it to MP 3, and, then half of those make it to MP 4. Your mix for consistency requires *eight times* as many of your sales calls to be in MP 1 than in MP 4. (See Exhibit 9-8.)

Exhibit 9-8. The right balance for sales calls.

Phase	Planting Seeds		Watering	Harvesting	
	MP 1 (via telephone)	MP 2	MP 3	MP 4	Total
Number of in-person sales calls	8 phone calls	4 sales calls	2 sales calls	1 sales call	7 sales calls
Approximate % in each phase		57%	28%	15%	100%

It is easy to understand why you want to manage your selling efforts in a measurable manner. You can manage your sales activities by recording how many open sales opportunities fall into these groupings. The productivity equation later in this chapter takes into account the varying sales factors that determine your optimal balance.

Note: Customers also set limits on the numbers of sales calls they will spend with a salesperson before they must know the price of your products or the measurable benefits of their goals. Which one do you want to happen first?

Using a Monthly Sales Call Planner

To help you plan and manage your selling activities, use a monthly sales call planner. It motivates you to think about where you want to invest your limited sales resources—your in-person sales calls. You use this sales tool (see Exhibit 9-9) to plan your sales calls one month in advance. (This tool can be found as an Excel spreadsheet at www.measuremax.com.)

You decide how many sales calls you need to make to practice account or opportunity management effectively. No magic number exists other than what you think you require to be successful. You

Exhibit 9-9. Example of a monthly sales call planner.

Account	Opportunity Name	Contact Name	Position	Planned, In-Person Calls/Month	Actual	Current Phase
Advanced Computer Company	West End facilities upgrade	Tom James	director of engineering	2	3	MP 2
Advanced Computer Company	West End facilities upgrade	Becky Barr	CEO	2	1	MP 2
Advanced Computer Company	Martinville maintenance agreement	William Thomas	plant supervisor	1	1	MP 2
Positron	Central Plant upgrade	Olivia Ontime	VP of manufacturing	3	2	MP 3
Positron	Central Plant upgrade	Ron Reuters	CEO	2	1	MP 3
Star Computers	Unknown	Gary Bryant	VP of engineering	1	0	MP 1
Star Computers	Unknown	Deborah Dietz	CFO	1	1	MP 1
PC Power Ltd.	Addition to 888 Market Street	Arthur Stein	plant manager	2	3	MP 4
Total Planned Calls:	14					
Nonscheduled, Reactive Calls:	8					
Total Monthly Calls:	22					

are not scheduling specific dates to visit, but rather specific numbers of planned sales calls. You can also use the monthly sales call planner to solicit advice from your peers or sales management team, but before your month begins, not after. Another benefit of the planner is that it lets you evaluate how well you know who the different players are and their role in the decision-making process.

A monthly sales call planner should have the following format:

- *Account.* The name of the account you are seeing that month.
- *Opportunity Name.* The name of the opportunity.
- *Contact.* The name of the person you plan on seeing. List all the decision makers you think are in important in that account, regardless of whether you plan on seeing him. You can then reuse your monthly sales planner by saving it as the next month's planner and updating it.
- *Position.* The title of the contact.
- *Planned, In-Person Sales Calls/Month.* Self-explanatory.
- *Actual.* The number of sales calls you actually made.
- *Current Phase.* In which Measurable Phase did you make the sales call?
- *Total Planned Calls.* Self-explanatory.
- *Nonscheduled Reactive Calls.* The number of sales calls you make on a reactive basis rather than on a planned one. Try to make sure your reactive calls (such as customer requests, unexpected bids or opportunities that surface, and customer problems that arise) are less than a third of your total sales calls. It's difficult to react your way to sales superstar status.
- *Total Monthly Calls.* Self-explanatory.

Note: If you do not use customer relationship management (CRM) software to record your selling activities or a day timer, then use scheduling software programs such as Lotus Notes or Outlook to record in their calendars where you made in-person, sales calls. Compare the number from your calendar to your monthly sales call planner to evaluate your performance.

Set Limits on Sales Calls to Increase Productivity

Another way to improve productivity is to limit the number of sales calls in each of the MPs. In a given sales opportunity, decide how many calls you are willing to invest without obtaining an MPC in each selling phase. When you reach a certain limit, it is time to call it quits. Otherwise, hope springs eternal—along with wasted efforts.

Setting limits provides an objective and measurable mechanism to motivate you to identify and handle potential hinges or smokescreens. Limits also trigger create-and-wait (Chapter 4) responses sooner so you pursue more productive and high-return opportunities. As discussed, if you end the sales process at this time, let the customers know why. Also, if possible, explain to them that if certain goals or filters change you can provide them with more benefits and value than they currently receive. Q sheets chart the number of sales calls you make in each MP. (See Exhibit 9-10.)

Use a Quote Inventory to Increase Productivity

A quote inventory is easy to create. The quote inventory encompasses the law of diminishing returns. Every MP 3: Cement Solution quote (proposal) you add over a certain number of outstanding ones, the harder it becomes for you to handle them proficiently. Therefore, set a maximum number on your MP 3: Cement Solution quotes. Typically, salespeople can effectively manage between eight and fifteen quotes. Do not count proposals made outside of the MeasureMax process (*public bids*) in your numbers, just the MP 3 ones that occur within it. You know public bid outcomes most often depend on low price to win the sale.

Exhibit 9-10. Setting limits to improve productivity.

Compete Against Yourself and You Always Win

MP 1: Spark Interest & MP 2: Measure Potential	MP 3: Cement Solution	MP 4: Implement Agreement

Establish a Personal Baseline That Limits Your In-Person Sales Calls for Each Phase--and Productivity Will Boom!

When you exceed this limit, take one quote out of inventory and insert it in an inactive file. Bring the oldest quote first back into inventory when you fall below your maximum level. Purchase orders and, regrettably, lost sales provide room to add quotes into your inventory.

Question why your MP 3: Cement Solution proposals are not sales yet. When the agreed-upon budget or start dates arrive without purchase orders, ask customers why. After all, the MPC 3: Solution Confirmed supposedly validated that your proposed solutions met their conditional commitments. Depending on their answers, review the "Handling Hinges" section in Chapter 8 to determine the best strategy to use. As a preventative measure, remember that the stronger the measurable benefits are in MP 3, the more likely MPC 4 will occur at the same time.

Set up a quote log to track your outstanding MP 3: Cement Solution proposals by budget and decision dates of the proposals, dollar amounts, and gross margins. Again, Q sheets record this information. (See Exhibit 9-11.)

Exhibit 9-11. Manageable quote limit.

MANAGEABLE QUOTE LIMIT

Newest

MP 3 Proposals

Oldest

Set a Limit on Your Inventory of Golden Opportunities (*MP 3 Proposals*); Move One In Past the Limit, Move One Out

Note: When customers view your products as commodities, your input become less important after you provide them with quotes, which they often view as official price tags. With value-driven sales, your input is just important after the quote as before.

Compete Against Yourself and Productivity Explodes

As discussed, one of your greatest strengths is your ability to influence sales performance. Traditionally, you or your sales manager judged performance solely on dollars sold. The logic ran that volume is the only thing that matters. Yet, other things matter because they help you to reach dollars sold. The productivity equation is important because it *quantifies and improves* your sales skills and productivity on an annual basis.

Sales productivity is an equation. Total dollars sold is the part that comes after the equal sign. Yet, dollars sold tells you only past results, not current or future trends. Therefore, the key to influencing performance is to look at the five variables that come before the equal sign and the selling skills they reflect. As in any equation, the variables affect each other. The equation is shown in Exhibit 9-12 and Exhibit 9-13.

Exhibit 9-12. The productivity equation.

Of Calls / Quote Ratio x Closure Rate x Average Order Size x Average Gross Margin %
= Total Gross Margin $ Sold

Exhibit 9-13. Using the productivity equation as your personal benchmark.

THE PRODUCTIVITY EQUATION ALLOWS YOU TO GET TO "DOLLARS SOLD"

1. Calculate the number of in-person sales calls you make in a year.
2. Divide that number by your Quote Ratio (the number of calls it takes to generate a quote). You calculate this number by dividing your annual sales calls by your annual number of proposals.
3. Multiply this number by your Closure Rate (the percent of proposals you close). You calculate this number by dividing your annual number of orders by your annual number of proposals.
4. Multiply this number by your Average Order Size (the average dollar value of an order). You calculate this number by dividing your annual sales volume by your annual number of orders.
5. Multiply this number by your Average Gross Margin % (the average profit margin of an order). You calculate this number by dividing your annual profit dollars by your annual sales volume.
6. These calculations will equal your total gross margin for the year.

THE FIVE VARIABLES

1. *Number of Sales Calls.* The quantity of in-person sales calls you make to all customers. They are the power cells that fuel sales production. (Do not include telephone calls in this figure.) **Reflects:** Your planning and time management skills.

    For example, four hundred in-person sales calls in a year might indicate good planning. However, whether they are productive calls still needs to be determined by the four other variables.

2. *Quote Ratio.* The number of sales calls it takes to generate one quote. Taking your total number of sales calls and dividing that sum by your total number of quotes calculates this ratio. **Reflects:** Your ability to identify market segments that have goals achievable by your products and services. It also reflects both your technical (products) and market segments—that is, filters or systems of evaluations—knowledge to recognize and seize opportunities. The *lower* the number, the greater your skills.

    For example, you generate 114 proposals. Your *quote ratio* is 3.5 (400 calls ÷ 114 proposals). It took you 3.5 calls to generate a quote.

3. *Closure Rate.* This is the number of quotes it takes to obtain one purchase order. Calculate this percentage by taking the number of orders and dividing it by your total quantity of quotes. **Reflects:** Your ability to qualify customers and to obtain and build on the sequence of the MPCs. It also highlights whether you are in negotiated (higher rate) or bid markets (lower rate). Most important, it shows whether you made the order nothing more than the logical conclusion to a series of engineered agreements—the MPCs.

    For example, you sold forty-six orders. Your *closure rate* is 40 percent (46 orders ÷ 114 proposals). You receive orders on four out of every ten sales opportunities you quoted.

4. *Average Order Size.* The total dollar value of your orders divided by the total number of purchase orders. **Reflects:** Your technical skills and industry knowledge in identifying customers' goals, measurable benefits, and SOEs rather than just ability to respond to customers' needs or pains. It also illustrates the ability to package products and services.

    For example, your total sales are $1,150,000. Your *average order size* is $25,000 ($1,150,000 ÷ 46 orders).

5. *Average Gross Margin Percentage.* This is the profit level of a sale, which only includes its direct labor, material, and overhead costs. The sell price minus direct labor, material, and overhead costs equals gross margin dollars. Dividing the gross margin dollars by dollars sold gives you the percentage. **Reflects:** Whether your sales are price- or value-

driven. Bid sales represent the former, negotiated sales the latter. Did customers seek low-cost products or did you build goal-oriented and high-value solutions? Did you make the dollar value of Column 2 larger than Column 1?

For example, if you generated $550,000 gross margin dollars, your *average gross margin percentage* is 47.8 ($550, 000 ÷ $1,150,000).

Total gross margin dollars sold, as opposed to just total dollars sold, more accurately reflects your ability to have customers compensate you for providing more value than competitors. Do not stop at dollars sold to make any judgments about performance without accounting for gross margins (value).

Managing the Productivity Equation

Set up your productivity equation for the year. Compare your results to each variable. MeasureMax's focus is on the numbers that precede the equal's sign and on improving each variable.

View the trends to determine how your sales, marketing skills, and the effects of any new strategies or training are working (including MeasureMax.) Regardless of whether you chart this information or not, it is beneficial to be aware of how the measurable variables can influence your sales productivity.

Productivity equations also let you review the results of trade-offs. If you make fewer proposals but qualify better, will your *closure rate* go up? If you make more calls, will your *quote ratio* become worse? If you work the bid market more, will your *closure rate* go down but your *average order size* increase? What happens to *average gross margins*? The list of questions is endless.

If you keep a sales productivity equation, even an informal one, you have more objective questions to ask yourself. In addition, it gives you the means to perform a *test of reasonableness* to determine whether your planned selling efforts can achieve your targeted sales results.

Note: Do not fall into an analysis-paralysis trap. The numbers do not provide answers; they only point you to what questions you should be asking yourself about how to improve performance management expectations.

Getting the Process Rolling

As a minimum, use a Q sheet or the Pulled-Through test on your next sales call or proposal that falls under the *two-plus* category (two or more in-person sales calls, two or more decision makers). Big deal if you only get a few measurable goals, filters, or conditional commitments. So what if you mention specific products during MP 1: Spark Interest or MP 2: Measure Potential.

The real objective is to change your customers' systems of evaluation of value by altering yours. Make the next call or proposal measurably better than the last, and the details will work themselves out. Who knows? You might even classify market segments by the number of goals or filters you make measurable. Let the measurable benchmarks of the sales tools enable you to tap the creative strengths of all your selling resources (marketing group, sales management, other salespeople on your team, and the like).

What Happens When You Cannot Use MeasureMax?

Sometimes, in spite of your good efforts and intentions, customers do not conduct business within the framework of your sales process. They do not provide you with the specifics of their goals and filters. They are unwilling to make conditional commitments. Does this mean you walk away from potential business opportunities? No!

Yet, without this data, a significant number of goals and filters remains unknown and decreases the probability of successful outcomes. Therefore, your best course of action is to determine how much time, effort, and resources to invest with the risks involved. Obviously, the larger the business opportunity, the more time you are willing to expend—and the greater the risks of unknowns you are willing to accept.

Such risks are typical of bid sales. If customers' goals are low price or fast delivery, concentrate on making their other filters measurable. Benefit from having fewer unknowns with which to contend. Although, you may discover after MP 1 and MP 2 that customers' goals are still lowest price or fastest delivery, so be it. The outcome for these particular sales might not change, but your mind-set for other sales opportunities has in powerful and productive ways.

The challenge is to ensure that the majority of your sales opportunities do not depend on working outside known and measurable customers' goals, filters, and SOEs. If need be, invest more selling time with value-driven decision makers or market segments than you do with your current customers. After all, you did not invest all this time, energy, and resources to acquire a new sales perspective, tools, and set of skills merely to do the same type of selling as before. Ask yourself, "What new markets or customers do I pursue knowing I have value-driven business tools and sales perspectives my competition do not have?"

Some Final Thoughts

Condition yourself, as discussed in Chapter 1, to initially view every sale as a negotiated opportunity. Help customers identify goals with measurable value and SOEs that connect them to your features and unique strengths. There is nothing magical; there are no tricks. You do not need to be a great detective to eliminate the unknowns that surround your potential to sell value. Just use the various tools of the MeasureMax selling system in a manner that suits your styles and personalities. The time you invest will not only provide you and customers with fair returns but also exponential ones.

In the final analysis, while knowledge may be power, applying knowledge is the key to success. Change the way you sell to change the way customers buy—measurably better, of course. Greatness awaits those who constantly measure, manage, and maximize their performance. Greatness awaits you!

SUMMARY

- Increase the quality, not only the quantity, of your sales calls; make fewer calls to get more orders, not visa versa.
- Use the following five steps to set MeasureMax in motion:
  1. Create Product Profile sheets on a pay-as-you-go basis.
  2. Create Market Profile sheets the same way.
  3. Use Quick-Entry Sales Management (Q) sheets.
  4. Use Connecting Value sheets.
  5. Use the Pulled-Through test.
- Q sheets are the most important documents in the sales process. Use them instead of loose-leaf paper. They guide you through every

step of the sales process by providing you with measurable feedback. Regardless of what sales methods you use, Q sheets are your report cards on how effectively they work.

- A quick way to keep your results consistent is to see how many of your sales calls fall within the four MPs. MP 1: Spark Interest and MP 2: Measure Potential are the *planting seeds* portion; MP 3: Cement Solution is the *watering crops* portion; and MP 4: Implement Agreement is the *harvesting crops* portion.

- A quote inventory limits you to a specific number of *manageable* MP 3: Cement Solution proposals. If you bring in a new one, remove the oldest.

- Placing a maximum limit of sales calls to obtain MPCs helps you to invest your time wisely and pursue better opportunities if necessary.

- The productivity equation assigns numerical values to your skills and progress over time so that you influence, not just judge, performance.

- Use measurable competitive analysis to determine whether you receive higher gross margins for providing more value than competitors.

- Use account management to protect and grow your existing base of positive customers. Use measurable value to make relationships stronger both professionally and personally.

- Market development converts neutral or negative customers into positive ones.

- Always view a sales opportunity as value driven, not price driven, to change your mind-set and increase your productivity and profitability.

Glossary

80/20 Rule—conventional (and highly inefficient) sales wisdom that states that 80 percent of your sales comes from only 20 percent of your customers.

80/80 Law—Highly productive MeasureMax concept that states—with measurable information—you can make 80 percent of filled-out quick entry sales management sheets generate proposals that produce 80 percent of your sales.

account management—The selling strategy that focuses on creating sales from your existing positive customers.

active listening—Ability to acknowledge receipt and understanding of customers' comments.

active questioning—Ability to ask for specifics concerning customers' goals, measurable benefits, filters, and systems of evaluation.

advocate—The individual whose goals your products help achieve the most in an organization. This person's opinion carries the most credence with final decision makers.

advocating—Salespeople who do not listen for customers' comments concerning goals, benefits, filters, and systems of evaluation. Instead, they constantly think about how to force product discussions into their sales calls.

alternatives—One of the five influencer filters. Besides any products you recommend, it also encompasses the other options or competitive offerings that customers are considering to achieve their goals.

analogies—Explaining method used to simplify technical details to customers by paralleling them to everyday occurrences.

anticipating—The ability to listen for clues as to where speakers are heading concerning goals, filters, measurable benefits, and systems of evaluation. You use those clues to formulate your follow-up questions.

assuming—Guessing where speakers' comments are heading based on personal prejudices, emotions, and experiences.

attainment measurement—This is the most important of the four prerequisite filters. It combines decision makers' prerequisites of dates and funding with their systems of evaluation and measurable benefits to set the conditions for determining if they achieve their goals.

average order size—One of the five variables of the productivity equation. It is the dollar value of your average order. You calculate its value by dividing your dollars sold by the number of orders sold.

benchmarks—The second step of MP 3: Cement Solution. In this step, you select and connect the features of your products to the measurable benefits of the customers' goals.

beneficiaries—The individuals in an organization who benefit the most from the goals your solutions achieve.

benefits—The value customers derive from the features of products or services achieving their goals.

bid system—Sale opportunities where customers view products as commodities. They invite competitors to bid on purchasing specifications. The lowest price or fastest deliveries in Column 1 usually wins the sale.

brinkmanship selling—Selling mode you use with new prospects to quickly qualify or disqualify them as potential sales opportunities.

budget, decision, start, and complete Dates—One of the four prerequisite filters. These deadlines determine when customers must achieve their goals and sense of urgency.

business question—Question that seeks answers about goals, filters, benefits, and systems of evaluation. Other questions serve limited business value.

C level—The level refers to executive suite of decision makers such as chief executive officer (CEO), chief financial officer (CFO), chief operating officer (COO), chief information officer (CIO).

call for action—A recommendation you make to customers to implement measurable activities (issuing purchase orders, arranging meetings, or conducting surveys) to prove a Measurable Phase Change occurred.

capital investment—Funding for a sale that occurs outside of customers' operating budgets. It usually requires multilevel approvals and special allocations.

clarifying—Questioning process by which you seek to gather details about customers' goals, measurable benefits, filters, and systems of evaluation.

clearer—The second tier of a customer's response pattern that provides more details to the salesperson, usually in response to a clarifying question.

closure rate—One of the five variables of the productivity equation. The percentage of orders you obtain as compared with the number of proposals or quotes you make. Divide the number of orders by the number of proposals to calculate your percentage.

Column 1—The first of two columns that customers use to weigh out their purchasing decisions. Both of these columns have items with actual or perceived dollar figures assigned to them. Customers then add up the items and use the totals of the two columns to decide whether they will buy something and from whom. Column 1 contains four items that customers—on their own—assign dollar values to: (1) purchase prices, (2) delivery dates, (3) personal relationships, and (4) the costs of changing to new suppliers or products and services.

Column 2—The second of the two columns customers use to weigh out their purchasing decisions. It encompasses the measurable benefits in dollars that customers receive from achieving their goals. Salespeople must make sure this column gets filled out to outweigh the perceived dollar value of Column 1.

commodity—Products that customers consider the same except for price and delivery differences. Lowest price or fastest delivery wins the sale.

compensated value—The ability to provide more measurable benefits than competitors and receive your expected profit margins for doing so.

competitor's product profile—Sales tool that evaluates the unique strengths of competitive offerings.

conditional commitment—Customers' acknowledgment they want to achieve their goals within their attainment measurements. It is not a trial close; you do not ask for a commitment to a specific product.

conditions met—The sixth step of MP 3: Cement Solution. Salespeople demonstrate how features connect to customers' measurable benefits.

connect the dots—The fifth step of MP 3: Cement Solution. You explain how the features of your products achieve the customers' measurable benefits and conditional commitments.

connecting value sheet—The sales tool you use to select the features that connect to the measurable benefits of the customers' goals.

contact level—Decision-making level at which you make initial contact with customers.

costs of doing nothing—The system of evaluation that helps customers assign a cost on a per day basis for not pursuing specific goals.

countercyclical—The economic condition where the market segment goes in the opposite direction to the general economy. If the economy is booming, the market segment slows down. If the economy slows down, the market segments grow.

courtship selling—Selling mode you use with new customers to find out whether they will become long-term customers or occasional ones.

create-and-wait—Strategy you use when customers express satisfaction with their existing suppliers. It focuses on communicating to customers' over a period of one year or less how your strengths connect to their goals.

current situation—One of the five influencer filters. It involves what customers currently do to achieve their goals.

customer—Anyone with goals that your products or services fulfill within their conditional commitment.

customer expert—Knowing customers' goals, measurable benefits, and systems of evaluation used in their industry. Salespeople who build products from customers' goals down, not from their features up.

customer goal categories—Broad grouping of objectives that an organization goals fall within.

customer-generated proposals—Motivated customers seek proposals to find out how your solutions achieve their goals.

customer-oriented—Sales approach that focuses first on customers' goals, measurable benefits, filters, and systems of evaluation, not products.

cyclical—The economic condition where the market segment follows the general economy. If the economy is booming, so is the market segment. If the economy slows down, so does the market segment.

D level—This level refers to the second tier of decision makers such as department level heads and directors of operations, engineering, accounting, finance, and so forth.

damage report—First of the four steps in handling hinges. Salespeople evaluate the impact of the hinge before attempting to address it.

deal—The first step of MP 4: Implement Agreement. Salespeople verify that customers are ready to implement their proposals.

decision maker—Individual involved with deciding whether a supplier's products and services will be purchased, and from whom. See *gatekeeper, advocate,* and *final decision maker.*

decommoditizing the sale—Making the value of your products more than a function of price and delivery.

defining value—The process salespeople use to make their products and services produce perceived or measurable value using product profile sheets.

dialoguing—The questioning process you use to create an initial comfort level between you and customers unrelated to anyone's business objectives.

diluting feature—The features that do not connect to customers' goals and diminish value instead of creating it.

direct savings—Immediate financial benefits with measurable results.

don't shoot yourself—One of the six active questioning tactics. It involves making sure that you do not agree with a negative comment when you rephrase a question.

downplay—The last step in handling hinges. It involves verifying the removal of the hinge before returning to the appropriate Measurable Phase by using *explaining, outweighing,* or *revising* strategies.

economic sensitivity—A measure of how a market segment (and the customers within it) will react to changing economic conditions. See *cyclical, countercyclical,* and *noncyclical.*

eliminate unknowns—The third step in MP 2: Measure Potential. It involves making the customers' goals, benefits, filters, and systems of evaluation measurable.

explaining—Conveying factual details about how your proposed products and services achieve customers' goals within their conditional commitments. One of the three steps in the downplay step to handle hinges.

external focus—Benefits customers of your customers receive from your products.

feature—A characteristic of a product or service that defines its traits or image, which produces either perceived or measurable benefits.

feature value rating—Numerical value given to a feature to calculate its competitiveness. A unique strength receives a 5 while a regular feature receives a 1 rating.

features creatures—Salespeople who believe the most features win.

filters—The nine purchasing considerations (5 influencers, 4 prerequisites) that influence and determine whether customers can achieve their goals via your products and services.

final decision maker—Individual who approves the attainment measurements, systems of evaluation, and allocates or releases funds for achieving goals.

following the customer's lead—One of the six active questioning tactics. It involves using questions to bridge customers' response to your next question to better understand their goals, filters, measurable benefits, or and systems of evaluation.

funding—One of the four prerequisite filters. It determines how much in financial resources customers can allocate to achieve their goals and its source. See *capital investment* and *operating budget.*

gatekeeper—Customer contact who cannot give a final yes but can give an initial no to any proposed solution. Gatekeeper initially approves any proposed products if they fall within their operational, technical, or financial expertise.

go for measurable specific—Mnemonics to help you remember the purpose of goals, filters, measurable benefits, and systems of evaluation.

goal motivation—One of the five influencer filters. It conveys whether the driving forces behind customers' goals are to avoid negative results or achieve positive ones.

goals—Prioritized objectives customers want to achieve because of the benefits they could derive from them.

gross margin percentage—One of the five variables of the productivity equation. Gross margin dollars divided by the total dollars sold provides this percentage.

gross margin dollars—The sell price of the product or service minus its direct labor and material costs.

gutter ball hinge—Customers perceive your proposed solution as not achieving their conditional commitments. This hinge prevents salespeople from attaining MPC 3: Solution Confirmed.

harvesting crops—The selling stage associated with the number of in-person sales calls invested in MP 4: Implement Agreement to close orders.

hidden costs—Costs or expenses that customers do not normally associate with the manufacturing of your products or services.

hidden hinge—Either natural or leveraged hinges that customers do not want to disclose to you. They feel it creates a negative impression of them or their company, or your products or company.

hinges—The actions or comments of customers that prevent you from continuing the Measurable Phases in the prescribed sequence; an inability to obtain Measurable Phase Changes via your call for action.

How's Zat?—The two most powerful words used to handle hinges. Different versions of "how does that" affect the customers' ability to achieve their goals. One of the four basic steps in handling hinges by asking a clarifying question concerning the hinge's impact on the customers' goals.

iceberg ahead hinge—Customers disclose a filter that impedes their or your ability to achieve their goals.

indirect savings—Financial benefits derived from long-term and perceived results.

influencers—The five filters or purchasing constraints that influence your ability and the customer's to achieve its goals.

in-person sales calls—Sales calls that involve face-to-face meetings with customers. These sales calls are your currency. You only have so many you can invest, and each one must provide a return to warrant further ones with the same customers. They are the power cells that fuel sales production.

internal focus—Benefits the purchasers of your products receive.

joint planning level—This level refers to the epitome of account management where you help the C-level set to achieve its long-term goals. You also help the D level do the same.

keys to previous successes/failures—One of the five influencer filters. It describes why customers approved or rejected past goals.

leveraged hinge—Customers leverage their concerns against a specific product. It occurs before salespeople know customers' goals, measurable benefits, filters, and systems of evaluation. Salespeople cannot obtain a Measurable Phase Change and their associated calls for action.

life-cycle analysis—System of evaluation used to identify the costs associated with products over their life. These costs help offset lower-priced products by showing how they really cost more over their life.

logistics—The last step of MP 4: Implement Agreement. It involves knowing the details necessary to start and complete the sale on time.

lose the battle; win the war—One of the handling hinge tactics. Salespeople build credibility by acknowledging that customers' concerns are accurate, but not sales stoppers. It involves using the downplay step.

market development—The selling strategy that focuses on generating business from new prospects and customers.

market focus—The first step in MP 2: Measure Potential. It involves displaying your knowledge of customers' market segments by citing relevant facts about their company and industry.

market profile—Sales tool that analyzes your market segments in terms of how the benefits of customers' goals connect to features of your products via systems of evaluation.

market segment—A group of customers that share the same organizational characteristics and goals, and react the same way to the same offer.

measurable phase changes (MPC)—Customers' agreements that end a Measurable Phase while providing objective feedback of your progress and chances of success.

measurable phases—The four selling phases that indicate where you are in the sales process, and what you must do to provide more value to customers than competitors and receive compensation for doing so.

measurable value—The worth of a benefit determined by objective, proven, and documented criteria expressed in dollars.

MP 1: Spark Interest—The first Measurable Phase that motivates customers to pursue further their opportunities to achieve confirmed goals. Salespeople verify that customers are members of their targeted market segment.

MP 2: Measure Potential—The second Measurable Phase that determines how customers' measurable benefits, filters, systems of evaluation, and conditional commitments affect their and your ability to achieve stated goals.

MP 3: Cement Solution—The third Measurable Phase that explains how your solutions achieve their goals within their conditional commitments.

MP 4: Implement Agreement—The fourth Measurable Phase where the order becomes the logical conclusion to a series of previously engineered agreements (MPCs).

MPC 1: Interest Confirmed—The first Measurable Phase Change that ends MP 1: Spark Interest. Salespeople confirm customers' interest in achieving general goals.

MPC 2: Potential Confirmed—The second Measurable Phase Change that ends MP 2: Measure Potential. Salespeople confirm customers' capability to achieve their goals.

MPC 3: Solution Confirmed—The third Measurable Phase Change that ends MP 3: Cement Solution. Salespeople confirm customers agree their solution achieves their goals.

MPC 4: Agreement Confirmed—The fourth Measurable Phase Change that ends MP 4: Implement Agreement. Salespeople confirm formal agreement to purchase products or services.

natural hinge—The potential concerns that arise naturally during the active questioning phase of MP 2: Measure Potential. Without any specific products mentioned, customers having nothing to adversely react to, or for salespeople to defend.

needs—Well-established problems or pain where customers feel they know the specific products required to solve them. Customers with expressed needs often view products and salespeople as commodities.

needs-satisfaction selling—Salespeople react to customers' requests for specific products without knowing their goals, measurable benefits, filters, and systems of evaluation. The antithesis of MeasureMax's selling strategy that centers on defining customers' goals and planning, not reacting to sales opportunities.

negative customers—Organizations or individuals that have preferred in the past, currently prefer, and are likely in the future to prefer to conduct business with competitors. When purchasing decisions involve perceived value, they always choose existing suppliers. Demonstrating the measurable value they can receive from achieving their goals via your products can convert them to positive customers.

neutral customers—Organizations or individuals that do not prefer a specific company, and conduct business on what appears to be a random basis.

no blanks—The first step in MP 3: Cement Solution. It involves using your Q sheets to determine what measurable details and specifics about goals and filter are still missing—and how it will affect the sale.

no echoes—One of the six active questioning tactics. It involves using questions to rephrase, not parrot customers' responses.

no loose ends—One of the six active questioning tactics. It involves making sure customers' goals, filters, benefits, and systems of evaluation are measurable before pursuing the next one.

no return—Explaining tactic where you exhaust all measurable benefits and their features before going to the next one. Do not go back and speak more about a benefit that you have already covered.

noncyclical—The economic condition where the market segment includes companies with both manufacturing and service business units. Therefore, these market segments will redirect their investments (that is, sales opportunities) depending on the direction and condition of the economy.

number of calls—Actual number of in-person sales calls, which are salespeople's limited currency. Only so many sales call in a year; each one requires a good return. See *in-person sales calls*.

objective decision making—One of two components that make up customers' decision making. It focuses on measurable facts. You want this component to proceed, not follow the subjective one.

one up, one down—Strategy in which you meet with your contacts' immediate boss and subordinate. You use these meetings to ensure they understand the measurable goals you achieved for their organization in case your contact leaves.

oops!—The third step in MP 3: Cement Solution. Salespeople prepare themselves to explain any misses of conditional commitments.

operating budget—Goals achieved through funding from existing budgets, which do not require specific allocations. Lowers decision making levels.

options—A broad array of features offered to customers with unclear goals or filters.

order—The logical conclusion to a series of previously engineered agreements known as Measurable Phase Changes.

organizational characteristics—Primary attributes that influence the way an organization views itself. They help to establish a customer's core values, priorities, and goals.

outvalue—When you provide more measurable value than competitors and receive higher profit margins for doing so.

outweighing—The third step in *downplay* to handle hinges by showing how your proposed solution's benefits more than offset any perceived liabilities.

owners—Individuals who fund the purchases of products and services—and who place a high premium on the dollar value of Column 2.

packaging—Combining the unique strengths or features of various products in a manner so customers view them as a single entity.

pain—Obvious needs customers want to address with specific products or services. See *needs-satisfaction selling.*

partner—Salesperson who focuses on helping customers make sure that any short-term solutions are consistent with their long-term goals.

Pat from *Saturday Night Live*—A tactic for handling hinges. It determines whether a perceived obstacle is really nothing more than a request for more information, a better explanation, or more documentation.

perceived value—Customers subjectively determine the worth derived from achieving their goals by individual preferences, background, and experiences, not by measurable criteria.

personal relationships—The friendly bonds that develop over time between salespeople and customers that increase their trust levels. Make your professional relationships as strong as your personal ones.

plans—One of the five influencer filters that describes what the customers' plans are to achieve their goals.

planting seeds—The selling stage associated with the number of in-person sales calls invested in MP 1: Spark Interest and MP 2: Measure Potential to quantify the potential of sales opportunities.

position—The roles and responsibilities of customers in their organizations, which plays a major influence in determining the goals they seek to achieve.

positive customers—Organizations that have preferred in the past, currently prefer, and are likely in the future to prefer to do business with you. They always choose your perceived value over that of your competitors.

power words—Explaining tactic that uses terms to express confidence.

prerequisites—The four filters of attainment measurement, dates, funding, and decision makers that require satisfaction for a sale to occur.

product—Any goods or services that you sell.

product expert—A salesperson whose expertise lies in the features and benefits of his or her products, not the customers' goals.

product profile—Sales tool used to define your products by their features benefits, value, focus, rating, and unique strengths.

productivity equation—Formula you use to measure selling and marketing skills, and predict trends that help you influence performance.

product-oriented—Sales mentality that starts with the initial focus on features and benefits of your product, and not on the customers' goals.

professional relationships—The business bonds that develop when salespeople document how they help customers achieve measurable goals, not a function of time.

progress—The rate at which you obtain Measurable Phase Changes that concluded with MPC 4: Agreement Confirmed.

proposal—A written document that outlines the business and legal conditions under which you will provide your products and services to a customer.

pulled-through proposal—Customers wanting to achieve their goals are the major catalysts for generating proposals.

pulse check hinge—Customers show no interest in any goals or potential benefits you described in your spark interest statement.

purpose and goals—The second step in MP 2: Measure Potential. It involves confirming that the meeting's purpose is to understand the customer's ability to achieve his or her goals.

purpose and summary—The fourth step in MP 3: Cement Solution. It involves explaining to the customer that the purpose of the meeting is to demonstrate how your proposed solutions achieve their conditional commitments and measurable benefits.

pushed-through proposal—Salespeople, not customers, are the major catalyst for generating a proposal.

qualifying—Questioning process used to gather initial information about customers goals, benefits, filters, and systems of evaluation.

quick entry sales management (Q) sheet—Sales tool that records, guides, and measures the progress of salespeople to help them manage and maximize their sales opportunities.

quote—See *proposal.*

quote inventory—Process by which you limit yourself to a set number of MP 3 proposals. If you bring in a new one, take out the oldest one.

quote ratio—The number of calls needed to generate a quote. The total number of calls divided by the total number of written proposals calculates its value.

receiving value—The process by which you demonstrate how your products and services achieve customers' measurable goals.

relationship selling—The selling mode used with long-term customers who freely discuss their goals, benefits, filters, and systems of evaluation.

requests for proposal—Bid documents with technical specifications sent to competitors to solicit their products and services. Lowest price or fastest delivery usually wins this type of sale.

research and membership—First step of MP 1: Spark Interest. This step conveys to customers specifics of their organizational characteristics and positions. It lets customers know that you selected them for valid business reasons rather than on a random basis.

revising—One of the three steps in *downplay* to handle hinges. It involves trying to change a filter or product selection to satisfy unfavorable requirements.

rip-off hinge—Customers consider the price of a proposed solution excessive even though it meets their conditional commitments.

safety zone—Questioning process and strategy in which you reference your filter questions to customers' goals.

scope of work—Detailed list of proposed solutions sent to customers for them to review. Customers comment on whether the outlined products and services achieve their goals within their conditional commitments. They then return the list to the salesperson for corrective action (if necessary). A scope of work does not include price or delivery information and occurs before making formal MP 3: Cement Solution presentations.

silence is golden—Tactic to handle hinges by pausing and not saying anything for five seconds, as you analyze the impact of the customers' comments.

simple—Explaining tactic where you use customers' jargon and terms to help them understand how features achieve their measurable benefit.

smokescreen—A hinge that a customer does not feel comfortable to disclose for fear of embarrassing himself or you.

solution—Goods and services that achieve customers' goals within their conditional commitments in MP 3: Cement Solution.

strategy-driven—Sales process where established plans and benchmarks drive the structure and tactics of your sales calls.

subjective decision making—One of two components that make up customers' decision making. It focuses on emotions. You want this component to follow, not precede, the objective component.

supplier—Salesperson who focuses on providing solutions that help customers achieve short-term goals.

sway—Amount of influence a contact exerts on the purchasing decision.

systems of evaluation (SOEs)—The methods customers use to calculate value they receive from achieving their goals.

tactics-driven—Sales approach where tactics and techniques dictate your sales strategy on a random basis.

take your pick—Second step of MP 1: Spark Interest. You let customers choose goals that might interest them from a broad array.

target confirmed—The third step in handling hinges. Salespeople verify they understand the impact of the hinges before attempting to remedy them.

test of reasonableness—Customers test if they can achieve their goals within their conditional commitments during MP 2: Measure Potential.

think positively—One of the six active questioning tactics. It involves using questions where you make positive assumptions, not negative ones.

third-party intermediaries—Owners' representatives and seasoned practitioners of the bid system. They place a high premium on the dollar value of price and delivery in Column 1.

top-five buzzing—Overview letter sent to the top five decision makers to generate initial interest. It outlines the company goals you could help them achieve.

track record—The third step of MP 1: Spark Interest. You provide references of your successes in similar or the same market segments.

trial close—Process where salesperson asks for a product purchase commitment from customers if certain conditions are met. It indicates a lack of understanding of customers' goals, measurable benefits, filters, and systems of evaluations—and obtaining Measurable Phase Changes.

two-plus sales—Opportunities that involves two or more decision makers and in-person sales calls. When both of these situations occur, they present the best opportunity for you to provide more value than competitors and receive higher profits for doing so.

unique strengths—The features only your product, service, or company possesses that produce measurable benefits to a specific marketplace.

universal feature—Any feature created at the organizational level (not at the product or service level) such as size in dollars or employees, years in business, number of distribution centers, and number of customers. A universal feature should only be used if it helps a customer achieve a measurable benefit of his or her goals.

vague—The first tier of customers' responses that provides nonspecific answers to salespeople, usually in response to qualifying questions.

value—Perceived or measurable benefits that customers derive from the features of products as it relates to the achievement of their goals.

vendor—Salesperson who focuses on satisfying customers' requests for specific products and services to satisfy specific needs.

verifying—Process that uses yes-or-no questions to validate and confirm complete understanding and agreement of goals or filters.

vivid—Explaining tactic that uses descriptions to create powerful images.

watering crops—The selling stage associated with the number of in-person sales calls invested in MP 3: Cement Solution.

"What do they do for you?" trap—The tactic and common sales mistake that occurs when salespeople find out that a customer does business with a competitor. They ask customers to tell them what a competitor's products or services do for them. The focus is now on the difference between your features and competitors—which leaves out how your products help customers achieve their goals.

wish lists—What customers think they want to achieve without understanding their goals and filters. You find these lists in *needs-satisfaction selling*.

yellow light—The fourth step of MP 2: Measure Potential. It involves a summary of the measurable benefits of the customers' goals and the attainment of the conditional commitments.

"You can only manage what you can measure"—Powerful business axiom that fuels the MeasureMax selling system.

Bibliography

Alessandra, Tony, Ph.D., Jim Cathcart, and John Monoky, Ph.D. *Be Your Own Sales Manager*. New York: Fireside, 1992.

Arnold, John. *The Art of Decision Making*. New York: AMACOM, 1978.

Bosworth, Michael. *Solution Selling*. New York: McGraw-Hill, 1995.

Conrad, Jay. *Guerrilla Selling*. Boston: Houghton Mifflin Company, 1992.

Drucker, Peter E. *Innovation and Entrepreneurship*. New York: Harper and Row Publishers, 1985.

Gellerman, Saul. *Motivation and Productivity*. New York: AMACOM, 1963.

Groder, Martin G. *Business Games: How to Recognize the Players and Deal with Them*. New York: Boardroom Classics, 1980.

Hanan, Michael, J. Cribben, and H. Heiser. *Consultative Selling*. New York: AMACOM, 1973.

Heiman, Stephen, Diane Sanchez, and Tad Tuleja. *The New Strategic Selling*. New York: Warner Books, 1998.

Holden, Jim. *World Class Selling*. New York: John Wiley and Sons, Inc., 1999.

Katz, Jack. *How Emotions Work*. Chicago: University of Chicago Press, 1999.

McConkey, David. *How to Manage by Results*. New York: AMACOM, 1976.

Peters, Thomas, and Robert Waterman, Jr. *In Search of Excellence*. New York: Harper and Row, 1982.

Rackham, Neil. *Rethinking the Sales Force.* New York: McGraw-Hill Trade, 1999.

Rackham, Neil. *Spin Selling.* New York: McGraw-Hill, 1988.

Sant, Tom. *Persuasive Business Proposals.* New York: AMACOM, 1992.

Schiffman, Stephan. *Asking Questions, Winning Sales.* New York: DEI Management, 1996.

Shonka, Mark, and Dan Kosch. *Beyond Selling Value.* Chicago: Dearborn Trade Publishing, 2002.

Werth, Jacques, and Nicholas Reuben. *High Probability Selling.* Philadelphia: ABBA Publishing Company, 1999.

Index

About the Author

In 1978, Josh Costell started using his radical "selling is a science" theory. Within three years, he went from a rookie salesperson to a sales superstar to a national sales manager of a billion-dollar Fortune 500 company. Along the way, Costell won every top sales and profitability award given to salespeople. This ascent was a direct result of his early MeasureMax concepts.

In 1984, the success of his selling program at York International Corporation attracted media attention. A three-page feature article titled "The Costell Sell" appeared in *Sales and Marketing Management* magazine. He changed careers to become president and CEO of a fledgling electronic controls company. Using his selling theories, Costell grew the company into a multimillion-dollar business selling products in more than twenty countries worldwide.

During a seventeen-year period, he participated in more than a thousand joint sales calls. He gained first-hand opportunities to apply, test, analyze, and fine-tune his sales and marketing theories on a local, national, and worldwide scale. He has since returned to his fiercest passion—articulating and teaching the sales process so that both buyer and seller benefit from having common, not competing, goals.

Twenty years later, Costell finished the book he started writing in 1981 at the urging of his former associates and customers. He founded Applying Knowledge Systems (AKS), a consulting and training firm for sales professionals, in January 1998 to allow him to fulfill his career-long passion. His mission is to convert selling from psychobabble to science, to increase sales productivity, and to ensure that customers exceed their measurable expectations.

LaVergne, TN USA
30 November 2009
165480LV00008B/34/P